Fixed Asset Accounting

Fifth Edition

Steven M. Bragg

For more information about AccountingTools® products, visit our Web site at www.accountingtools.com.

ISBN-13: 978-1-64221-035-4

Printed in the United States of America

Table of Contents

Preface

Fixed Asset Accounting describes every aspect of the accounting for fixed assets under both the GAAP and IFRS accounting frameworks, and illustrates key concepts with numerous examples. There are also dozens of tips throughout the text. The book is designed for both practicing accountants and students, since both can benefit from its detailed descriptions of fixed asset budgeting, acquisition, disposition, and more. *Fixed Asset Accounting* addresses four major fixed asset accounting topics, which are:

- Part I – Accounting for Fixed Assets. Chapters 1 through 9 cover the complete range of accounting activities related to fixed assets, including capital budgeting, asset recognition, interest capitalization, asset retirement obligations, depreciation, impairment, and disposal.
- Part II – Special Accounting for Fixed Assets. Chapter 10 notes the various financial statement disclosures associated with fixed assets, while Chapter 11 delves into special considerations for the not-for-profit entity.
- Part III – Fixed Asset Systems. Given the high cost of fixed assets, you need to surround them with a strong control system, which is addressed in four chapters. Chapter 12 describes fixed asset record keeping, while Chapter 13 delves into a variety of controls over all aspects of fixed asset usage. Chapter 14 itemizes many policies and procedures for fixed asset transactions. Finally, Chapter 15 addresses a number of available fixed asset tracking technologies.
- Part IV – Related Topics. There are several ancillary areas that may be of interest to the fixed asset practitioner. Chapter 16 describes a number of ratios that can be used to monitor fixed assets. Chapter 17 gives an overview of the procedures that auditors typically follow during the fixed asset portion of an audit, and describes the information they will request as part of this audit.

There is also an appendix that contains templates for the journal entries used in most fixed asset transactions, as well as a comprehensive glossary of fixed asset terms.

Fixed Asset Accounting gives you a complete grounding in every aspect of the accounting systems needed for fixed assets. As such, it may earn a place on your book shelf as a reference tool for years to come.

Centennial, Colorado
December, 2019

About the Author

Steven Bragg, CPA, has been the chief financial officer or controller of four companies, as well as a consulting manager at Ernst & Young. He received a master's degree in finance from Bentley College, an MBA from Babson College, and a Bachelor's degree in Economics from the University of Maine. He has been a two-time president of the Colorado Mountain Club, and is an avid alpine skier, mountain biker, and certified master diver. Mr. Bragg resides in Centennial, Colorado. He has written the following books and courses:

7 Habits of Effective CEOs	Change Management
7 Habits of Effective CFOs	Closing the Books
7 Habits of Effective Controllers	Coaching and Mentoring
Accountant Ethics [for multiple states]	Conflict Management
Accountants' Guidebook	Constraint Management
Accounting Changes and Error Corrections	Construction Accounting
Accounting Controls Guidebook	Corporate Bankruptcy
Accounting for Breweries	Corporate Cash Management
Accounting for Casinos and Gaming	Corporate Finance
Accounting for Derivatives and Hedges	Cost Accounting (college textbook)
Accounting for Earnings per Share	Cost Accounting Fundamentals
Accounting for Income Taxes	Cost Management Guidebook
Accounting for Intangible Assets	CPA Firm Mergers and Acquisitions
Accounting for Inventory	Credit & Collection Guidebook
Accounting for Investments	Crowdfunding
Accounting for Leases	Developing and Managing Teams
Accounting for Managers	Effective Collections
Accounting for Mining	Effective Employee Training
Accounting for Retirement Benefits	Effective Innovation
Accounting for Stock-Based Compensation	Effective Negotiation
Accounting for Vineyards and Wineries	Effective Time Management
Accounting Information Systems	Employee Onboarding
Accounting Procedures Guidebook	Enterprise Risk Management
Activity-Based Costing	Entertainment Industry Accounting
Activity-Based Management	Ethical Frameworks in Accounting
Agricultural Accounting	Ethical Responsibilities
Auditor Independence	Excel Charts and Visualizations
Behavioral Ethics	Excel Data Analysis Tools
Bookkeeping Guidebook	Excel Data Management
Budgeting	Excel Formulas and Functions
Business Combinations and Consolidations	Fair Value Accounting
Business Insurance Fundamentals	Fiduciary Accounting
Business Ratios	Financial Analysis
Business Strategy	Financial Forecasting and Modeling
Business Valuation	Fixed Asset Accounting
Capital Budgeting	Foreign Currency Accounting
CFO Guidebook	Franchise Accounting

Fraud Examination
Fraud Schemes
GAAP Guidebook
Governmental Accounting
Guide to Analytical Procedures
Guide to Audit Sampling
Guide to Audit Working Papers
Guide to Auditor Legal Liability
Guide to Data Analytics for Audits
Health Care Accounting
Hospitality Accounting
How to Audit Cash
How to Audit Equity
How to Audit Fixed Assets
How to Audit for Fraud
How to Audit Inventory
How to Audit Liabilities
How to Audit Payroll
How to Audit Procurement
How to Audit Receivables
How to Audit Revenue
How to Conduct a Compilation
How to Conduct a Review
How to Conduct an Audit Engagement
How to Run a Meeting
Human Resources Guidebook
IFRS Guidebook
Interpretation of Financial Statements
Introduction to Excel
Inventory Management
Investor Relations Guidebook
Key Performance Indicators
Law Firm Accounting
Lean Accounting Guidebook
Mergers & Acquisitions

Money Laundering
New Controller Guidebook
New Manager Guidebook
Nonprofit Accounting
Oil & Gas Accounting
Optimal Accounting for Cash
Optimal Accounting for Payables
Optimal Accounting for Payroll
Partnership Accounting
Payables Management
Payroll Management
Performance Appraisals
Persuasive Presentations
Project Accounting
Project Management
Property Management Accounting
Public Company Accounting
Purchasing Guidebook
Real Estate Accounting
Records Management
Recruiting and Hiring
Revenue Management
Revenue Recognition
Sales and Use Tax Accounting
Succession Planning
The Balance Sheet
The Income Statement
The MBA Guidebook
The Soft Close
The Statement of Cash Flows
The Year-End Close
Treasurer's Guidebook
Unethical Behavior
Working Capital Management

On-Line Resources by Steven Bragg

Steven maintains the accountingtools.com web site, which contains continuing professional education courses, the Accounting Best Practices podcast, and thousands of articles on accounting subjects.

Chapter 1
Introduction to Fixed Assets

Introduction

Why is a fixed asset different from other expenditures that are charged to expense right away? And how do we classify these fixed assets? This chapter introduces the concept of the fixed asset, describes when to classify an expenditure as a fixed asset, and provides further references to additional information about various fixed asset concepts that we will deal with later in this book.

What are Fixed Assets?

The vast majority of the expenditures that a company makes are for consumables, such as office supplies, wages, or products that it sells to customers. The effect of these items pass through the company quickly – they are used or sold and converted to cash, and they are recorded as expenses immediately, or with a slight delay (if they involve inventory). Thus, the benefits they generate are short-lived.

Fixed assets are entirely different. These are items that generate economic benefits over a long period of time. Because of the long period of usefulness of a fixed asset, it is not justifiable to charge its entire cost to expense when incurred. Instead, the *matching principle* comes into play. Under the matching principle, recognize both the benefits and expenses associated with a transaction (or, in this case, an asset) at the same time. To do so, we convert an expenditure into an asset, and use depreciation to gradually charge it to expense.

By designating an expenditure as a fixed asset, we are shifting the expenditure away from the income statement, where expenditures normally go, and instead place it in the balance sheet. As we gradually reduce its recorded cost through depreciation, the expenditure flows from the balance sheet to the income statement. Thus, the main difference between a normal expenditure and a fixed asset is that the fixed asset is charged to expense over a longer period of time.

The process of identifying fixed assets, recording them as assets, and depreciating them is time-consuming, so it is customary to build some limitations into the process that will route most expenditures directly to expense. One such limitation is to charge an expenditure to expense immediately unless it has a useful life of at least one year. Another limitation is to only recognize an expenditure as a fixed asset if it exceeds a certain dollar amount, known as the *capitalization limit* (see the Initial Fixed Asset Recognition chapter). These limits keep the vast majority of expenditures from being classified as fixed assets, which reduces the work of the accounting department.

EXAMPLE

Henderson Industrial incurs expenditures for three items, and must decide whether it should classify them as fixed assets. Henderson's capitalization limit is $2,500. The expenditures are:

- It buys a used mold for its plastic injection molding operation for $5,000. Henderson expects that the mold only has two months of useful life left, after which it should be scrapped. Since the useful life is so short, Henderson elects to charge the expenditure to expense immediately.
- It buys a laptop computer for $1,500, which has a useful life of three years. This expenditure is less than the capitalization limit, so Henderson charges it to expense.
- It buys a 10-ton injection molding machine for $50,000, which has a useful life of 10 years. Since this expenditure has a useful life of longer than one year and a cost greater than the capitalization limit, Henderson records it as a fixed asset, and will depreciate it over its 10-year useful life.

An alternative treatment of the $5,000 mold in the preceding example would be to record it under the Other Assets account in the balance sheet, and charge the cost to expense over two months. This is a useful alternative for expenditures that have useful lives of greater than one accounting period, but less than one year. It is a less time-consuming alternative for the accounting staff, which does not have to create a fixed asset record or engage in any depreciation calculations.

The "Fixed Asset" Designation

The "fixed asset" name is used in this book to describe the group of assets that generate economic benefits over a long period of time. The accounting literature and common usage have derived a somewhat longer name for the same assets, which is "property, plant, and equipment" (PP&E). You will find fixed assets listed as property, plant, and equipment in many balance sheets. The PP&E term is not used in this book for two reasons:

- The name describes a subset of all fixed assets, since it only implies the existence of land, buildings, and machinery.
- The PP&E name is simply too long.

Thus, we are using the more all-encompassing "fixed assets" term throughout the book.

Fixed Asset Classifications

If an expenditure qualifies as a fixed asset, it will be necessary to decide what its proper account classification should be. Account classifications are used to aggregate fixed assets into groups, in order to apply the same depreciation methods and useful lives to them.

General ledger accounts are usually created by classification, so that fixed asset transactions are stored within the classifications to which they belong (as described further in the Fixed Asset Record Keeping chapter). Here are the most common classifications used:

- *Buildings*. This account may include the cost of acquiring a building, or the cost of constructing one (in which case it is transferred from the Construction in Progress classification, described below). If the purchase price of a building includes the cost of land, apportion some of the cost to the Land account (which is not depreciated).
- *Computer equipment*. This classification can include a broad array of computer equipment, such as routers, servers, and backup power generators. It is useful to set the capitalization limit higher than the cost of desktop and laptop computers, in order to avoid tracking these items as assets.
- *Construction in progress*. This account is a temporary one, and is intended to store the ongoing cost of constructing a building; once completed, shift the balance in this account to the Buildings account, and then start depreciating it. Besides the materials and labor required for construction, architecture fees, the cost of building permits, and so forth can also be stored in this account.
- *Equipment*. This category includes production equipment, materials handling equipment, molds, the more expensive tools, and similar items.
- *Furniture and fixtures*. This is one of the broadest categories of fixed assets, since it can include such diverse assets as warehouse storage racks, office cubicles, and desks.
- *Intangible assets*. This is a non-physical asset, examples of which are trademarks, customer lists, literary works, broadcast rights, and patented technology.
- *Land*. This is the only asset that is not depreciated, because it is considered to have an indeterminate useful life. Include in this category all expenditures to prepare the land for its intended purpose, such as demolishing an existing building, or grading the land.
- *Land improvements*. Include any expenditures that add functionality to a parcel of land, such as irrigation systems, fencing, and landscaping.
- *Leasehold improvements*. These are improvements to leased space that are made by the tenant, and typically include office space, air conditioning, telephone wiring, and related permanent fixtures.
- *Office equipment*. This account contains such equipment as copiers, printers, and video equipment. Some companies elect to merge this classification into the furniture and fixtures classification, especially if they have few office equipment items.
- *Software*. Includes larger types of departmental or company-wide software, such as enterprise resources planning software or accounting software. Many desktop software packages are not sufficiently expensive to exceed the corporate capitalization limit.

- *Vehicles.* This account contains automobiles, tractors, trucks, and similar types of rolling stock.

A capital lease is not usually identified as a separate asset, since a lease merely identifies a form of financing; it does not identify the type of asset. Consequently, record the asset side of a capital lease in one of the above classifications. The liability side of the capital lease should be identified as a capital lease. See the Initial Fixed Asset Recognition chapter for more information.

> **Tip:** Do not create too many sub-classifications of fixed assets, such as automobiles, vans, light trucks, and heavy trucks within the main "vehicles" classification. If the classification system is too finely divided, there will inevitably be some "crossover" assets that could fall into several classifications. Also, having a large number of classifications requires extra tracking work by the accounting staff.

EXAMPLE

Henderson Industrial decides to construct a new production facility. It purchases land for $2 million, updates the land with irrigation systems and a parking lot for $300,000, and constructs the building for $5 million. It then purchases production equipment for the facility for $8 million, office equipment for $100,000, and furniture and fixtures for $400,000. It aggregates these purchases into the following fixed asset classifications:

Expenditure Item	Classification	Useful Life	Depreciation Method
Building - $5 million	Building	30 years	Straight line
Furniture and fixtures - $400,000	Furniture and fixtures	7 years	Straight line
Irrigation, parking lot - $300,000	Land improvements	15 years	Straight line
Land - $2 million	Land	Indeterminate	None
Office equipment - $100,000	Office equipment	5 years	Straight line
Production equipment - $8 million	Equipment	15 years	Straight line

> **Tip:** The local government that charges a company a personal property tax may require the completion of its tax forms using certain asset classifications. It may make sense to contact the government to see which classifications under which it wants the business to report, and adopt these classifications as the company's official classification system. By doing so, it will not be necessary to re-aggregate assets for personal property tax reporting.

Applicable Accounting Frameworks

The accounting for fixed assets is not uniform throughout the world. There are two primary accounting frameworks in use. One is Generally Accepted Accounting Principles (GAAP), which was founded in the United States, and which uses an extremely detailed, rules-oriented approach to mandating the treatment of accounting transactions. The other framework is International Financial Reporting Standards (IFRS), which has a greater orientation toward issuing higher-level guidelines than specific rules. IFRS is rapidly gaining acceptance outside of the United States, and it will likely become the dominant accounting framework at some point in the future.

Working committees from the organizations that create and update GAAP and IFRS meet regularly to resolve the differences in their approaches to fixed assets, but there are still variations in the two frameworks. Because of these differences, we are presenting both the GAAP and IFRS requirements for fixed asset accounting in the following chapters.

Accounting for Fixed Assets

There are several key points in the life of a fixed asset that require recognition in the accounting records; these are the initial recordation of the asset, the recognition of any asset retirement obligations, depreciation, subsequent changes in the recorded cost of the asset, impairment, and the eventual derecognition of the asset. We describe these general concepts below, and include a reference to the more comprehensive treatment in later chapters:

- *Initial recognition.* There are a number of factors to consider when initially recording a fixed asset, such as the base unit, which costs to include, and when to stop capitalizing costs. These issues are dealt with in the Initial Fixed Asset Recognition chapter, along with special situations involving capital leases, non-monetary exchanges, and business combinations.
- *Interest capitalization.* If an asset is being constructed, or it is requiring some time to bring a fixed asset to the condition and location intended for its use, it may be possible to capitalize the cost of the interest associated with the purchase. There are very specific rules for the use of interest capitalization, which are covered in the Interest Capitalization chapter.
- *Asset retirement obligations.* There are situations where it is possible to calculate the costs associated with retiring an asset, such as environmental remediation for a strip mine. These costs are known as *asset retirement obligations*, and their costs are recognized as part of the initial recordation of an asset. The Asset Retirement Obligations chapter addresses this topic.
- *Depreciation.* The cost of a fixed asset should be gradually charged to expense over time, using depreciation. There are a variety of depreciation methods available, which are described further in the Depreciation and Amortization chapter.
- *Subsequent changes.* Under limited circumstances under IFRS, it is allowable to revalue fixed assets, which has special accounting and disclosure requirements. This option, as well as the capitalization of subsequent expenditures, is discussed in the Subsequent Fixed Asset Measurement chapter.

- *Impairment.* If the fair value of a fixed asset falls below its recorded cost at any point during its useful life, one should reduce its recorded cost to its fair value, and recognize a loss for the difference between the two amounts. The Fixed Asset Impairment chapter delves into this accounting, as well as the options for reversing impairment if the fair value of a fixed asset subsequently rises.
- *Derecognition.* When an asset comes to the end of its useful life, a company will likely sell or otherwise dispose of it. At this time, it is removed from the accounting records, while a gain or loss (if any) is recorded on the final disposal transaction. This issue is discussed in the Fixed Asset Disposal chapter.

The accounting transactions noted above can involve a wide range of journal entries. Though the entries are integrated into the text of each chapter, they are also itemized in a journal entries appendix.

Accounting for Intangible Assets

The bulk of this book deals with *tangible* fixed assets – that is, assets having a physical presence. However, there are also *intangible* fixed assets, such as patents and copyrights, which have no physical substance. An intangible asset derives its value from the rights or privileges to which they entitle the entity that owns them. They are largely accounted for in the same manner as tangible fixed assets. When there is a unique accounting treatment for intangible assets, we make note of it, usually in a separate section within a chapter.

Accounting for Not-for-Profit Fixed Assets

An entity that is designated as a not-for-profit business may receive quite a large number of fixed assets as donations, which means that it does not incur a cost to obtain its assets. Since the initial recognition of a fixed asset is normally at its acquisition cost, how is a donated asset recorded? Or is it not recorded at all? This accounting is addressed in the Not-for-Profit Fixed Asset Accounting chapter.

Fixed Asset Disclosures

Fixed assets can comprise a large part of the assets listed on a company's balance sheet, so it is no surprise that both GAAP and IFRS require extensive disclosures of a variety of issues involving fixed assets, including:

- Asset impairment
- Asset retirement obligations
- Assets held for sale
- Capitalized interest
- Changes in accounting estimate
- Depreciation

- Estimates of recoverable amounts
- Intangible assets

GAAP and IFRS have different disclosure requirements, so we separately list their requirements in the Fixed Asset Disclosures chapter.

Fixed Asset Controls

Fixed assets can be quite expensive, and are also more mobile than the designation "fixed" assets would imply. Thus, there is a risk that they will be lost, damaged, or stolen. There are a number of controls over fixed assets that result in a close watch being maintained over them, such as asset tags, radio frequency identification tags that trigger an alarm if they pass a building exit, and assigning responsibility for each asset to a designated manager. Further, there is a risk that a fixed asset will be sold off without permission, or that the proceeds from the sale will be diverted. The controls for all of these issues and more are addressed in the Fixed Asset Controls chapter.

Fixed assets must be properly maintained to ensure that they remain usable through their useful lives. This calls for the use of ongoing preventive maintenance, but it is also possible to install controls in the form of sensors to warn of any impending equipment failures. These sensors, as well as location tracking sensors, are described in the Fixed Asset Tracking chapter.

As just noted, fixed assets can be quite expensive, so controls are needed over how they are approved for initial purchase or construction. This is an elaborate analysis and permission system called capital budgeting, and we cover it in the Capital Budgeting Analysis chapter.

Fixed Asset Policies and Procedures

There are many transactions involved in the life of a fixed asset, including such activities as capital budgeting, determining the correct costs to capitalize upon initial asset recognition, impairment testing, asset revaluation, and asset disposal. If these transactions are not handled in a consistent manner, the accuracy and reliability of the accounting records will likely suffer, and auditors will have an extremely difficult time verifying fixed asset records. The consistency of fixed asset record keeping can be greatly improved by formulating and closely adhering to a set of policies and procedures that address the most common fixed asset transactions. The Fixed Asset Policies and Procedures chapter contains a baseline set of policies and procedures that can be modified to meet the specific requirements of a business.

Fixed Asset Record Keeping

The preceding list of accounting activities should make it clear that a large amount of record keeping is required over the life span of a fixed asset. At a minimum, this includes the proper classification of asset classes, and setting up account numbers in the general ledger for assets, accumulated depreciation, and depreciation. It may also include more specialized accounting for construction projects. Furthermore, different types of records should be maintained for buildings, equipment, land, and leases, and decide how long to retain these documents. It is also useful to aggregate fixed asset information into the following reports:

- *Asset replacement report.* Includes information about each asset that allows for the prediction of when a fixed asset should be replaced.
- *Audit report.* Gives descriptive and location information for selected assets, in order to more easily locate them.
- *Depreciation report.* Summarizes the periodic depreciation and accumulated depreciation for each fixed asset.
- *Maintenance report.* Aggregates the scheduled and unscheduled maintenance associated with each asset, and links it to capacity utilization.
- *Responsibility report.* Notes the name of the person responsible for each asset, as well as the location of the asset.

All of the record keeping issues noted here, as well as the reports just described, are addressed in considerably more detail in the Fixed Asset Record Keeping chapter.

Fixed Asset Auditing

If a company has a loan outstanding with a lender, or is publicly held, it will likely undergo an annual audit. If the company has a large investment in fixed assets, the audit team will spend a considerable amount of time reviewing a selection of the fixed asset accounting transactions. The accounting, procedures, and controls already noted will probably cover the majority of the issues the auditors would normally find. Nonetheless, it is useful to know what specific items auditors ask for as part of an audit, as well as the audit steps normally included in their audit procedures. The Fixed Asset Auditing chapter provides this information.

Fixed Asset Measurements

A good management team wants to measure all aspects of a business, in order to maximize its efficiency, cash usage, and profits. The Fixed Asset Measurements chapter shows how to calculate the metrics that appear in the following table.

Sample Fixed Asset Measurements

Measurement	Reason for Use
Accumulated depreciation to fixed assets ratio	Determine whether asset replacement levels are changing over time
Bottleneck utilization	Determine the level of utilization of a constrained resource
Cash flow to fixed asset requirements ratio	Determine whether a business has sufficient cash flow to pay for planned fixed asset purchases
Repairs and maintenance expense to fixed assets ratio	Determine whether a company has unusual proportions of old assets or utilization levels
Return on assets employed	Calculate the return on all assets (not just fixed assets)
Return on operating assets	Calculate the return on all assets that are being actively used to create revenue
Sales to fixed assets ratio	Determine fixed asset usage levels compared to those of competitors
Unscheduled machine downtime	Determine the extent to which unscheduled machine downtime is interfering with production

Summary

This chapter has provided an overview of the nature of fixed assets, how to account for them, and a variety of other topics related to their management. We also provided references to the chapters later in this book that address these topics in much greater detail. In addition, a complete listing of the journal entries that may be needed to record transactions over the life of a fixed asset are noted in the Journal Entries appendix. Also, if there is any uncertainty about the meaning of a term, definitions are provided in the glossary at the end of the book.

Chapter 2
Capital Budgeting Analysis

Introduction

Capital budgeting is a series of analysis steps followed to justify the decision to purchase an asset, usually including an analysis of the costs, related benefits, and impact on capacity levels of the prospective purchase. In this chapter, we will address a broad array of issues to consider when deciding whether to recommend the purchase of a fixed asset, including constraint analysis, the lease versus buy decision, and post-acquisition auditing.

> **Related Podcast Episodes:** Episodes 45, 144, 145, and 147 of the Accounting Best Practices Podcast discuss throughput analysis, evaluating capital budgeting proposals, capital budgeting with minimal cash, and net present value analysis, respectively. The episodes are available at: **accountingtools.com/podcasts** or **iTunes**

Overview of Capital Budgeting

The normal capital budgeting process is for the management team to request proposals to acquire fixed assets from all parts of the company. Managers respond by filling out a standard request form, outlining what they want to buy and how it will benefit the company. The financial analyst or accountant then assists in reviewing these proposals to determine which are worthy of an investment. Any proposals that are accepted are included in the annual budget, and will be purchased during the next budget year. Fixed assets purchased in this manner also require a certain number of approvals, with more approvals required by increasingly senior levels of management if the sums involved are substantial.

These proposals come from all over the company, and so are likely not related to each other in any way. Also, the number of proposals usually far exceeds the amount of funding available. Consequently, management needs a method for ranking the priority of projects, with the possible result that some proposals are not accepted at all. The traditional method for doing so is net present value (NPV) analysis, which focuses on picking proposals with the largest amount of discounted cash flows.

The trouble with NPV analysis is that it does not account for how an investment might impact the profit generated by the entire system of production; instead, it tends to favor the optimization of specific work centers, which may have no particular impact on overall profitability. Also, the results of NPV are based on the future projections of cash flows, which may be wildly inaccurate. Managers may even tweak their cash flow estimates upward in order to gain project approval, when they know that actual cash flows are likely to be lower. Given these issues, we favor constraint analysis over NPV, though NPV is also discussed later in this chapter.

A better method for judging capital budget proposals is constraint analysis, which focuses on how to maximize use of the bottleneck operation. The bottleneck operation is the most constricted operation in a company; if the intent is to improve the overall profitability of the company, concentrate all attention on management of that bottleneck. This has a profound impact on capital budgeting, since a proposal should have some favorable impact on that operation in order to be approved.

There are two scenarios under which certain project proposals may avoid any kind of bottleneck or cash flow analysis. The first is a legal requirement to install an item. The prime example is environmental equipment, such as smokestack scrubbers, that are mandated by the government. In such cases, there may be some analysis to see if costs can be lowered, but the proposal *must* be accepted, so it will sidestep the normal analysis process.

The second scenario is when a company wants to mitigate a high-risk situation that could imperil the company. In this case, the emphasis is not on profitability at all, but rather on the avoidance of a situation. If so, the mandate likely comes from top management, so there is little additional need for analysis, other than a review to ensure that the lowest-cost alternative is selected.

A final scenario is when there is a sudden need for a fixed asset, perhaps due to the catastrophic failure of existing equipment, or due to a sudden strategic shift. These purchases can happen at any time, and so usually fall outside of the capital budget's annual planning cycle. It is generally best to require more than the normal number of approvals for these items, so that management is made fully aware of the situation. Also, if there is time to do so, they are worthy of an unusually intense analysis, to see if they really must be purchased at once, or if they can be delayed until the next capital budgeting approval period arrives.

Once all items are properly approved and inserted into the annual budget, this does not end the capital budgeting process. There is a final review just prior to actually making each purchase, with appropriate approval, to ensure that the company still needs each fixed asset.

The last step in the capital budgeting process is to conduct a post-implementation review, in which the actual costs and benefits of each fixed asset are summarized and compared to the initial projections included in the original application. If the results are worse than expected, this may result in a more in-depth review, with particular attention being paid to avoiding any faulty aspects of the original proposal in future proposals.

Bottleneck Analysis

Under constraint analysis, the key concept is that an entire company acts as a single system, which generates a profit. Under this concept, capital budgeting revolves around the following logic:

1. Nearly all of the costs of the production system do not vary with individual sales; that is, nearly every cost is an operating expense; therefore,

2. Maximize the throughput (which is sales minus all variable costs) of the *entire* system in order to pay for the operating expense; and
3. The only way to increase throughput is to maximize the throughput passing through the bottleneck operation.

Consequently, give primary consideration to those capital budgeting proposals that favorably impact the throughput passing through the bottleneck operation.

This does not mean that all other capital budgeting proposals will be rejected, since there are a multitude of possible investments that can reduce costs elsewhere in a company, and which are therefore worthy of consideration. However, throughput is more important than cost reduction, since throughput has no theoretical upper limit, whereas costs can only be reduced to zero. Given the greater ultimate impact on profits of throughput over cost reduction, any non-bottleneck proposal is simply not as important.

Net Present Value Analysis

Any capital investment involves an initial cash outflow to pay for it, followed by a mix of cash inflows in the form of revenue, or a decline in existing cash flows that are caused by expense reductions. We can lay out this information in a spreadsheet to show all expected cash flows over the useful life of an investment, and then apply a discount rate that reduces the cash flows to what they would be worth at the present date. This calculation is known as *net present value*.

Net present value is the traditional approach to evaluating capital proposals, since it is based on a single factor – cash flows – that can be used to judge any proposal arriving from anywhere in a company.

EXAMPLE

Milford Sound, a manufacturer of audio equipment, is planning to acquire an asset that it expects will yield positive cash flows for the next five years. Its cost of capital is 10%, which it uses as the discount rate to construct the net present value of the project. The following table shows the calculation:

Year	Cash Flow	10% Discount Factor	Present Value
0	-$500,000	1.0000	-$500,000
1	+130,000	0.9091	+118,183
2	+130,000	0.8265	+107,445
3	+130,000	0.7513	+97,669
4	+130,000	0.6830	+88,790
5	+130,000	0.6209	+80,717
		Net Present Value	-$7,196

The net present value of the proposed project is negative at the 10% discount rate, so Milford should not invest in the project.

In the "10% Discount Factor" column, the factor becomes smaller for periods further in the future, because the discounted value of cash flows are reduced as they progress further from the present day. The discount factor is widely available in textbooks, or can be derived from the following formula:

$$\text{Present value of a future cash flow} = \frac{\text{Future cash flow}}{(1 + \text{Discount rate})^{\text{squared by the number of periods of discounting}}}$$

To use the formula for an example, if we forecast the receipt of \$100,000 in one year, and are using a discount rate of 10 percent, the calculation is:

$$\text{Present value} = \frac{\$100,000}{(1+.10)^1}$$

Present value = \$90,909

A net present value calculation that truly reflects the reality of cash flows will likely be more complex than the one shown in the preceding example. It is best to break down the analysis into a number of sub-categories, to see exactly when cash flows are occurring and with what activities they are associated. Here are the more common contents of a net present value analysis:

- *Asset purchases.* All of the expenditures associated with the purchase, delivery, installation, and testing of the asset being purchased.
- *Asset-linked expenses.* Any ongoing expenses, such as warranty agreements, property taxes, and maintenance, that are associated with the asset.
- *Contribution margin.* Any incremental cash flows resulting from sales that can be attributed to the project.
- *Depreciation effect.* The asset will be depreciated, and this depreciation shelters a portion of any net income from income taxes, so note the income tax reduction caused by depreciation.
- *Expense reductions.* Any incremental expense reductions caused by the project, such as automation that eliminates direct labor hours.
- *Tax credits.* If an asset purchase triggers a tax credit (such as for a purchase of energy-reduction equipment), note the credit.
- *Taxes.* Any income tax payments associated with net income expected to be derived from the asset.

- *Working capital changes.* Any net changes in inventory, accounts receivable, or accounts payable associated with the asset. Also, when the asset is eventually sold off, this may trigger a reversal of the initial working capital changes.

By itemizing the preceding factors in a net present value analysis, it is easier to review and revise individual line items.

We have given priority to bottleneck analysis over net present value as the preferred method for analyzing capital proposals, because bottleneck analysis focuses on throughput. The key improvement factor is throughput, since there is no upper limit on the amount of throughput that can be generated, whereas there are only so many operating expenses that can be reduced. This does not mean that net present value should be eliminated as a management tool. It is still quite useful for operating expense reduction analysis, where throughput issues are not involved.

The Payback Method

The most discerning method for evaluating a capital budgeting proposal is its impact on the bottleneck operation, while net present value analysis yields a detailed analysis of cash flows. The simplest and least accurate evaluation technique is the payback method. This approach is still heavily used, because it provides a very fast "back of the envelope" calculation of how soon a company will earn back its investment. This means that it provides a rough measure of how long a company will have its investment at risk, before earning back the original amount expended. Thus, it is a rough measure of risk. There are two ways to calculate the payback period, which are:

1. *Simplified.* Divide the total amount of an investment by the average resulting cash flow. This approach can yield an incorrect assessment, because a proposal with cash flows skewed far into the future can yield a payback period that differs substantially from when actual payback occurs.
2. *Manual calculation.* Manually deduct the forecasted positive cash flows from the initial investment amount, from Year 1 forward, until the investment is paid back. This method is slower, but ensures a higher degree of accuracy.

EXAMPLE

Milford Sound has received a proposal from a manager, asking to spend $1,500,000 on equipment that will result in cash inflows in accordance with the following table:

Year	Cash Flow
1	+$150,000
2	+150,000
3	+200,000
4	+600,000
5	+900,000

The total cash flows over the five-year period are projected to be $2,000,000, which is an average of $400,000 per year. When divided into the $1,500,000 original investment, this results in a payback period of 3.75 years. However, the briefest perusal of the projected cash flows reveals that the flows are heavily weighted toward the far end of the time period, so the results of this calculation cannot be correct.

Instead, the accountant runs the calculation year by year, deducting the cash flows in each successive year from the remaining investment. The results of this calculation are:

Year	Cash Flow	Net Invested Cash
0		-$1,500,000
1	+$150,000	-1,350,000
2	+150,000	-1,200,000
3	+200,000	-1,000,000
4	+600,000	-400,000
5	+900,000	0

The table indicates that the real payback period is located somewhere between Year 4 and Year 5. There is $400,000 of investment yet to be paid back at the end of Year 4, and there is $900,000 of cash flow projected for Year 5. The accountant assumes the same monthly amount of cash flow in Year 5, which means that he can estimate final payback as being just short of 4.5 years.

The payback method is not overly accurate, does not provide any estimate of how profitable a project may be, and does not take account of the time value of money. Nonetheless, its extreme simplicity makes it a perennial favorite in many companies.

Discounted Payback

The accuracy of the payback method can be improved by incorporating the time value of money into the cash flows expected in each future year, which is known as discounted payback. However, doing so increases the complexity of this analysis method. To apply the time value of money to the calculation, follow these steps:

1. Create a table in which is listed the expected cash outflow related to the investment in Year 0.
2. In the following lines of the table, enter the cash inflows expected from the investment in each subsequent year.
3. Multiply the expected annual cash inflows in each year in the table by the applicable discount rate, using the same interest rate for all of the periods in the table. No discount rate is applied to the initial investment, since it occurs at once.
4. Create a column on the far right side of the table that lists the cumulative discounted cash flow for each year. The calculation in this final column is to add back the discounted cash flow in each period to the remaining negative balance from the preceding period. The balance is initially negative because it includes the cash outflow to fund the project.
5. When the cumulative discounted cash flow becomes positive, the time period that has passed up until that point represents the payback period.

EXAMPLE

We will continue with the preceding example. Milagro has a cost of capital of 7%, so the present value factor for 7% is included in the payback table, with the following results:

Year	Cash Flow	7% Present Value Factor	Cash Flow Present Value	Net Invested Cash
0				-$1,500,000
1	+$150,000	0.9346	+$140,190	-1,359,810
2	+150,000	0.8734	+131,010	-1,228,800
3	+200,000	0.8163	+163,260	-1,065,540
4	+600,000	0.7629	+457,740	-607,800
5	+900,000	0.7130	+641,700	-33,900

The discounted payback calculation reveals that the payback period will be slightly longer than the five years of cash flows presented in the manager's original proposal.

The concept of discounted payback does have some value, for it indicates the point in time at which the initial investment has been recouped on a discounted basis. If a project is still expected to have a significant useful life after this point has been reached, then there is ample opportunity for additional returns to be generated. Alternatively, if the discounted payback is late in the useful life of an investment, then there is a substantial risk that no positive returns will ever be generated. From this viewpoint, a project with (for example) a discounted payback of two years with two additional years remaining in its useful life could be a better investment than a project with a discounted payback of three years with one additional year remaining thereafter in its useful life.

Capital Budget Proposal Analysis

Reviewing a capital budget proposal does not necessarily mean passing judgment on it exactly as presented. A variety of suggestions can be attached to an analysis of a proposal, which management may incorporate into a revised proposal. Here are some examples:

- *Asset capacity*. Does the asset have more capacity than is actually needed under the circumstances? Is there a history of usage spikes that call for extra capacity? Depending on the answers to these questions, consider using smaller assets with less capacity. If the asset is powered, this may also lead to reductions in utility costs, installation costs, and floor space requirements.
- *Asset commoditization*. Wherever possible, avoid custom-designed machinery in favor of standard models that are readily available. By doing so, it is easier to obtain repair parts, and there may even be an aftermarket for disposing of the asset when the company no longer needs it.
- *Asset features*. Managers have a habit of wanting to buy new assets with all of the latest features. Are all of these features really needed? If an asset is being replaced, it is useful to compare the characteristics of the old and new assets, and examine any differences between the two to see if they are really needed. If the asset is the only model offered by the supplier, would the supplier be willing to strip away some features and offer it at a lower price?
- *Asset standardization*. If a company needs a particular asset in large quantities, adopt a policy of always buying from the same manufacturer, and preferably only buying the same asset every time. By doing so, the maintenance staff becomes extremely familiar with maintenance requirements, and only has to stock replacement parts for one model.
- *Bottleneck analysis*. As noted earlier in this chapter, assets that improve the amount of throughput in a production operation are usually well worth the investment, while those not impacting the bottleneck require substantially more justification, usually in the direction of reducing operating expenses.
- *Extended useful life*. A manager may be applying for an asset replacement simply because the original asset has reached the end of its recommended useful life. But is it really necessary to replace the asset? Consider conducting a formal review of these assets to see if they can still be used for some additional period of time. There may be additional maintenance costs involved, but this will almost certainly be lower than the cost of replacing the asset.
- *Facility analysis*. If a capital proposal involves the acquisition of additional facility space, consider reviewing any existing space to see if it can be compressed, thereby eliminating the need for more space. For example, shift storage items to less expensive warehouse space, shift from offices to more

17

space-efficient cubicles, and encourage employees to work from home or on a later shift. If none of these ideas work, at least consider acquiring new facilities through a sublease, which tends to require shorter lease terms than a lease arranged with the primary landlord.

- *Monument elimination.* A company may have a large fixed asset around which the rest of the production area is configured; this is called a monument. If there is a monument, consider adopting a policy of using a larger number of lower-capacity assets. By doing so, the risk of having a single monument asset go out of service and stopping all production is avoided, in favor of having multiple units, among which work can be shifted if one unit fails.

The sponsors of capital proposals frequently do *not* appreciate this additional review of their proposals, since it implies that they did not consider these issues themselves. Nonetheless, the savings can be substantial, and so are well worth the aggravation of dealing with annoyed managers.

If the additional review indicates some promising alternatives that may substantially reduce the cost of a proposal, if not eliminate it entirely, it may be politically wise to route the proposed changes through the controller or chief financial officer, who may have the clout to force a serious review of the alternatives by the project sponsor.

The Outsourcing Decision

It may be possible to avoid a capital purchase entirely by outsourcing the work to which it is related. By doing so, the company may be able to eliminate all assets related to the area (rather than acquiring more assets), while the burden of maintaining a sufficient asset base now shifts to the supplier. The supplier may even buy the company's assets related to the area being outsourced. This situation is a well-established alternative for high technology manufacturing, as well as for information technology services, but is likely not viable outside of these areas.

If outsourcing is a possibility, the likely cash flows resulting from doing so will be highly favorable for the first few years, as capital expenditures vanish. However, the supplier must also earn a profit and pay for its own infrastructure, so the cost over the long term will probably not vary dramatically from what a company would have experienced if it had kept a functional area in-house. There are three exceptions that can bring about a long-term cost reduction. They are:

- *Excess capacity.* A supplier may have such a large amount of excess capacity already that it does not need to invest further for some time, thereby potentially depressing the costs that it would otherwise pass through to its customers. However, this excess capacity pool will eventually dry up, so it tends to be a short-term anomaly.
- *High volume.* There are some outsourcing situations where the supplier is handling such a massive volume of activity from multiple customers that its

costs on a per-unit basis decline below the costs that a company could ever achieve on its own. This situation can yield long-term savings to a company.

- *Low costs.* A supplier may locate its facility and work force in low-cost countries or regions within countries. This can yield significant cost reductions in the short term, but as many suppliers use the same technique, it is driving up costs in all parts of the world. Thus, this cost disparity is useful for a period of time, but is gradually declining as a long-term option.

There are also risks involved in shifting functions to suppliers. First, a supplier may go out of business, leaving the company scrambling to shift work to a new supplier. Second, a supplier may gradually ramp up prices to the point where the company is substantially worse off than if it had kept the function in-house. Third, the company may have so completely purged the outsourced function from its own operations that it is now completely dependent on the supplier, and has no ability to take it back in-house. Fourth, the supplier's service level may decline to the point where it is impairing the ability of the company to operate. And finally, the company may have entered into a multi-year deal, and cannot escape from the arrangement if the business arrangement does not work out. These are significant issues, and must be weighed as part of the outsourcing decision.

The cautions noted here about outsourcing do not mean that it should be avoided as an option. On the contrary, a rapidly growing company that has minimal access to funds may cheerfully hand off multiple operations to suppliers in order to avoid the up-front costs associated with those operations. Outsourcing is less attractive to stable, well-established companies that have better access to capital.

In summary, outsourcing is an attractive option for rapidly growing companies that do not have sufficient cash to pay for capital expenditures, but also carries with it a variety of risks involving shifting key functions to a supplier over which a company may not have a great deal of control.

The Capital Budgeting Application Form

Most companies require managers to fill out a standardized form for all capital budgeting proposals. The type of information included in the form will vary, depending on whether the approval decision is based on bottleneck considerations or the results of a net present value analysis. However, the header section of the form will likely be the same in all circumstances. It identifies the project, its sponsor, the date on which it was submitted, and a unique product identification number that is filled in by the recipient. A sample header is:

Sample Application Header

Project name:	50 Ton plastic injection molder		
Project sponsor:	E. R. Edison		
Submission date:	May 28	Project number:	2020-14

If a proposal is for a legal requirement or a risk mitigation issue, it is absolved from most analysis, and will likely move to the top of the approved project list. Consequently, the form should contain a separate section for these types of projects, and should involve a different set of approvers. The corporate attorney may be involved, as well as anyone involved in risk management. A sample block in the application form for legal and risk mitigation issues follows.

Sample Legal and Risk Mitigation Block

		Required Approvals	
Initial cash flow:	-$250,000	All proposals	*Susan Lafferty*
Year 1 cash flow:	-10,000		Attorney
Year 2 cash flow:	-10,000		
Year 3 cash flow:	-10,000	< $100,000	*George Mason*
			Risk Officer
Describe legal or risk mitigation issue:			
Replanting of pine forest on southern property, with annual forestry review, per new zoning requirements		$100,000+	*Fred Scurry*
			President

If the election is made to focus on bottleneck considerations for capital budgeting approvals, include the following block of text in the application form. This block focuses on the changes in cash flow that are associated with a capital expenditure. The block requests an itemization of the cash flows involved in the purchase (primarily for finance planning considerations), followed by requests for information about how the investment will help the company – via an improvement in throughput, a reduction in operating costs, or an increase in the return on investment. In the example, note that the primary improvement used as the basis for the proposal is the improvement in throughput. This also leads to an enhancement of the return on investment. There is an increase in the total net operating cost, which represents a reduction in the positive effect of the throughput, and which is caused by the annual $8,000 maintenance cost associated with the investment.

The approvals for a bottleneck-related investment change from the ones shown previously for a legal or risk mitigation investment. In this case, a process analyst verifies the information include in the block, to ensure that the applicant's claims are correct. The supervisor in whose area of responsibility the investment falls should also sign off, thereby accepting responsibility for the outcome of the investment. A higher-level manager, or even the board of directors, approves any really large investment proposals.

Sample Bottleneck Approval Block

		Required Approvals	
Initial cash flow:	-$125,000	All proposals	*Monica Byers*
Year 1 cash flow:	-8,000		Process Analyst
Year 2 cash flow:	-8,000		
Year 3 cash flow:	-8,000	< $100,000	*Al Rogers*
			Responsible Supervisor
Net throughput change:*	+$180,000		
		$100,000+	*Fred Scurry*
Net operating cost change:*	+$8,000		President
Change in ROI:*	+0.08%		

* On an annual basis

If a bottleneck-oriented application is not used, then the following block may be useful in the application. It is based on the more traditional analysis of net present value. Consider using this block as a supplement to the bottleneck block just noted, in case some managers prefer to work with both sets of information.

Sample Net Present Value Approval Block

Year	Cash Out (payments)	Cash In (Revenue)	Incremental Tax Effect	Totals
0	-$1,000,000			-$1,000,000
1	-25,000	+$200,000	+$8,750	+183,750
2	-25,000	+400,000	-61,250	+313,750
3	-25,000	+400,000	-61,250	+313,750
4	-25,000	+400,000	-61,250	+313,750
5	-25,000	+400,000	-61,250	+313,750
Totals	-$1,125,000	+$1,800,000	-$236,250	+$438,750
			Tax Rate:	35%
			Hurdle Rate:	12%
			Net Present Value:	+$13,328

The net present value block requires the presentation of cash flows over a five-year period, as well as the net tax effect resulting from this specific transaction. The tax effect is based on $25,000 of maintenance expenses in every year shown, as well as $200,000 of annual depreciation, and a 35% incremental tax rate. Thus, in Year 2, there is $400,000 of revenue, less $225,000 of depreciation and maintenance expenses, multiplied by 35%, resulting in an incremental tax effect of $61,250.

The block then goes on to state the corporate hurdle rate, which is 12% in the example. We then discount the stream of cash flows from the project at the hurdle rate of 12%, which results in a positive net present value of $13,328. Based on just the net present value analysis, this appears to be an acceptable project.

A variation on the rather involved text just shown is to shift the detailed cash flow analysis to a backup document, and only show the resulting net present value in the application form.

The text blocks shown here contain much of the key information that management should see before it decides whether to approve a capital investment. In addition, there should be a considerable amount of supporting information that precisely describes the nature of the proposed investment, as well as backup information that supports each number included in the form.

The Post Installation Review

It is very important to conduct a post installation review of any capital expenditure project, to see if the initial expectations for it were realized. If not, the results of this review can be used to modify the capital budgeting process to include better information.

Another reason for having a post installation review is that it provides a control over those managers who fill out the initial capital budgeting proposals. If they know there is no post installation review, they can wildly overstate the projected results of their projects with impunity, just to have them approved. Of course, this control is only useful if it is conducted relatively soon after a project is completed. Otherwise, the responsible manager may have moved on in his career, and can no longer be tied back to the results of his work.

It is even better to begin a post installation review while a project is still being implemented, and especially when the implementation period is expected to be long. This initial review gives senior management a good idea of whether the cost of a project is staying close to its initial expectations. If not, management may need to authorize more vigorous management of the project, scale it back, or even cancel it outright.

If the post implementation review results in the suspicion that a project proposal was unduly optimistic, this brings up the question of how to deal with the responsible manager. At a minimum, the proposal reviews can flag any future proposals by this reviewer as suspect, and worthy of especially close attention. Another option is to tie long-term compensation to the results of these projects. A third possibility is to include the results of these project reviews in personnel reviews, which may lead to a reduction in employee compensation. A really catastrophic result may even be grounds for the termination of the responsible party.

EXAMPLE

Milford Sound has just completed a one-year project to increase the amount of production capacity at its speaker production work center. The original capital budgeting proposal was for an initial expenditure of $290,000, resulting in additional annual throughput of $100,000 per year. The actual result is somewhat different. The accountant's report includes the following text:

> **Findings:** The proposal only contained the purchase price of the equipment. However, since the machinery was delivered from Germany, Milford also incurred $22,000 of freight charges and $3,000 in customs fees. Further, the project required the installation of a new concrete pad, a breaker box, and electrical wiring that cost an additional $10,000. Finally, the equipment proved to be difficult to configure, and required $20,000 of consulting fees from the manufacturer, as well as $5,000 for the materials scrapped during testing. Thus, the actual cost of the project was $350,000.

> Subsequent operation of the equipment reveals that it cannot operate without an average of 20% downtime for maintenance, as opposed to the 5% downtime that was advertised by the manufacturer. This reduces throughput by 15%, which equates to a drop of $15,000 in throughput per year, to $85,000.

> **Recommendations:** To incorporate a more comprehensive set of instructions into the capital budgeting proposal process to account for transportation, setup, and testing costs. Also, given the wide difference between the performance claims of the manufacturer and actual results, to hire a consultant to see if the problem is caused by our installation of the equipment; if not, we recommend not buying from this supplier in the future.

The Lease or Buy Decision

Once the asset acquisition decision has been made, management still needs to decide if it should buy the asset outright, or lease it. In a leasing situation, a lessor buys the asset and then allows the lessee to use it in exchange for a monthly fee. Depending on the terms of the lease, it may be treated in one of two ways:

- *Capital lease.* The lessee records the leased asset on its books as a fixed asset and depreciates it, while recording interest expense separately.
- *Operating lease.* The lessor records the leased asset on its books as a fixed asset and depreciates it, while the lessee simply records a lease payment.

The decision to use a lease may be based on management's unwillingness to use its line of credit or other available sources of financing to buy an asset. Leases can be easier to obtain than a line of credit, since the lease agreement always designates the asset as collateral.

There are a multitude of factors that a lessor includes in the formulation of the monthly rate that it charges, such as the down payment, the residual value of the asset at the end of the lease, and the interest rate, which makes it difficult to break out and examine each element of the lease. Instead, it is much easier to create separate net present value tables for the lease and buy alternatives, and then compare the results of the two tables to see which is the better alternative.

EXAMPLE

Milford Sound is contemplating the purchase of an asset for $500,000. It can buy the asset outright, or do so with a lease. Its cost of capital is 8%, and its incremental income tax rate is 35%. The following two tables show the net present values of both options.

Buy Option

Year	Depreciation	Income Tax Savings (35%)	Discount Factor (8%)	Net Present Value
0				-$500,000
1	$100,000	$35,000	0.9259	32,407
2	100,000	35,000	0.8573	30,006
3	100,000	35,000	0.7938	27,783
4	100,000	35,000	0.7350	25,725
5	100,000	35,000	0.6806	23,821
Totals	$500,000	$175,000		$360,258

Lease Option

Year	Pretax Lease Payments	Income Tax Savings (35%)	After-Tax Lease Cost	Discount Factor (8%)	Net Present Value
1	$135,000	47,250	$87,750	0.9259	$81,248
2	135,000	47,250	87,750	0.8573	75,228
3	135,000	47,250	87,750	0.7938	69,656
4	135,000	47,250	87,750	0.7350	64,496
5	135,000	47,250	87,750	0.6806	59,723
Totals	$675,000	$236,250	$438,750		$350,351

Thus, the net purchase cost of the buy option is $360,258, while the net purchase cost of the lease option is $350,351. The lease option involves the lowest cash outflow for Milford, and so is the better option.

Leasing Concerns

There is an undeniable attraction to acquiring assets with a lease, since it replaces a large up-front cash outflow with a series of monthly payments. However, before signing a lease agreement, be aware of the following issues that can increase the cost of the arrangement:

- *Buyout price*. Many leases include an end-of-lease buyout price that is inordinately high. If the lessee wants to continue using a leased asset, the buyout price may be so outrageous that the only realistic alternative is to continue making lease payments, which generates outsized profits for the lessor. Therefore, always negotiate the size of the buyout payment before signing a lease agreement. If the buyout is stated as the "fair market value" of the asset at the end of the lease term, the amount can be subject to interpretation, so include a clause that allows for arbitration to determine the amount of fair market value.
- *Deposit*. The lessor may require that an inordinately large deposit be made at the beginning of the lease term, from which the lessor can then earn interest over the term of the lease.
- *Deposit usage*. The terms of a lease may allow the lessor to charge any number of fees against the up-front deposit made by the lessee, resulting in little of the deposit being returned at the end of the lease.
- *Lease fee*. The lessor may charge a lease fee, which is essentially a paperwork charge to originate the lease. It may be possible to reduce or eliminate this fee.
- *Rate changes*. The lessor may offer a low lease rate during the beginning periods of a lease, and then escalate the rates later in the lease term. Be sure to calculate the average lease rate to see if the implicit interest rate is reasonable. In these sorts of arrangements, a rate ramp-up usually indicates an average interest rate that is too high.
- *Return fees*. When the lease term is over, the lessor may require that the leased asset be shipped at the lessee's cost to a distant location, and sometimes even in the original packaging.
- *Termination notification*. The lease agreement may require the lessee to notify the lessor in writing that it intends to terminate the lease as of the termination date stated in the contract. If the lessee does not issue this notification in a timely manner, it is obligated to continue leasing the asset, or to pay a large termination fee. Whenever this clause appears in a lease agreement, always negotiate it down to the smallest possible termination notification period.
- *Wear-and-tear standards*. A lease agreement may contain unreasonable standards for assigning a high rate of wear-and-tear to leased assets when they have been returned to the lessor, resulting in additional fees being charged to the lessee.

In short, many lessors rely upon obfuscation of the lease terms to generate a profit, so it makes sense to delve into every clause in a lease agreement and to be willing to bargain hard for changes to the terms. Also, have a well-managed system in place for retaining lease agreements and monitoring when the key dates associated with each lease will arise. Finally, conduct a cost review after each lease agreement has been terminated, to determine the total out-of-pocket cost and implicit interest rate; the result may be the discovery that certain lessors routinely gouge the company, and should not be used again.

In addition to the issues just noted, the lessee also loses access to any favorable changes in the residual value of leased assets, since the lessor usually retains ownership of the assets. Also, the lessee cannot take advantage of the tax benefits of depreciation when a lease is classified as an operating lease; instead, the lessor records the depreciation and takes advantage of the related tax benefits. This latter issue may not be a concern if the lessee has minimal taxable income that could be reduced by a depreciation charge, and does not expect to be able to use a net operating loss carryforward in future years.

The list of concerns with leasing arrangements may appear formidable. However, they also have a number of advantages, as explained in the next section.

Leasing Advantages

The leasing concerns just described should introduce a note of caution into dealings with lessors, since a careful analysis of lease terms may reveal an inordinately high cost. However, there are also a number of advantages to leasing, which include:

- *Asset servicing.* The lessor may have a sophisticated asset servicing capability. Though the cost of this servicing may be high, it can result in fast servicing intervals and therefore extremely high equipment usage levels. In some cases, the presence of a servicing capability may be the main attraction of a leasing deal.
- *Competitive lease rates.* A lessor can offer quite competitive lease rates. This situation arises when a lessor buys assets in such high volumes that it can obtain volume purchase discounts from suppliers, some of which it may pass along to lessees. The lessor may also be able to borrow funds at a lower rate than the lessee, and can share some of the cost differential.
- *Financing accessibility.* A lessor is more likely to enter into a leasing arrangement with a company that is experiencing low profitability than a traditional lender. This is because the leased asset is collateral for the lessor, which can take the asset back if the lessee is unable to continue making timely lease payments. Conversely, a traditional lender might have a considerably more difficult time accessing company assets, and so would be less inclined to lend funds for the purchase of assets.
- *New technology.* A non-monetary advantage of leasing is that a company is continually swapping out old equipment for newer and more technologically advanced equipment. This can present a competitive advantage in those cases where the equipment is being used within a core function, or used to enhance products or services.
- *Off-balance sheet transaction.* Depending on the terms of a leasing arrangement, it may be possible for a lessee to avoid having to state its re-

maining lease payment liabilities on its balance sheet. By doing so, the balance sheet shows the company as having fewer obligations than is really the case, and so the business appears more solvent. However, it may still be necessary to reveal the annual amount of future lease payments in the accompanying financial statement disclosures.

- *Reserve available debt.* The company can reserve room on its existing line of credit by instead using a lease to buy an asset.
- *Short-term usage.* A leasing arrangement can be an effective alternative for those assets that are expected to have little value by the end of their lease terms, or for which the company expects to install a replacement asset at about the time of the lease termination.

Capital Budgeting with Little Cash

This chapter has been about deciding how to allocate cash to prospective purchases of fixed assets. But what if there is little cash on hand with which to buy any fixed assets? This could involve a startup company, or any business that has fallen on hard times. In this situation, the main principle to follow is to conserve cash, which means that the capital budgeting objectives change to the sole pursuit of the conservation of cash. A business in this position needs to figure out ways to get the maximum return on investment as fast as possible, while spending next to nothing. Here are some options:

- *Repair existing equipment.* Repair what the business already has, or root around in the warehouse and see if there is old equipment that can be repaired. Repairs are usually far less expensive than buying new equipment. This repaired equipment may be less inefficient than newer machines, but since the investment is minimal, the loss in efficiency is acceptable.
- *Extend operating hours.* Extend the operating hours of the existing equipment. It can be much less expensive to have a few people work an extra shift – even if they are not very efficient – than to buy new equipment. Better yet, do not just work two shifts – run the machinery for *three* shifts. Efficiency will absolutely go down if this is done, because the equipment will need more maintenance time – but it still saves cash.
- *Outsource.* Focus hard on outsourcing instead of capital purchases. Even if the returns are a bit worse by shifting work to a supplier, that is still better than investing cash in new equipment. The situation – hopefully – will improve at some point in the future, so keep options open for bringing production back in house. This might mean signing off on just a short-term deal with a supplier.
- *Buy second-hand equipment.* Old equipment may not be overly efficient, and it may be in need of repair, and it may have a short useful life; but if it requires little cash, consider this type of purchase.
- *Lease equipment.* The company may not be in very good financial condition, but it can still be possible to persuade a leasing company to issue a lease,

since it can use the value of the leased equipment as collateral. Doing so delays the outflow of cash by shifting to monthly lease payments.

There are also ways to enhance incoming cash flows through certain types of fixed asset purchases. The focus needs to be on providing an immediate inflow of cash. If it is possible to acquire equipment that can generate revenue at once, that is better than acquiring equipment that takes so long to set up that the business cannot use it to generate cash flow for months.

A variation on the immediate cash inflow concept is to completely avoid any purchases for which product sales are uncertain. Instead, there should be customer orders in hand or promised before any cash expenditure is made for fixed assets. This is no time to be taking chances on speculative revenues.

This discussion did not address any net present value analysis, because the point was to focus on businesses that are in pure survival mode. When a company is in this position, it does not need to concern itself with multi-year returns on investment. Instead, the point is to survive for another day, so net present value is not overly relevant.

Some of the investment paths recommended in this section may not result in the most efficient operations. In particular, the business is likely to have acquired an odd assemblage of assets that may not work together very well. That is acceptable in the short term, but should be addressed if the company can survive for a longer period of time, when there will hopefully be more money to enhance operations. If the company can last that long, consider selling off the older machines in a few years and using the excess cash to buy what management wanted in the first place.

Summary

This chapter addressed a variety of issues to consider when deciding whether to recommend the purchase of a fixed asset. We put less emphasis on net present value analysis, which has been the primary capital budgeting tool in industry for years, because it does not take into consideration the impact on throughput of a company's bottleneck operation. The best capital budgeting analysis process is to give top priority to project proposals that have a strong favorable impact on throughput, and then use net present value to evaluate the impact of any remaining projects on cost reduction.

Chapter 3
Initial Fixed Asset Recognition

Introduction

The basic process of recognizing a newly-acquired fixed asset in a company's accounting records may at first appear quite simple – just record the acquisition cost. This simple rule will apply to the majority of a company's fixed assets. However, there are also some special situations that complicate the accounting, such as the appropriate designation of a base unit, acquired assets, capital leases, and asset exchanges. Further, International Financial Reporting Standards (IFRS) are somewhat different from Generally Accepted Accounting Principles (GAAP). In this chapter, we deal with not only the basic initial recordation of a fixed asset under GAAP and IFRS, but also the variety of special scenarios just noted.

The Capitalization Limit

One of the most important decisions to be made in the initial recognition of a fixed asset is what minimum cost level to use, below which an expenditure is recorded as an expense in the period incurred, rather than recording it as a fixed asset and depreciating it over time. This capitalization limit, which is frequently abbreviated as the *cap limit*, is usually driven by the following factors:

- *Asset tracking*. If an expenditure is recorded as a fixed asset, the fixed asset tracking system may impose a significant amount of control over the newly-recorded fixed asset. This can be good, in order to know where an asset is at any time. Conversely, there is not usually a tracking system in place for an expenditure that is charged to expense, since the assumption is that such items are consumed at once, and so require no subsequent tracking.
- *Fixed asset volume*. The number of expenditures that will be recorded as fixed assets will increase dramatically as the cap limit is lowered. For example, there may only be one fixed asset if the cap limit is $100,000, 50 assets if the cap limit is $10,000, and 500 assets if the cap limit is $1,000. Analyze historical expenditures to estimate a cap limit that will prevent the accounting staff from being deluged with additional fixed asset records.
- *Profit pressure*. Senior management may have a strong interest in reporting the highest possible profit levels right now, which means that they want a very low cap limit that shifts as many expenditures as possible into capitalized assets. Since this pressure can result in a vast number of very low-cost fixed assets, this issue can create a significant work load for the accounting staff.

- *Record keeping cost.* What is the lowest asset cost at which it becomes burdensome to track an individual fixed asset? There is a labor cost associated with each fixed asset, which includes depreciation, derecognition, impairment, and auditing transactions.
- *Tax requirements.* Some government entities require that fixed assets be reported, so that they can charge a personal property tax that is calculated from the reported fixed asset levels. Clearly, a high cap limit will reduce the number of reported fixed assets, and therefore the tax paid. However, government entities may require a minimum cap limit in order to protect their tax revenues.

From an efficiency or tax liability perspective, a high cap limit is always best, since it greatly reduces the work of the accountant and results in lower personal property taxes. From a profitability or asset tracking perspective, you would want the reverse, with a very low cap limit. These conflicting objectives call for some discussion within the management team about the most appropriate cap limit – it should not simply be imposed on the company by the accounting department.

EXAMPLE

Nascent Corporation is reviewing its capitalization limit, which is currently set at $1,000. A review of this limit reveals that the company has capitalized several hundred laptop computers, none of which it actively tracks, and which it replaces as per company policy every three years. There are also a number of servers that were acquired for its data storage facility, each of which cost about $5,000. These servers are occasionally subject to failure, and so are monitored closely. Finally, there are several large astronomical installations around the world, with each installation costing several million dollars.

Upon review of this information, the company concludes that it should re-set the capitalization limit to $4,000, so that it excludes all laptop computers, but continues to include the servers that it has more interest in tracking. This change in policy will also eliminate roughly 40 percent of all assets tracked, which will reduce the cost of record keeping. Though there will be an additional expense associated with immediately charging new laptop purchases to expense, the increase is considered immaterial to the company's overall profitability.

Note: GAAP does not mention the capitalization concept, so theoretically, the minimum threshold for recognizing an expenditure as a fixed asset does not exist. However, auditors recognize the need to impose a cap limit in order to reduce the accounting work load, and so will accept a reasonable cap limit. Discuss the issue with the auditors before imposing a cap limit or changing an existing one.

The Base Unit

There is no specific guidance in either GAAP or IFRS about the unit of measure for a fixed asset. This unit of measure, or *base unit*, is essentially the company's definition of what constitutes a fixed asset. Since there is no prescribed definition, it can be created. This definition can be formalized into a policy, so that it is applied consistently over time. Here are several issues to consider when creating a definition of a base unit:

- *Aggregation.* Should individually insignificant items be aggregated into a fixed asset, such as a group of desks? This increases the administrative burden, but does delay recognition of the expense associated with the items.

Tip: If a supplier is billing for several assets on a single invoice, do not record everything on the invoice as a single fixed asset. Instead, determine the base unit for each asset, and allocate the freight and tax for the entire invoice to the individual fixed assets that are recognized.

- *Asset control.* If control over an asset cannot be exercised, do not designate it as a base unit. For example, hand tools are constantly being used throughout the production shop, and may not be adequately controlled. Similarly, laptop computers are moved around constantly, and so might also not be a good choice for a base unit. In both of these examples, the cost of the items involved may be so low that they would fall under the company capitalization limit, and so would not be a valid base unit in any case.
- *Component replacement.* Is it likely that large components of an asset will be replaced during its useful life? If so, designate the smaller units as the most appropriate base unit to track in the accounting records. This decision may be influenced by the probability of these smaller components actually being replaced over time.
- *Costs are assignable.* Each base unit should be linked with an invoiced supplier cost (if acquired elsewhere). Otherwise, too much time will be spent apportioning invoiced costs between multiple base units.
- *Identification.* Is it possible to identify an asset that has been designated as a base unit, or at least attach an asset tag to it? If not, it will not be possible to subsequently track it, so it should not be designated as a base unit. This is a particular problem with highly complex machinery that contains a variety of equipment that may require replacement at different intervals; even if you might want to track these components separately, it may not be possible to disentangle the assets sufficiently to do so.
- *Legal description.* If there is a legal description of an asset, such as is stated on a tax billing for a specific parcel of land, this can form the basis for a base unit, since you can then associate future expenses billed by a government entity to the base unit.

- *Safety equipment.* Some items may be so important to the safety of employees or facilities that they must be tracked as base units. In this case, the monitoring capabilities of a fixed asset system may be of great importance in ensuring that these assets are in the proper locations at all times. See the Fixed Asset Tracking chapter for more information.
- *Tax treatment.* Is there a tax advantage in separately accounting for the components of a major asset? This may be the case where the useful life of a component is shorter than that of a major asset of which it is a part, so that it can be more quickly depreciated.
- *Useful life.* The useful lives of the components of a base unit should be similar, so that the entire unit can be eliminated or replaced at approximately the same time.
- *Value of information.* At what level of asset aggregation is the information collected the most valuable? If you need to track the useful lives of major asset components, consider setting the base unit at the level of those components. Conversely, if it is only necessary to comply with the accounting standards and there is no other need for fixed asset information collected, it may make sense to create base units for assets at a high expenditure level.

> **Tip:** Do not confuse the collection of information needed for accounting records with information collected for maintenance records. The accounting database does not normally include any maintenance information, so do not set base units due to the need for maintenance information.

EXAMPLE

Nascent Corporation owns and operates a number of wide-field telescopes around the world, which are used for tracking near-earth objects that might enter the atmosphere. Each telescope contains optics that must be removed and recoated every 20 years, as well as a drive mechanism that should be replaced every five years, and a massive concrete mount that realistically requires no maintenance or replacement of any kind for the foreseeable future. The observatory dome has a thirty-year useful life.

Given these differing useful lives and replacement requirements, Nascent elects to designate the optics, drive mechanism, mount, and dome as separate base units.

EXAMPLE

Fireball Flight Services operates a high-altitude solar telescope from a small business jet. Fireball elects to designate the air frame, telescope, jet engines, radio equipment, and GPS triangulation system as separate base units, since each one has a different useful life to which costs can be clearly assigned.

GAAP: The Initial Measurement of a Fixed Asset

Initially record a fixed asset at the historical cost of acquiring it, which includes the costs to bring it to the condition and location necessary for its intended use. If these preparatory activities will occupy a period of time, you can also include in the cost of the asset the interest costs related to the cost of the asset during the preparation period (see the Interest Capitalization chapter for more information).

The activities involved in bringing a fixed asset to the condition and location necessary for its intended purpose include the following:

- Physical construction of the asset
- Demolition of any preexisting structures
- Renovating a preexisting structure to alter it for use by the buyer
- Administrative and technical activities during preconstruction for such activities as designing the asset and obtaining permits
- Administrative and technical work after construction commences for such activities as litigation, labor disputes, and technical problems

---

EXAMPLE

Nascent Corporation constructs a solar observatory. The project costs $10 million to construct. Also, Nascent takes out a loan for the entire $10 million amount of the project, and pays $250,000 in interest costs during the six-month construction period. Further, the company incurs $500,000 in architectural fees and permit costs before work begins.

All of these costs can be capitalized into the cost of the building asset, so Nascent records $1.75 million as the cost of the building asset.

Patent Measurement

When initially measuring the amount of a patent that can be capitalized, it should include the registration, documentation, and other legal fees associated with the application. If the company instead bought a patent from another party, the purchase price is the initial asset cost. Note that the research and development (R&D) costs required to develop the idea being patented cannot be included in the capitalized cost of a patent. These R&D costs are instead charged to expense as incurred; the basis for this treatment is that R&D is inherently risky, without assurance of future benefits, so it should not be considered an asset.

Interpretive Commentary

Readers have posed a number of questions regarding what to do in circumstances where the initial GAAP guidance is unclear or does not exist. In the following bullet points, we provide interpretive commentary that may assist in deciding whether to record costs as part of a fixed asset:

- *Architectural fees.* A company incurs architect's fees for the design of a leased space. These fees are considered consulting fees, which are commonly charged to expense as incurred. However, GAAP states that one can capitalize the cost of administrative and technical activities during preconstruction for such activities as designing the asset. Thus, it is possible that these fees could be capitalized into the leasehold improvement asset.
- *Consultant cost.* A company is having trouble setting up new equipment, and hires a consultant to assist them. The cost of this consultant can be capitalized, since the outcome is intended to bring the asset to its intended condition.
- *Employee transport of assets.* An employee is transporting a part to a fixed asset that will be installed and capitalized as part of the fixed asset. Employee compensation related to the transport function is typically charged to expense as incurred, and not capitalized.
- *Energy conservation credits.* A company purchases energy efficient windows and will later claim energy conservation credits because of this investment. The exact amount of the credit is not known at the time of the investment, and the credit is granted by the utility company, not the supplier that sold the company the windows. In this case, record the full cost of the windows as part of the fixed asset; do not net the energy credits against the fixed asset cost.
- *Investigative costs.* A company is investigating properties that it may want to purchase, and incurs costs for soil testing, legal fees, and on-site visits. Since there is no actual asset to capitalize at this stage, all of these costs are charged to expense as incurred.
- *Meals.* A company pays for meals related to business meetings during the development phase of a property. Meals are considered an operational cost of a business, and so are charged to expense as incurred.
- *Movement of facilities.* A company is moving a laboratory from one location to another. It incurs costs to terminate old phone lines, rent moving trucks, set up a new network, install cabling, and install equipment. These are all moving costs, and should be charged to expense as incurred.
- *Off-site management.* A company has a corporate management oversight team that makes decisions for multiple projects regarding which bids/proposals to use, and answers the questions of site managers. These are overhead activities that are typically charged to expense as incurred.
- *Operator training.* A company installs new equipment and must then incur training costs to ensure that its machine operators and maintenance staff can operate and fix the equipment. This training cost should be charged to expense as incurred, since they are an operating cost of the business.
- *Qualification costs.* A company installs new equipment and must run several batches of product to ensure that the equipment is running in accordance with specifications. This is a cost needed to bring a fixed asset to its intended condition, and so can be capitalized.

- *Relocation of existing assets.* A company is prepping a site for the installation of new equipment; this involves relocating existing machinery to other locations. Only the cost of preparation for the new equipment can be capitalized. The relocation cost for the existing equipment should be charged to expense as incurred.
- *Temporary office space.* A company is undergoing a building renovation and has had to move several employees to temporary office space during the construction period. The cost of this temporary space must be charged to expense as incurred, since it does not contribute to the inherent value of the renovation that takes place in their absence.
- *Travel costs - construction.* A company incurs travel costs to transport employees to a construction site where a fixed asset is being constructed. This cost falls outside of the normal cluster of cost categories associated with a fixed asset, and so is difficult to justify as part of a fixed asset. It is better to charge this cost to expense as incurred.
- *Travel costs – product placement.* A company incurs travel costs to send employees to new store locations to stock the stores with goods. This is an operational cost, and should be charged to expense as incurred.

It is quite common to have questions arise over the proper recordation of certain costs that are tangentially related to fixed assets. When in doubt, consult with the company's external auditors for advice.

GAAP: The Measurement of Assets Acquired in a Business Combination

If a company acquires fixed assets as part of a business combination, it should recognize all identifiable assets, including such identifiable intangible assets as a patent, customer relationship, or a brand. Record these fixed assets at their fair values as of the acquisition date.

EXAMPLE

Nascent Corporation acquires Stellar Designs for $40 million. It allocates $10 million of the purchase price among current assets and liabilities at their book values, which approximate their fair values. Nascent also assigns $22 million to identifiable fixed assets and $4 million to a customer relationships intangible asset. This leaves $4 million that cannot be allocated, and which is therefore assigned to a goodwill asset.

GAAP: The Measurement of Assets Acquired in a Finance Lease

If the business is a lessee and the lease qualifies as a finance lease (formerly known as a capital lease), record the asset being leased as a fixed asset. A lease qualifies as a finance lease if it meets any one of the following four criteria:

- *Ownership transfer*. Ownership of the underlying asset is shifted to the lessee by the end of the lease term.
- *Ownership option*. The lessee has a purchase option to buy the leased asset, and is reasonably certain to use it.
- *Lease term*. The lease term covers the major part of the underlying asset's remaining economic life. This is considered to be 75% or more of the remaining economic life of the underlying asset. This criterion is not valid if the lease commencement date is near the end of the asset's economic life, which is considered to be a date that falls within the last 25% of the underlying asset's total economic life.
- *Present value*. The present value of the sum of all lease payments and any lessee-guaranteed residual value matches or exceeds the fair value of the underlying asset. The present value is based on the interest rate implicit in the lease.
- *Specialization*. The asset is so specialized that it has no alternative use for the lessor following the lease term. In this situation, there are essentially no remaining benefits that revert to the lessor.

A central concept of the accounting for leases is that the lessee should recognize the assets and liabilities that underlie each leasing arrangement. This concept results in the following recognition in the balance sheet of the lessee as of the lease commencement date:

- Recognize a liability to make lease payments to the lessor
- Recognize a right-of-use asset that represents the right of the lessee to use the leased asset during the lease term

As of the commencement date of a lease, the lessee measures the liability and the right-of-use asset associated with the lease. These measurements are derived as follows:

- *Lease liability*. The present value of the lease payments, discounted at the discount rate for the lease. This rate is the rate implicit in the lease when that rate is readily determinable. If not, the lessee instead uses its incremental borrowing rate.
- *Right-of-use asset*. The initial amount of the lease liability, plus any lease payments made to the lessor before the lease commencement date, plus any initial direct costs incurred, minus any lease incentives received.

EXAMPLE

Inscrutable Corporation enters into a five-year lease, where the lease payments are $35,000 per year, payable at the end of each year. Inscrutable incurs initial direct costs of $8,000. The rate implicit in the lease is 8%.

At the commencement of the lease, the lease liability is $139,745, which is calculated as $35,000 multiplied by the 3.9927 rate for the five-period present value of an ordinary annuity. The right-of-use asset is calculated as the lease liability plus the amount of the initial direct costs, for a total of $147,745.

GAAP: Non-Monetary Exchanges

What if a fixed asset is acquired through an exchange of assets? Follow this sequence of decisions to decide upon the correct cost at which to record the asset received:

1. Measure the asset acquired at the fair value of the asset surrendered to the other party.
2. If the fair value of the asset received is more clearly evident than the fair value of the asset surrendered, measure the acquired asset at its own fair value.

In either case, recognize a gain or loss on the difference between the recorded cost of the asset transferred to the other party and the recorded cost of the asset that has been acquired.

If it is not possible to determine the fair value of either asset, record the asset received at the cost of the asset relinquished in order to obtain it. Use this later approach under any of the following circumstances:

- The fair value of either asset cannot be determined within reasonable limits;
- The transaction is intended to facilitate a sale to a customer other than the parties to the asset exchange; or
- The transaction does not have commercial substance.

EXAMPLE

Nascent Corporation exchanges a color copier with a carrying amount of $18,000 with Declining Company for a print-on-demand publishing station. The color copier had an original cost of $30,000, and had incurred $12,000 of accumulated depreciation as of the transaction date. No cash is transferred as part of the exchange, and Nascent cannot determine the fair value of the color copier. The fair value of the publishing station is $20,000.

Nascent can record a gain of $2,000 on the exchange, which is derived from the fair value of the publishing station that it acquired, less the carrying amount of the color copier that it gave up. Nascent uses the following journal entry to record the transaction:

	Debit	Credit
Publishing equipment	20,000	
Accumulated depreciation	12,000	
Copier equipment		30,000
Gain on asset exchange		2,000

A transaction is considered to have commercial substance under GAAP if a company expects that its future cash flows will change significantly as a result of the transaction. A cash flow change is considered significant if the risk, timing, or amount of future cash flows of the asset received differ significantly from those of the asset given up; alternatively, a cash flow change is considered significant if there is a significant difference in the entity-specific values of the assets exchanged. *Entity-specific value* can vary from fair value, if the company plans to use assets for a less-than-optimal activity. Thus, entity-specific value can be less than fair value.

EXAMPLE

Nascent Corporation and Starlight Inc. swap spectroscopes, since the two devices have different features that the two companies need. The spectroscope given up by Nascent has a carrying amount of $25,000, which is comprised of an original cost of $40,000 and accumulated depreciation of $15,000. Both spectroscopes have identical fair values of $27,000.

Nascent's controller tests for commercial substance in the transaction. She finds that there is no difference in the fair values of the assets exchanged, and that Nascent's cash flows will not change significantly as a result of the swap. Thus, she concludes that the transaction has no commercial value, and so should account for it at book value, which means that Nascent cannot recognize a gain of $2,000 on the transaction, which is the difference between the $27,000 fair value of the spectroscope and the $25,000 carrying amount of the asset given up. Instead, she uses the following journal entry to record the transaction, which does not contain a gain or loss:

	Debit	Credit
Spectroscope (asset received)	25,000	
Accumulated depreciation	15,000	
Spectroscope (asset given up)		40,000

What if there is an exchange of cash between the two parties, in addition to a non-monetary exchange? The accounting varies if the amount of cash, or *boot*, paid as part of the asset exchange is relatively small (which is defined under GAAP as less than 25 percent of the fair value of the exchange), or if it is larger.

In the case of a small amount of boot, the recipient of the cash records a gain to the extent that the amount of cash received exceeds a proportionate share of the cost of the surrendered asset. This proportionate share is calculated as the ratio of the cash paid to the total consideration received (which is the cash received plus the fair value of the asset received); if the amount of the consideration received is not clearly evident, then use the fair value of the asset surrendered to the other party. The calculation is:

$$\frac{\text{Boot}}{\text{Boot} + \text{Fair value of asset received}} \times \text{Total gain} = \text{Gain recognized}$$

What is the accounting from the perspective of the party paying cash as part of the transaction? This entity records the asset received as the sum of the cash paid to the other party plus the recorded amount of the asset surrendered. If the transaction results in a loss, record the entire amount of the loss at once. Under no circumstances is it allowable to record a gain on such a transaction.

EXAMPLE

Nascent Corporation is contemplating the exchange of one of its heliographs for a catadioptric telescope owned by Aphelion Corporation. The two companies have recorded these assets in their accounting records as follows:

	Nascent (Heliograph)	Aphelion (Catadioptric)
Cost	$82,000	$97,000
Accumulated depreciation	22,000	27,000
Net book value	$60,000	$70,000
Fair value	$55,000	$72,000

Under the terms of the proposed asset exchange, Nascent must pay cash (boot) to Aphelion of $17,000. The boot amount is 24 percent of the fair value of the exchange, which is calculated as:

$17,000 Boot ÷ ($55,000 Fair value of heliograph + $17,000 Boot) = 24%

The parties elect to go forward with the exchange. The amount of boot is less than 25 percent of the total fair value of the exchange, so Aphelion should recognize a pro rata portion of the $2,000 gain (calculated as the $72,000 total fair value of the asset received - $70,000 net book value of the asset received) on the exchange using the following calculation:

24% portion of boot to total fair value received × $2,000 Gain = $480 Recognized gain

Nascent uses the following journal entry to record the exchange transaction:

	Debit	Credit
Telescope (asset received)	72,000	
Accumulated depreciation	22,000	
Loss on asset exchange	5,000	
Cash		17,000
Heliograph (asset given up)		82,000

Nascent's journal entry includes a $5,000 loss; the loss is essentially the difference between the book value and fair value of the heliograph on the transaction date.

Aphelion uses the following journal entry to record the exchange transaction:

	Debit	Credit
Heliograph (asset received)	53,480	
Accumulated depreciation	27,000	
Cash	17,000	
Gain on asset exchange		480
Telescope (asset given up)		97,000

Aphelion is not allowed to recognize the full value of the heliograph at the acquisition date because of the boot rule for small amounts of cash consideration; this leaves the heliograph undervalued by $1,520 (since its fair value is actually $55,000).

The accounting is different if the amount of boot is 25 percent or more of the fair value of the exchange. In this situation, both parties should record the transaction at its fair value.

EXAMPLE

Nascent Corporation exchanges a wide field CCD camera for a Schmidt-Cassegrain telescope owned by Aphelion Corporation. The two companies have recorded these assets in their accounting records as follows:

	Nascent (Camera)	Aphelion (Schmidt-Cassegrain)
Cost	$50,000	$93,000
Accumulated depreciation	(30,000)	(40,000)
Net book value	$20,000	$53,000
Fair value	$24,000	$58,000

Under the terms of the agreement, Nascent pays $34,000 cash (boot) to Aphelion. This boot amount is well in excess of the 25 percent boot level, so both parties can now treat the deal as a monetary transaction.

Nascent uses the following journal entry to record the exchange transaction, which measures the telescope acquired at the fair value of the camera and cash surrendered:

	Debit	Credit
Telescope (asset received)	58,000	
Accumulated depreciation	30,000	
Gain on asset exchange		4,000
Cash		34,000
CCD camera (asset given up)		50,000

The gain recorded by Nascent is the difference between the $24,000 fair value of the camera surrendered and its $20,000 book value.

Aphelion uses the following journal entry to record the exchange transaction, which measures the camera acquired at the fair value of the telescope surrendered less cash received:

	Debit	Credit
Camera (asset received)	24,000	
Accumulated depreciation	40,000	
Cash	34,000	
Gain on asset exchange		5,000
Telescope (asset given up)		93,000

The gain recorded by Aphelion is the difference between the $58,000 fair value of the telescope surrendered and its $53,000 book value.

GAAP: Internal-Use Software

Companies routinely develop software for internal use, and want to understand how these development costs are to be accounted for. Software is considered to be for internal use when it has been acquired or developed *only* for the internal needs of a business. Examples of situations where software is considered to be developed for internal use are:

- Accounting systems
- Cash management tracking systems
- Membership tracking systems
- Production automation systems

Further, there can be no reasonably possible plan to market the software outside of the company. A market feasibility study is not considered a reasonably possible marketing plan. However, a history of selling software that had initially been developed for internal use creates a reasonable assumption that the latest internal-use product will also be marketed for sale outside of the company.

The accounting for internal-use software varies, depending upon the stage of completion of the project. The relevant accounting is:

- *Stage 1: Preliminary*. All costs incurred during the preliminary stage of a development project should be charged to expense as incurred. This stage is considered to include making decisions about the allocation of resources, determining performance requirements, conducting supplier demonstrations, evaluating technology, and supplier selection.
- *Stage 2: Application development*. Capitalize the costs incurred to develop internal-use software, which may include coding, hardware installation, and testing. Any costs related to data conversion, user training, administration, and overhead should be charged to expense as incurred. Only the following costs can be capitalized:
    - Materials and services consumed in the development effort, such as third party development fees, software purchase costs, and travel costs related to development work.
    - The payroll costs of those employees directly associated with soft-ware development.
    - The capitalization of interest costs incurred to fund the project.

- *Stage 3. Post-implementation*. Charge all post-implementation costs to expense as incurred. Samples of these costs are training and maintenance costs.

Any allowable capitalization of costs should begin *after* the preliminary stage has been completed, management commits to funding the project, it is probable that the project will be completed, and the software will be used for its intended function.

The capitalization of costs should end when all substantial testing has been completed. If it is no longer probable that a project will be completed, stop capitalizing the costs associated with it, and conduct impairment testing on the costs already capitalized. The cost at which the asset should then be carried is the lower of its carrying amount or fair value (less costs to sell). Unless there is evidence to the contrary, the usual assumption is that uncompleted software has no fair value.

A business may purchase software for internal use. If the purchase price of this software includes other elements, such as training and maintenance fees, only capitalize that portion of the purchase price that relates to the software itself.

In addition, any later upgrades of the software can be capitalized, but only if it is probable that extra system functionality will result from the upgrade. The costs of maintaining the system should be charged to expense as incurred. If the maintenance is provided by a third party and payment is made in advance for the services of that party, amortize the cost of the maintenance over the service period.

Once costs have been capitalized, amortize them over the expected useful life of the software. This is typically done on a straight-line basis, unless another method more clearly reflects the expected usage pattern of the software. Amortization should begin when a software module is ready for its intended use, which is considered to be when all substantial system testing has been completed. If a software module cannot function unless other modules are also completed, do not begin amortization until the related modules are complete.

It may be necessary to regularly reassess the useful life of the software for amortization purposes, since technological obsolescence tends to shorten it.

The capitalized cost of internal-use software should be periodically reviewed for impairment, as described in the Fixed Asset Impairment chapter. The following are all indicators of the possible presence of asset impairment:

- The software is not expected to be of substantive use
- The manner in which the software was originally intended to be used has now changed
- The software is to be significantly altered
- The development cost of the software significantly exceeded original expectations

Once a business has developed software for internal use, management may decide to market it for external use by third parties. If so, the proceeds from software licensing, net of selling costs, should be applied against the carrying amount of the software asset. For the purposes of this topic, selling costs are considered to include commissions, software reproduction costs, servicing obligations, warranty costs, and installation costs. The business should not recognize a profit on sales of the software until the application of net sales to the carrying amount of the software asset have reduced the carrying amount to zero. The business can recognize all further proceeds as revenue.

The guidance noted in this section is identical for the fees paid by a customer in a cloud computing arrangement (where software and/or data are being hosted on the systems of a third party). In this situation, capitalized implementation costs are ratably charged to expense over the term of the hosting arrangement.

GAAP: Website Development Costs

A company may allocate significant funding to the development of a company website in such areas as coding, graphics design, the addition of content, and site operation. The accounting for website development varies, depending upon the stage of completion of the project. The relevant accounting is:

- *Stage 1: Preliminary.* Charge all site planning costs to expense as incurred. This stage is considered to include project planning, the determination of site functionality, hardware identification, technology usability, alternatives analysis, supplier demonstrations, and legal considerations.

- *Stage 2: Application development and infrastructure.* The accounting matches what was just described in the last section for internal-use software. In essence, capitalize these costs. More specifically, capitalize the cost of obtaining and registering an Internet domain, as well as the procurement of software tools, code customization, web page development, related hardware, hypertext link creation, and site testing. Also, if a site upgrade provides new functions or features to the website, capitalize these costs.
- *Stage 3: Graphics development.* For the purposes of this topic, graphics are considered to be software, and so are capitalized, unless they are to be marketed externally. Graphics development includes site page design and layout.
- *Stage 4: Content development.* Charge data conversion costs to expense as incurred, as well as the costs to input content into a website.
- *Stage 5: Site operation.* The costs to operate a website are the same as any other operating costs, and so should be charged to expense as incurred. The treatment of selected operating costs associated with a website are:
  - ○ Charge website hosting fees to expense over the period benefited by the hosting
  - ○ Charge search engine registration fees to expense as incurred, since they are advertising costs

IFRS: Initial Inclusions in a Fixed Asset

Under IFRS, there are some differences from the GAAP requirements for the initial recognition of a fixed asset, so we are presenting a detailed review of the IFRS requirements.

Under IFRS, only recognize an item as a fixed asset if there will probably be future economic benefits associated with the item that will flow to the owning entity, and the cost of the item can be reliably measured. Thus, it is possible to legitimately record major spare parts and stand-by equipment as fixed assets if they are expected to be used during more than one accounting period. Further, if you can only use spare parts and servicing equipment in connection with a specific fixed asset, they can be legitimately recorded as fixed assets.

Tip: Do not take the preceding advice literally, and record items as fixed assets for just a few months! The work required to track such assets will far exceed any resulting improvement in the accuracy of reported financial results.

The costs that can be included in a fixed asset are the cost initially incurred to acquire or construct the asset, as well as any costs incurred at a later date to add to, replace part of, or service it. When applying this concept, be aware of the following three situations:

- *Repair and maintenance activities.* Charge to expense in the period incurred the costs of routine servicing of a fixed asset (typically the costs of labor and consumables).
- *Replacement parts.* If parts of a fixed asset are replaced, derecognize the parts being replaced, and recognize as fixed assets those parts being added to the fixed asset. An example of this situation is replacing a motor in a machine, or the interior seating in an aircraft. This rule only applies if there will probably be future economic benefits associated with the replacement, and the cost of the replacement can be measured.

EXAMPLE

Nova Corporation needs to replace the motor drive on its deep field scanning telescope. The new drive costs $25,000. The original motor drive cost $20,000 and was depreciated over a five-year period, of which four years have expired. Nova records the following entry to derecognize the old motor drive:

	Debit	Credit
Loss on asset derecognition	4,000	
Accumulated depreciation	16,000	
Motor drive		20,000

Nova then records the new motor drive as a fixed asset with the following entry:

	Debit	Credit
Motor drive	25,000	
Cash		25,000

- *Major inspections.* If it is necessary to perform a major inspection to continue operating a fixed asset, record the cost of the inspection as a fixed asset and derecognize any remaining cost associated with the preceding inspection. If the cost of the preceding inspection had not been capitalized, you must still derecognize an amount based on an estimate of what the preceding inspection would have cost, based on the future cost of a similar inspection. This rule only applies if there will probably be future economic benefits associated with a major inspection, and the cost of the inspection can be measured.

EXAMPLE

Fireball Flight Services operates a high-altitude solar telescope from a small business jet. The airframe is rated for 6,000 hours of flight time, after which the Federal Aviation Administration will lock down the jet unless it undergoes a major inspection. The plane reaches its 6,000-hour limitation, and Fireball pays $75,000 for a major inspection. There is a future economic benefit associated with this inspection, since the plane would otherwise be restricted from flying.

Fireball acquired the jet in used condition, and this is the first time it has performed a major inspection since its acquisition of the plane. Fireball's maintenance manager estimates that the cost of a previous major inspection would have been similar to the cost of the most recent one, so Fireball records the following journal entry to remove the estimated cost of the previous major inspection from the cost of the jet:

	Debit	Credit
Accumulated depreciation	75,000	
Jet aircraft		75,000

Fireball then records the following journal entry to capitalize the cost of the most recent major inspection as a component of the jet:

	Debit	Credit
Jet aircraft (inspection cost)	75,000	
Cash		75,000

Fireball plans to depreciate the cost of the major inspection fixed asset over the next 6,000 flight hours logged by the jet.

Derecognition is the process of removing a transaction from the accounting records of an entity. Thus, in the case of a fixed asset, this is the removal of the asset and any accumulated depreciation from the accounting records, as well as the recognition of any associated gain or loss.

IFRS: Initial Cost of a Fixed Asset

The amount that is initially capitalized for a fixed asset is its cost. The capitalized cost of a fixed asset can include the following items:

- Purchase price
- Import duties
- Non-refundable taxes on the purchase transaction

- Costs incurred that are directly attributable to bringing the asset to the location and condition necessary for it to be operated as intended. Examples of these directly attributable costs are:
  - Assembly and installation
  - Delivery and handling
  - Employee benefits arising directly from the construction or acquisition of the asset
  - Site preparation
  - Testing to ascertain functionality
- Professional fees
- Interest costs incurred that relate to asset construction during the construction period
- The initial estimate of the cost to be incurred to dismantle and remove the asset, as well as to restore the site on which it was placed
- Less: trade discounts and rebates
- Less: proceeds from samples produced during testing

Do *not* capitalize any of the following costs:

- Opening a new facility
- Introducing a new product or service (and any related marketing costs)
- Conducting business in a new location
- Conducting business with a new customer or class of customer
- Administration and general overhead

Stop capitalizing costs into a designated fixed asset when the asset is in the location and condition for it to operate as intended. Due to this restriction, do not capitalize any *subsequent* costs to use or redeploy a fixed asset. Examples of costs *not* to capitalize are:

- Costs incurred after an asset is in the location and condition for it to operate as intended, but it is still not operational or operating at full capacity
- Costs to relocate or reorganize some portion or all of a company's operations
- Initial operating losses

There are several special cost situations under IFRS that pertain to fixed assets, though they will not apply in most situations. They are:

- If a company is self-constructing an asset, charge any abnormal costs of wasted material, labor, or other such items to expense as incurred.
- If a company's payment for a fixed asset is deferred beyond common credit terms, charge a portion of the payment to interest expense to account for the long-term credit being granted by the supplier. The amount of interest charged to expense is the difference between the price paid and the price the

company would have paid under normal credit terms. Depending on the situation, this interest cost may be capitalized as part of the fixed asset (see the Interest Capitalization chapter for more information).

EXAMPLE

Hubble Corporation builds a new observatory to measure the declining orbits of satellites and plot the trajectories of incoming debris. The following table shows whether it can capitalize costs incurred or charge them to expense:

Item	Cost	Capitalize	Charge to Expense
Administrative overhead	$80,000		$80,000
Architectural fees	45,000	$45,000	
Balancing certification	10,000	10,000	
Construction contractor fees	430,000	430,000	
Construction loan interest	40,000	40,000	
Import fees on telescope mount	4,000	4,000	
Landscaping	35,000	35,000	
Move staff to new location	60,000		60,000
Observatory dome	390,000	390,000	
Opening day marketing	15,000		15,000
Sales taxes on equipment	70,000	70,000	
Scrapped concrete foundation	25,000		25,000
Telescope mount	190,000	190,000	
Testing labor	5,000	5,000	
Utilities	8,000		8,000
Wide field telescope	580,000	580,000	
Zoning application	12,000	12,000	
Totals	$1,999,000	$1,811,000	$188,000

IFRS: The Measurement of Assets Acquired in a Business Combination

In a business combination, the acquiring entity measures the tangible and intangible assets acquired at their fair values as of the acquisition date. If the acquirer designates any acquired assets as held for sale as of the acquisition date, record them at their fair values, less any costs to sell.

An intangible asset acquired through a business combination is recorded at its fair value as of the acquisition date. If there is some uncertainty about the range of possible fair values, it may be necessary to use an average of the various possible valuations, weighted based on their probabilities.

EXAMPLE

Pulsed Laser Drilling Corporation acquires a competitor that has made a significant investment in the development of a high-powered laser for drilling oil wells. At the time of the acquisition, the competitor had signed a contract with a large oil and gas exploration company to use the laser drill for a total fee of £18,000,000. The discounted cash flows associated with this contract are £7,200,000, which is used as a substitute for fair value by Pulsed Laser in estimating the valuation of the project that it should record as an intangible asset.

Here are several additional rules that may apply to the recognition of intangible assets acquired in a business combination:

- *Linked asset.* If an intangible asset is linked to a contract or other specifically identifiable asset or liability, recognize the intangible asset as part of the related item.
- *Research and development projects.* It is allowable to recognize an in-process research and development project of an acquiree as an intangible asset, as long as the project meets the criteria for an intangible asset.
- *Similar assets.* Similar intangible assets can be combined into a single asset, though they must have useful lives of roughly the same duration.

Once a research and development project has been recognized as an intangible asset by the acquirer, the following rules apply to any additional expenditures made in association with that project:

- *Research expenditures.* Expenditures made on research activities are charged to expense as incurred.
- *Development expenditures.* Expenditures made on development activities are charged to expense as incurred, unless they satisfy all of the following capitalization requirements:
  - Future economic benefits are probable
  - Management intends to complete and use the asset, and has the ability to do so
  - Technical feasibility of the product has been demonstrated
  - The amount of the development expenditure can be reliably measured
  - There are adequate resources to complete the project

IFRS: The Measurement of Assets Acquired in a Finance Lease

A lease arrangement occurs when a lessor agrees to allow a lessee to control the use of identified fixed assets for a stated period of time or an amount of usage in exchange for one or more payments. When there is a lease, the lessee must recognize an asset and liability for all leases having a term of more than 12 months, unless the asset associated with the lease has a low value. The asset to be recognized is a right-of-use asset that represents the right of the lessee to use the asset during the lease term. The liability to be recognized is the obligation of the lessee to pay the lessor.

A lessee may elect not to record a right-of-use asset for a short-term lease (which has a term of 12 months or less) or a lease for which the associated asset is of low value. In this situation, the lessee recognizes the lease payments for those leases as an expense. This may be done on a straight-line basis over the term of the lease or on some other systematic basis. An alternative systematic basis is used if the alternative is more representative of the pattern of benefits enjoyed by the lessee.

The election to classify a leased asset as short-term is made for the class of assets to which the right of use relates. A class of assets is similar in nature and has a common use within the operations of the lessee. Conversely, the election to classify a leased asset as being of low value can be made by individual lease. Examples of low-value underlying assets are personal computers, telephones, lesser items of office furniture, and tablet computers.

As of the commencement date of a lease, the lessee measures the liability and the right-of-use asset associated with the lease. These measurements are derived as follows:

- *Lease liability.* The present value of the lease payments, discounted at the discount rate for the lease. This rate is the rate implicit in the lease when that rate is readily determinable. If not, the lessee instead uses its incremental borrowing rate. The lease payments encompassed by the lease liability measurement include the following items:
  - Payments made at the commencement date
  - Fixed payments, minus any lease incentives payable to the lessee
  - Variable lease payments that depend on an index or a rate (such as a consumer price index)
  - The exercise price of an option to purchase the underlying asset, if it is reasonably certain that the lessee will exercise the option
  - Penalty payments associated with an assumed exercise of an option to terminate the lease
  - Residual value guarantees, if it is probable that these amounts will be owed. Note that a lease provision requiring the lessee to pay for any deficiency in residual value that is caused by damage or excessive usage is not considered a guarantee of the residual value.

- *Right-of-use asset.* The initial amount of the lease liability, plus any lease payments made to the lessor before the lease commencement date, plus any initial direct costs incurred, minus any lease incentives received.

IFRS: Non-Monetary Exchanges

A company may acquire a fixed asset in exchange for a non-monetary asset or a mix of cash and non-monetary assets. Measure the cost of such an acquired item at its fair value, except under the following conditions:

- The transaction lacks commercial substance.
- The fair value of either asset exchanged cannot be reliably measured. An asset is considered to be reliably measurable when there is an insignificant variability in the range of reasonable fair value estimates, or when one can reasonably assess and use the probabilities in a range of fair value estimates to derive a fair value.

If an acquired asset cannot be measured at its fair value, instead use the fair value of the received asset. If neither fair value is available, use the carrying amount of the asset given up to acquire the asset.

EXAMPLE

Binary Brothers acquires a tractor for its rocket launching operation in an exchange of assets. The tractor has a fair value of $120,000. Binary gives up two liquid nitrogen fuel tankers in the exchange, which have an original cost of $200,000 and accumulated depreciation of $60,000. The other party also pays Binary $40,000 in cash. Binary records the following entry to eliminate the trucks from its books, record the tractor at its fair value, and record a gain on the transaction:

	Debit	Credit
Tractor	120,000	
Cash	40,000	
Accumulated depreciation	60,000	
Gain on asset exchange		20,000
Trailers		200,000

Binary records a $20,000 gain because the $160,000 fair value of the tractor and cash received exceeds the $140,000 carrying amount of the trailers surrendered in the transaction.

IFRS: Website Development Costs

A business may incur costs, both internally and from third parties, to develop and maintain a website on which it promotes and sells its products and services. IFRS considers such a website to be an internally generated intangible asset. Its development cost can only be capitalized if it complies with all of the following requirements:

- Future economic benefits are probable
- Management intends to complete and use the asset, and has the ability to do so
- Technical feasibility of the product has been demonstrated
- The amount of the development expenditure can be reliably measured
- There are adequate resources to complete the project

If these requirements cannot be met, all expenditures related to the website should be charged to expense as incurred.

Subject to the preceding requirements, development costs that can be capitalized include obtaining a domain name, acquiring hardware and software, installing applications, designing web pages, preparing and uploading information, and stress testing.

All other costs related to a website must be charged to expense as incurred. These costs include feasibility studies, defining specifications, evaluating alternatives, site hosting, advertising products and services on the site, and site maintenance.

When determining the useful life of a website for the purpose of amortizing related costs that have been capitalized, IFRS recommends that the useful life be "short."

EXAMPLE

The Close Call Company compiles the cost of its new website, which is used by customers to place orders for cross-town delivery services. The following table shows which items will be capitalized into an intangible asset and which will be charged to expense, on the assumption that the website meets the criteria for capitalization as an internally developed intangible asset:

Expenditure Type	Capitalize	Charge to Expense
Planning activities		
Feasibility study		$8,000
Hardware and software requirements specification		12,000
Product evaluation		18,000
Preference selection		5,000
Infrastructure development		
Obtain domain name	$20,000	
Develop operating system and application code	120,000	
Install developed applications	30,000	
Stress testing	15,000	
Graphical design		
Design web page layout	40,000	
Creating graphics files	20,000	
Operating		
Updates to site graphics		35,000
Addition of new site features		60,000
Registering site with search engines		3,000
Backing up data		7,000
Employee training on website usage		11,000
Totals	$245,000	$159,000

IFRS: Internally Developed Intangible Assets

It is possible under IFRS to recognize internally-generated intangible assets. To do so, split expenditures related to a prospective intangible asset into those incurred during the research and development phases of constructing the asset. All research-related expenditures are to be charged to expense as incurred. Examples of research-related expenditures are:

- Activities designed to acquire new knowledge

- The search for and application of research findings
- The search for and/or formulation of product or process alternatives

Expenditures related to development activities can be capitalized as intangible assets, but only if they meet the following criteria:

- Future economic benefits are probable
- Management intends to complete and use the asset, and has the ability to do so
- Technical feasibility of the product has been demonstrated
- The amount of the development expenditure can be reliably measured
- There are adequate resources to complete the project

Examples of development-related expenditures are:

- The design and testing for prototypes, or of alternative materials, processes, and so forth
- The design of tools, molds, and related items that involve new technology applications
- The design, construction, and operation of a pilot plant that is not intended for commercial production levels

IFRS does not allow the following internally-generated items or similar items to be recognized as intangible assets:

- Brands
- Customer lists
- Goodwill
- Mastheads
- Publishing titles

EXAMPLE

The Electronic Inference Corporation is developing a new manufacturing process for its electronic calculator line. The company expends £150,000 on the development of this process through the first half of 20X2, and is then able to demonstrate as of July 1 that the process meets the criteria for an intangible asset. The £150,000 expended prior to that date must be charged to expense.

The company estimates that the recoverable amount of knowledge embodied in the new process is £300,000. In the following four months, the company incurs an additional £330,000 of costs, which it capitalizes into an intangible asset. Since the capitalized amount is £30,000 higher than the recoverable amount, the controller writes off the difference as an asset impairment.

A number of items cannot be capitalized into intangible assets, and must instead be charged to expense as incurred. This situation arises because the expenditures do not meet the criteria listed earlier for development activities. Examples of expenditures that are rarely capitalized as intangible assets are those related to training activities, advertising and promotions, relocations, reorganizations, and start-up activities.

Summary

As noted in the introduction, the accountant will likely have a very easy time recording the initial acquisition of a fixed asset. Determination of the base unit is also fairly routine in most cases. There is a moderate increase in transactional complexity when dealing with assets acquired through a business combination, since fair values are used. Nonetheless, the accounting is not especially difficult. Capital leases require some additional analysis, since a discounted cash flow calculation must also be considered. The real complexity lies in the exchange of assets, where the rules are based on such factors as the proportional amount of cash paid and the uses to which assets are to be put. In this last case, it is best to closely review the applicable accounting standards before recording a transaction.

Chapter 4
Interest Capitalization

Introduction

When a fixed asset is recorded, part of the cost that may be included is the cost incurred to bring it to the condition and location of its intended use. If these activities require some time to complete, capitalize the cost of the interest incurred during that period that relate to the asset. This chapter describes the assets for which interest capitalization is allowable (or not), how to determine the capitalization period and the capitalization rate, and how to calculate the amount of interest cost to be capitalized.

Why and When Do We Capitalize Interest?

Interest is a cost of doing business, and if a company incurs an interest cost that is directly related to a fixed asset, it is reasonable to capitalize this cost, since it provides a truer picture of the total investment in the asset. Since a business would not otherwise have incurred the interest if it had not acquired the asset, the interest is essentially a direct cost of owning the asset.

Conversely, if you did not capitalize this interest cost and instead charged it to expense, you would be unreasonably reducing the amount of reported earnings during the period when the company incurred the expense, and increasing earnings during later periods, when you would otherwise have been charging the capitalized interest to expense through depreciation.

> **Tip:** If the amount of interest that may be applied to a fixed asset is minor, try to avoid capitalizing it. Otherwise, too much time will be spent documenting the capitalization, and the auditors will spend time investigating it – which may translate into higher audit fees.

The value of the information provided by capitalizing interest may not be worth the effort of the incremental accounting cost associated with it. Here are some issues to consider when deciding whether to capitalize interest:

- How many assets would be subject to interest capitalization?
- How easy is it to separately identify those assets that would be subject to interest capitalization?
- How significant would be the effect of interest capitalization on the company's reported resources and earnings?

Thus, only capitalize interest when the informational benefit derived from doing so exceeds the cost of accounting for it. The positive impact of doing so is greatest for construction projects, where:

- Costs are separately compiled
- Construction covers a long period of time
- Expenditures are large
- Interest costs are considerable

GAAP specifically does *not* allow for the capitalization of interest for inventory items that are routinely manufactured in large quantities on a repetitive basis.

Assets for Which Interest Must be Capitalized

Interest must be capitalized that is related to the following types of fixed assets:

- That are constructed for the company's own use. This includes assets built for the company by suppliers, where the company makes progress payments or deposits.
- That are constructed for sale or lease, and which are constructed as discrete projects.

EXAMPLE

Milford Sound builds a new corporate headquarters. The company hires a contractor to perform the work, and makes regular progress payments to the contractor. Milford should capitalize the interest expense related to this project.

Milford Sound creates a subsidiary, Milford Public Sound, which builds custom-designed outdoor sound staging for concerts and theatre activities. These projects require many months to complete, and are accounted for as discrete projects. Milford should capitalize the interest cost related to each of these projects.

If a company is undertaking activities to develop land for a specific use, capitalize interest related to the associated expenditures for as long as the development activities are in progress.

Assets for Which Interest Capitalization is Not Allowed

Do not capital interest that is related to the following types of fixed assets:

- Assets that are already in use or ready for their intended use.
- Assets not being used, and which are not being prepared for use.
- Assets not included in the company's balance sheet.
- Inventories that are routinely manufactured.

The Interest Capitalization Period

Capitalize interest over the period when there are ongoing activities to prepare a fixed asset for its intended use, but only if expenditures are actually being made during that time, and interest costs are being incurred.

EXAMPLE

Milford Public Sound is constructing an in-house sound stage in which to test its products. It spent the first two months designing the stage, and then paid a contractor $30,000 per month for the next four months to build the stage. Milford incurred interest costs during the entire time period.

Since Milford was not making any expenditures related to the stage during the first two months, it cannot capitalize any interest cost for those two months. However, since it was making expenditures during the next four months, it can capitalize interest cost for those months.

If a company stops essentially all construction on a project, stop capitalizing interest during that period. However, interest capitalization can be continued under any of the following circumstances:

- Brief construction interruptions
- Interruptions imposed by an outside entity
- Delays that are an inherent part of the asset acquisition process

---

EXAMPLE

Milford Public Sound is constructing a concert arena that it plans to lease to a local municipality upon completion. Midway through the project, the municipality orders a halt to all construction, when construction reveals that the arena is being built on an Indian burial ground. Two months later, after the burial site has been relocated, the municipality allows construction to begin again.

Since this interruption was imposed by an outside entity, Milford can capitalize interest during the two-month stoppage period.

Terminate interest capitalization as soon as an asset is substantially complete and ready for its intended use. Here are several scenarios showing when to terminate interest capitalization:

- *Unit-level completion*. Parts of a project may be completed and usable before the entire project is complete. Stop capitalizing interest on each of these parts as soon as they are substantially complete and ready for use.

- *Entire-unit completion*. All aspects of an asset may need to be completed before any part of it can be used. Continue capitalizing interest on such assets until the entire project is substantially complete and ready for use.
- *Dependent completion*. An asset may not be usable until a separate project has also been completed. Continue capitalizing interest on such assets until not only the specific asset, but also the separate project is substantially complete and ready for use.

EXAMPLE

Milford Public Sound is building three arenas, all under different circumstances. They are:

1. *Arena A*. This is an entertainment complex, including a stage area, movie theatre, and restaurants. Milford should stop capitalizing interest on each component of the project as soon as it is substantially complete and ready for use, since each part of the complex can operate without the other parts being complete.
2. *Arena B*. This is a single outdoor stage with integrated multi-level parking garage. Even though the garage is completed first, Milford should continue to capitalize interest for it, since the garage is only intended to service patrons of the arena, and so will not be operational until the arena is complete.
3. *Arena C*. This an entertainment complex for which Milford is also constructing a highway off-ramp and road that leads to the complex. Since the complex is unusable until patrons can reach the complex, Milford should continue to capitalize interest expenses until the off-ramp and road are complete.

Do not continue to capitalize interest when completion is being deliberately delayed, since the cost of interest then changes from an asset acquisition cost to an asset holding cost.

EXAMPLE

The CEO of Milford Sound wants to report increased net income for the upcoming quarter, so he orders the delay of construction on an arena facility that would otherwise have been completed, so that the interest cost related to the project will be capitalized. He is in error, since this is now treated as a holding cost – the related interest expense should be recognized in the period incurred, rather than capitalized.

The Capitalization Rate

The amount of interest cost to capitalize for a fixed asset is that amount of interest that would have been avoided if the asset had not been acquired.

To calculate the amount of interest cost to capitalize, multiply the capitalization rate by the average amount of expenditures that accumulate during the construction period.

The basis for the capitalization rate is the interest rates that are applicable to the company's borrowings that are outstanding during the construction period. If a specific borrowing is incurred in order to construct a specific asset, use the interest rate on that borrowing as the capitalization rate. If the amount of a specific borrowing that is incurred to construct a specific asset is less than the expenditures made for the asset, use a weighted average of the rates applicable to other company borrowings for any excess expenditures over the amount of the project-specific borrowing.

EXAMPLE

Milford Public Sound incurs an average expenditure over the construction period of an outdoor arena complex of $15,000,000. It has taken out a short-term loan of $12,000,000 at 9% interest specifically to cover the cost of this project. Milford can capitalize the interest cost of the entire amount of the $12,000,000 loan at 9% interest, but it still has $3,000,000 of average expenditures that exceed the amount of this project-specific loan.

Milford has two bonds outstanding at the time of the project, in the following amounts:

Bond Description	Principal Outstanding	Interest
8% Bond	$18,000,000	$1,440,000
10% Bond	12,000,000	1,200,000
Totals	$30,000,000	$2,640,000

The weighted-average interest rate on these two bond issuances is 8.8% ($2,640,000 interest ÷ $30,000,000 principal), which is the interest rate that Milford should use when capitalizing the remaining $3,000,000 of average expenditures.

These rules regarding the formulation of the capitalization rate are subject to some interpretation. The key guideline is to arrive at a *reasonable* measure of the cost of financing the acquisition of a fixed asset, particularly in regard to the interest cost that could have been avoided if the acquisition had not been made. Thus, use a selection of outstanding borrowings as the basis for a weighted average calculation. This may result in the inclusion or exclusion of borrowings at the corporate level, or just at the level of the subsidiary where the asset is located.

EXAMPLE

Milford Public Sound (MPS) has issued several bonds and notes, totaling $50,000,000, that are used to fund both general corporate activities and construction projects. It also has access to a low-cost 4% internal line of credit that is extended to it by its corporate parent, Milford Sound. MPS regularly uses this line of credit for short-term activities, and typically draws the balance down to zero at least once a year. The average amount of this line that is outstanding is approximately $10,000,000 at any given time.

Since the corporate line of credit comprises a significant amount of MPS's ongoing borrowings, and there is no restriction that prevents these funds from being used for construction projects, it would be reasonable to include the interest cost of this line of credit in the calculation of the weighted-average cost of borrowings that is used to derive MPS's capitalization rate.

Calculating Interest Capitalization

Follow these steps to calculate the amount of interest to be capitalized for a specific project:

1. Construct a table itemizing the amounts of expenditures made and the dates on which the expenditures were made.
2. Determine the date on which interest capitalization ends.
3. Calculate the capitalization period for each expenditure, which is the number of days between the specific expenditure and the end of the interest capitalization period.
4. Divide each capitalization period by the total number of days elapsed between the date of the first expenditure and the end of the interest capitalization period to arrive at the capitalization multiplier for each line item.
5. Multiply each expenditure amount by its capitalization multiplier to arrive at the average expenditure for each line item over the capitalization measurement period.
6. Add up the average expenditures at the line item level to arrive at a grand total average expenditure.
7. If there is project-specific debt, multiply the grand total of the average expenditures by the interest rate on that debt to arrive at the capitalized interest related to that debt.
8. If the grand total of the average expenditures exceeds the amount of the project-specific debt, multiply the excess expenditure amount by the weighted average of the company's other outstanding debt to arrive at the remaining amount of interest to be capitalized.
9. Add together both capitalized interest calculations. If the combined total is more than the total interest cost incurred by the company during the calculation period, reduce the amount of interest to be capitalized to the total interest cost incurred by the company during the calculation period.
10. Record the interest capitalization with a debit to the project's fixed asset account and a credit to the interest expense account.

EXAMPLE

Milford Public Sound is building a concert arena. Milford makes payments related to the project of $10,000,000 and $14,000,000 to a contractor on January 1 and July 1, respectively. The arena is completed on December 31.

For the 12-month period of construction, Milford can capitalize all of the interest on the $10,000,000 payment, since it was outstanding during the full period of construction. Milford can capitalize the interest on the $14,000,000 payment for half of the construction period, since it was outstanding during only the second half of the construction period. The average expenditure for which the interest cost can be capitalized is calculated in the following table:

Date of Payment	Expenditure Amount	Capitalization Period*	Capitalization Multiplier	Average Expenditure
January 1	$10,000,000	12 months	12/12 months = 100%	$10,000,000
July 1	14,000,000	6 months	6/12 months = 50%	7,000,000
				$17,000,000

* In the table, the capitalization period is defined as the number of months that elapse between the expenditure payment date and the end of the interest capitalization period.

The only debt that Milford has outstanding during this period is a line of credit, on which the interest rate is 8%. The maximum amount of interest that Milford can capitalize into the cost of this arena project is $1,360,000, which is calculated as:

8% Interest rate × $17,000,000 Average expenditure = $1,360,000

Milford records the following journal entry:

	Debit	Credit
Fixed assets – Arena	1,360,000	
Interest expense		1,360,000

Tip: There may be an inordinate number of expenditures related to a larger project, which could result in a large and unwieldy calculation of average expenditures. To reduce the workload, consider aggregating these expenses by month, and then assume that each expenditure was made in the middle of the month, thereby reducing all of the expenditures for each month to a single line item.

Do not capitalize more interest cost in an accounting period than the total amount of interest cost incurred by the business in that period. If there is a corporate parent, this rule means that the amount capitalized cannot exceed the total amount of interest cost incurred by the business on a consolidated basis.

Tip: Do not include the cost of asset retirement obligations in the expenditure total on which the interest capitalization calculation is based, since there is no up-front expenditure associated with such an obligation (see the Asset Retirement Obligations chapter for more information).

Derecognizing Capitalized Interest

Capitalized interest is considered to be an integral part of the cost of an asset, so account for it in the same manner as any other capitalized cost of a fixed asset. See the Asset Disposal chapter for more information.

Interest Capitalization under IFRS

Interest capitalization under International Financial Reporting Standards is addressed in IAS 23, *Borrowing Costs*. The IFRS rules are essentially the same as those required by GAAP. The key features of the IFRS rules related to interest capitalization, including some minor differences from GAAP, are:

- Capitalize interest costs that are directly attributable to the acquisition, construction, or production of a fixed asset into the cost of that asset.
- If a company is located in a hyperinflationary economy, charge that portion of interest costs to expense that compensates for inflation, rather than capitalizing it.
- Interest costs eligible for capitalization are those that would have been avoided if the asset had not been acquired.
- If using a specific borrowing to obtain an asset, capitalize the interest cost associated with that borrowing, less any investment income earned on the temporary investment of those borrowings (as may occur when the borrowed funds are received early in the project, but are not immediately needed).

EXAMPLE

Milford Public Sound issues a one-year note for $20,000,000 at 6% interest to pay for the construction of a new arena. At the end of the one-year period, Milford has incurred $1,200,000 in interest costs, but has also earned $250,000 on interest income from the temporary investment of funds received from the note. Thus, the maximum amount of interest expense that Milford can capitalize is $950,000 ($1,200,000 interest cost - $250,000 interest income).

- The capitalization rate to use for capitalizing the cost of interest is the rate on the borrowings incurred specifically for the project, after which the weighted average rate of other borrowings are used for any remaining expenditures. The amount of interest capitalized cannot exceed the total amount of borrowing costs incurred during the period.

- The start of interest capitalization is the *commencement date*, which is defined as the date when a company begins to incur expenditures for a project, *and* incurs borrowing costs, *and* begins to prepare the asset for its intended use or sale. Preparing an asset for its intended use or sale can encompass a variety of administrative activities prior to actual construction, such as designing the asset or obtaining construction permits.
- Suspend the capitalization of interest costs when there are extended periods when a company suspends the active development of an asset. However, interest may still be capitalized when there is a temporary delay, such as waiting for a construction permit to be granted.
- Terminate all interest capitalization when substantially all of the activities required to prepare the project for its intended use or sale are complete. This means that minor modifications and adjustments will not keep the interest capitalization from being terminated.
- If a portion of a project can be completed while construction continues on other parts of the project, stop capitalizing the cost of interest on that portion of the project.

Summary

The key issue with interest capitalization is whether to use it at all. It requires a certain amount of administrative effort to compile, and so is not recommended for smaller fixed assets. Instead, reserve its use for larger projects where including the cost of interest in an asset will improve the quality of the financial information reported by the entity. It should *not* be used merely to delay the recognition of interest expense.

If interest capitalization is chosen, adopt a procedure for determining the amount to be capitalized and closely adhere to it, with appropriate documentation of the results. This will result in a standardized calculation methodology that auditors can more easily review.

Chapter 5
Asset Retirement Obligations

Introduction

An asset retirement obligation (ARO) is a liability associated with the retirement of a fixed asset, such as a legal requirement to return a site to its previous condition. The concept of an ARO is dealt with in great detail within Generally Accepted Accounting Principles (GAAP), and is only referenced in passing within International Financial Reporting Standards (IFRS). Thus, nearly all of the discussion in this chapter concerns the GAAP requirements for asset retirement obligations. An example near the end of the chapter illustrates many of the concepts noted below. In addition, this chapter addresses when to record a liability associated with an environmental obligation, how to determine the amount of the liability and the types of costs that should be included in it.

The Liability for an Asset Retirement Obligation

A company usually incurs an ARO due to a legal obligation. It may also incur an ARO if a company promises a third party (even the public at large) that it will engage in ARO activities; the circumstances of this promise will drive the determination of whether there is an actual liability. This liability may exist even if there has been no formal action against the company. When making the determination of liability, base the evaluation on current laws, not on projections of what laws there may be in the future, when the asset retirement occurs.

EXAMPLE

Glow Atomic operates an atomic power generation facility, and is required by law to bring the property back to its original condition when the plant is eventually decertified. The company has come under some pressure by various environmental organizations to take the remediation one step further and create a public park on the premises. Because of the significant negative publicity generated by these groups, the company issues a press release in which it commits to create the park. There is no legal requirement for the company to incur this additional expense, so the company's legal counsel should evaluate the facts to determine if there is a legal obligation.

A business should recognize the fair value of an ARO when it incurs the liability, and if it can make a reasonable estimate of the fair value of the ARO.

EXAMPLE

Glow Atomic has completed the construction of an atomic power generation facility, but has not yet taken delivery of fuel rods or undergone certification tests. It will incur an ARO for decontamination, but since it has not yet begun operations, it has not begun to contaminate, and therefore should not yet record an ARO liability.

If a fair value is not initially obtainable, recognize the ARO at a later date, when the fair value becomes available. If a company acquires a fixed asset to which an ARO is attached, recognize a liability for the ARO as of the fixed asset acquisition date.

If there is not sufficient information available to reasonably estimate the fair value of an ARO, you may be able to use an expected present value technique that assigns probabilities to cash flows, thereby creating an estimate of the fair value of the ARO. Use an expected present value technique under either of the following scenarios:

- Other parties have specified the settlement date and method of settlement, so that the only uncertainty is whether the obligation will be enforced.
- There is information available from which to estimate the range of possible settlement dates and possible methods of settlement, as well as the probabilities associated with them.

Examples of the sources from which to obtain the information needed for the preceding estimation requirements are past practice within the company, industry practice, the stated intentions of management, or the estimated useful life of the asset (which indicates a likely ARO settlement date at the end of the useful life).

Tip: The ARO settlement date may be quite a bit further in the future than the useful life of an asset may initially indicate, if the company intends to prolong the useful life with asset upgrades, or has a history of doing so.

If there is an unambiguous requirement that causes an ARO, but there is a low likelihood of a performance requirement, a liability must still be recognized. When you incorporate the low probability of performance into the expected present value calculation for the ARO liability, this will likely reduce the amount of the ARO that is recognized. Even if there has been a history of non-enforcement of prior AROs for which there was an unambiguous obligation, do not defer the recognition of a liability.

The Initial Measurement of an Asset Retirement Obligation

In most cases, the only way to determine the fair value of an ARO is to use an expected present value technique. When constructing an expected present value of future cash flows, incorporate the following points into the calculation:

- *Discount rate.* Use a credit-adjusted risk-free rate to discount cash flows to their present value. Thus, the credit standing of a business may impact the discount rate used.
- *Probability distribution.* When calculating the expected present value of an ARO, and there are only two possible outcomes, assign a 50 percent probability to each one until there is additional information that alters the initial probability distribution. Otherwise, spread the probability across the full set of possible scenarios.

EXAMPLE

Glow Atomic is compiling the cost of a decontamination ARO several years in the future. It is uncertain of the cost, since supplier fees fluctuate considerably. It arrives at an expected weighted average cash flow based on the following probability analysis:

Cash Flow Estimates	Probability Assessment	Expected Cash Flows
$12,500,000	10%	$1,250,000
15,000,000	15%	2,250,000
16,000,000	50%	8,000,000
22,500,000	25%	5,625,000
	Weighted average cash flows	$17,125,000

Follow these steps in calculating the expected present value of an ARO:

1. Estimate the timing and amount of the cash flows associated with the retirement activities.
2. Determine the credit-adjusted risk-free rate.
3. Recognize any period-to-period increase in the carrying amount of the ARO liability as *accretion expense*. To do so, multiply the beginning liability by the credit-adjusted risk-free rate derived when the liability was first measured.
4. Recognize upward liability revisions as a new liability layer, and discount them at the current credit-adjusted risk-free rate.
5. Recognize downward liability revisions by reducing the appropriate liability layer, and discount the reduction at the rate used for the initial recognition of the related liability layer.

Accretion expense is an expense arising from an increase in the carrying amount of the liability associated with an asset retirement obligation. It is not interest expense. It is classified as an operating expense in the income statement.

When an ARO liability is initially recognized, also capitalize the related asset retirement cost by adding it to the carrying amount of the related fixed asset.

Subsequent Measurement of an Asset Retirement Obligation

It is possible that an ARO liability will not remain static over the life of the related fixed asset. Instead, the liability may change over time. If the liability increases, consider the incremental increase in each period to be an additional layer of liability, in addition to any previous liability layers. The following points will assist in the recognition of these additional layers:

- Initially recognize each layer at its fair value.

EXAMPLE

Glow Atomic has been operating an atomic power plant for three years. It initially recognized an ARO of $250 million for the eventual dismantling of the plant after its useful life has ended. In the fifth year, Glow detects groundwater contamination, and recognizes an additional layer of ARO liability for $20 million to deal with it. In the seventh year, a leak in the sodium cooling lines causes overheating and a significant release of radioactive steam that impacts 50 square miles of land downwind from the facility. Glow recognizes an additional layer of ARO liability of $150 million to address this issue.

- Systematically allocate the ARO liability to expense over the useful life of the underlying asset.
- Measure changes in the liability due to the passage of time, using the credit-adjusted risk-free rate when each layer of liability was first recognized. This cost is recognized as an increase in the liability. When charged to expense, this is classified as accretion expense.
- As the time period shortens before an ARO is realized, the assessment of the timing, amount, and probabilities associated with cash flows will improve. You will likely need to alter the ARO liability based on these changes in estimate. If an upward revision is made to the ARO liability, discount it using the current credit-adjusted risk-free rate. If a downward revision is made to the ARO liability, discount it using the original credit-adjusted risk-free rate when the liability layer was first recognized. If it is not possible to identify the liability layer to which the downward adjustment relates, use a weighted-average credit-adjusted risk-free rate to discount it.

Settlement of an Asset Retirement Obligation

An ARO is normally settled only when the underlying fixed asset is retired, though it is possible that some portion of an ARO will be settled prior to asset retirement.

If it becomes apparent that no expenses will be required as part of the retirement of an asset, reverse any remaining unamortized ARO to zero.

> **Tip:** If a company cannot fulfill its ARO responsibilities and a third party does so instead, this does not relieve the company from recording an ARO liability, on the grounds that it may now have an obligation to pay the third party instead.

EXAMPLE

Glow Atomic operates an atomic power generation facility, and is legally required to decontaminate the facility when it is decommissioned in five years. Glow uses the following assumptions about the ARO:

- The decontamination cost is $90 million.
- The risk-free rate is 5%, to which Glow adds 3% to reflect the effect of its credit standing.
- The assumed rate of inflation over the five-year period is four percent.

With an average inflation rate of 4% per year for the next five years, the current decontamination cost of $90 million increases to approximately $109.5 million by the end of the fifth year. The expected present value of the $109.5 million payout, using the 8% credit-adjusted risk-free rate, is $74,524,000 (calculated as $109.5 million × 0.68058 discount rate).

Glow then calculates the amount of annual accretion using the 8% rate, as shown in the following table:

Year	Beginning Liability	Accretion	Ending Liability
1	$74,524,000	$5,962,000	$80,486,000
2	80,486,000	6,439,000	86,925,000
3	86,925,000	6,954,000	93,879,000
4	93,879,000	7,510,000	101,389,000
5	101,389,000	8,111,000	109,500,000

Glow then combines the accretion expense with the straight-line depreciation expense noted in the following table to show how all components of the ARO are charged to expense over the next five years. Note that the accretion expense is carried forward from the preceding table. The depreciation is based on the $74,524,000 present value of the ARO, spread evenly over five years.

Year	Accretion Expense	Depreciation Expense	Total Expense
1	$5,962,000	$14,904,800	$20,866,800
2	6,439,000	14,904,800	21,343,800
3	6,954,000	14,904,800	21,858,800
4	7,510,000	14,904,800	22,414,800
5	8,111,000	14,904,800	23,015,800
			$109,500,000

After the plant is closed, Glow commences its decontamination activities. The actual cost is $115 million.

Here is a selection of the journal entries that Glow recorded over the term of the ARO:

	Debit	Credit
Facility decontamination asset	90,000,000	
Asset retirement obligation liability		90,000,000
To record the initial fair value of the asset retirement obligation		

	Debit	Credit
Depreciation expense	14,904,800	
Accumulated depreciation		14,904,800
To record the annual depreciation on the asset retirement obligation		

	Debit	Credit
Accretion expense	As noted in schedule	
Asset retirement obligation liability		As noted in schedule
To record the annual accretion expense on the asset retirement obligation liability		

	Debit	Credit
Loss on ARO settlement	5,500,000	
Remediation expense		5,500,000
To record settlement of the excess asset retirement obligation		

Overview of Environmental Obligations

There are a number of federal laws that impose an obligation on a business to remediate sites that contain environmentally hazardous conditions, as well as to control or prevent pollution. Remediation can include feasibility studies, cleanup costs, legal fees, government oversight costs, and restoration costs.

In total, these laws can create a serious liability for a business, to the extent of causing the business to go bankrupt. Consider, for example, the extent of liability associated with a Superfund site, where liability can be associated with:

- The current owner or operator of the site
- Previous owners or operators of the site at the time of disposal of hazardous substances
- Parties that arranged for the disposal of hazardous substances found at the site
- Parties that transported hazardous substances to the site

The level of liability imposed by other environmental laws may not be as all-encompassing as the Superfund liability, but the level of liability imposed can still be crushing. Accordingly, the accounting for environmental obligations must be well documented, in order to convey the full scope of the liability.

In general, a liability for an environmental obligation should be accrued if both of the following circumstances are present:

- It is probable that an asset has been impaired or a liability has been incurred. This is based on both of the following criteria:
  - An assertion has been made that the business bears responsibility for a past event; and
  - It is probable that the outcome of the assertion will be unfavorable to the business.

- The amount of the loss or a range of loss can be reasonably estimated.

It is recognized that the liability associated with environmental obligations can change dramatically over time, depending on the number and type of hazardous substances involved, the financial condition of other responsible parties, and other factors. Accordingly, the recorded liability associated with environmental obligations can change. Further, it may not be possible to initially estimate some components of the liability, which does not prevent other components of the liability from being recognized as soon as possible.

EXAMPLE

Glow Atomics has been notified by the government that it must conduct a remedial investigation and feasibility study for a Superfund site to which it sent uranium waste products in the past. There is sufficient information to estimate the cost of the study, for which Glow records an accrued liability. However, there is no way to initially determine the extent of any additional liabilities associated with the site until the study has at least commenced. Accordingly, Glow continually reviews the preliminary findings of the study, and updates the liability for its environmental obligation based on changes in that information.

Once there is information available regarding the extent of an environmental obligation, a business should record its best estimate of the liability. If it is not possible to create a best estimate, at least a minimum estimate of the liability should be recorded. The estimate is refined as better information becomes available.

In some cases, it is possible to derive a reasonable estimate of liability quite early in the remediation process, because it is similar to the remediation that a business has encountered at other sites. In these instances, recognize the full amount of the liability at once.

The costs associated with the treatment of environmental contamination costs should be charged to expense in nearly all cases. The sole exceptions are:

- The costs incurred will increase the capacity of the property, or extend its life, or improve its safety or efficiency
- The costs incurred are needed to prepare a property for sale that is currently classified as held for sale
- The costs improve the property, as well as mitigate or prevent environmental contamination that has yet to occur and that might otherwise arise from future operations

EXAMPLE

Armadillo Industries spends $250,000 to construct a concrete pad that is designed to prevent fluid leaks from causing groundwater contamination. Making this investment improves the safety of the property, while also preventing future environmental contamination. Consequently, Armadillo can capitalize the $250,000 cost of the concrete pad, and should depreciate it over the remaining useful life of the property.

Measurement of Environmental Obligations

In order to determine the extent of the liability associated with an environmental obligation, follow these steps:

1. Identify those parties likely to be considered responsible for the site requiring remediation. These potentially responsible parties may include the following:

   - Participating parties
   - Recalcitrant parties
   - Unproven parties
   - Unknown parties
   - Orphan share parties

2. Determine the likelihood that those parties will pay their share of the liability associated with site remediation, based primarily on their financial condition. There is a presumption that costs will only be allocated among

the participating responsible parties, since the other parties are less likely to pay their shares of the liability.

3. Based on the preceding steps, calculate the percentage of the total liability that the company should record. The sources for this information can include the liability percentages that the responsible parties have agreed to, or which have been assigned by a consultant, or which have been assigned by the Environmental Protection Agency (EPA). If the company chooses to record the liability in a different amount, it should be based on objective, verifiable information, examples of which are:

- Existing data about the types and amounts of waste at the site
- Prior experience with liability allocations in comparable situations
- Reports issued by environmental specialists
- Internal data that refutes EPA allegations

EXAMPLE

Armadillo Industries has been notified by the EPA that it is a potentially responsible party in a groundwater contamination case. The EPA has identified three companies as being potentially responsible. The three parties employ an arbitrator to allocate the responsibility for costs among the companies. The arbitrator derives the following allocations:

	Allocation Percentage
Armadillo Industries	40%
Boxcar Munitions	20%
Chelsea Chemicals	20%
	80%
Recalcitrant share (nonparticipating parties)	15%
Orphan share (no party can be identified)	5%
Total	100%

The total estimated remediation cost is estimated to be $5 million. Armadillo's direct share of this amount is $2 million (calculated as $5 million total remediation × 40% share). Also, Armadillo should record a liability for its share of those amounts allocated to other parties who are not expected to pay their shares, which is $500,000 (calculated as half of the total allocation for responsible parties × the cost allocated to the recalcitrant and orphan shares).

The costs that should be included in a company's liability for environmental obligations include the following:

- Direct remediation activity costs, such as investigations, risk assessments, remedial actions, activities related to government oversight, and post-remediation monitoring.
- The compensation and related benefit costs for those employees expected to spend a significant amount of their time on remediation activities.

When measuring these costs, do so for the estimated time periods during which activities will occur, which means that an inflation factor should be included for periods further in the future. It may also be possible to include a productivity factor that is caused by gaining experience with remediation efforts over time, and which may reduce mitigation costs. When it is not possible to estimate the costs of inflation, perhaps due to uncertainties about the timing of expenditures, it is acceptable to initially record costs at their current-cost estimates, and adjust them later, as more precise information becomes available.

Any costs related to routine environmental compliance activities, as well as any litigation costs associated with potential recoveries, are not considered part of the remediation effort, and so are not included in the environmental obligation liability. These costs are to be charged to expense as incurred.

Changes in the environmental liability are especially likely when there are multiple parties involved, since additional parties may be added over time, or the apportionment of liability between parties may change. Also, estimates of the exact amount of cost incurred will change continually. For these reasons, the amount of liability recorded for environmental obligations will almost certainly not be the exact amount that is eventually incurred, and so will have to be updated at regular intervals. If so, each update is treated as a change in estimate, which means that there is no retroactive change in the liability reported by a business; instead, the change is recorded only on a go-forward basis.

Recoveries Related to Environmental Obligations

It is possible that a business may contact other entities concerning the recovery of funds expended on environmental remediation, on the grounds that the other entities are liable for the remediation (or are liable because they are insurers).

The recognition of an asset related to the recovery of an environmental obligation should not be made unless recovery of the claimed amount is considered probable and the amount can be reasonably estimated. If a claim is currently the subject of litigation, it is reasonable to assume that recovery of the claim is not probable, and so should not be recognized.

A recovery can be recorded at its undiscounted amount if the liability is not discounted, and the timing of the recovery is dependent on the timing of the liability payment. This will be the case in most situations, so the recovery will generally be recorded at its undiscounted amount.

Asset Retirement Obligations under IFRS

IFRS has not yet given much attention to the concept of asset retirement obligations. IFRS merely states that you should include in the initial cost of a fixed asset the initial estimate of the costs of dismantling and removing an item and restoring the site on which it is located.

Since the cost of an asset is defined in IFRS as the cash price equivalent on the recognition date, we may infer that the cost of an ARO is actually the present value of the future cash flows associated with this action. If so, use as a discount rate the market rate at the time of recognition, adjusted for the risks specific to the ARO.

Summary

The accounting for an asset retirement obligation can be complex, especially if there are multiple liability layers and changes to those layers occur with some frequency. Because of the additional accounting effort required to track AROs, it makes sense to use every effort to avoid the recognition of an ARO within the boundaries set by GAAP. In many cases, the amount of an ARO will likely be so minimal as to not require recognition. However, in such industries as mining, chemicals, and power generation, the concept of the ARO is of great concern, and forms a significant proportion of a company's total liabilities.

Environmental obligations can strike any company, large or small, and can result in a massive liability. The accounting for this liability is not especially difficult. However, given its considerable impact on a company's financial results, it is necessary to thoroughly document the calculation of all recorded environmental liabilities, as well as the justification for *not* recording any additional liabilities.

Chapter 6
Depreciation and Amortization

Introduction

This chapter describes why we use depreciation and amortization, key terms, and the various methods for calculating depreciation and amortization, as well as the accounting entries associated with these calculations. We end the chapter with a review of the key depreciation concepts used in International Financial Reporting Standards.

The difference between depreciation and amortization is that amortization is associated with charging intangible assets to expense over their usage period, and depreciation is associated with charging tangible assets to expense over their usage period. A similar concept, *depletion*, involves charging the cost of natural resources to expense over their usage period.

The treatment of amortization is quite similar to the treatment of depreciation, so much of the discussion in this chapter pertaining to depreciation also applies to amortization.

The Purpose of Depreciation

The purpose of depreciation is to charge to expense a portion of an asset that relates to the revenue generated by that asset. This is called the matching principle, where revenues and expenses both appear in the income statement in the same reporting period, which gives the best view of how well a company has performed in a given accounting period. The trouble with this matching concept is that there is usually only a tenuous connection between the generation of revenue and a specific asset. Under the tenets of constraint analysis, all of the assets of a company should be treated as a single system that generates a profit; thus, there is no way to link a specific asset to specific revenue.

To get around this linkage problem, we usually assume a steady rate of depreciation over the useful life of each asset, so that we approximate a linkage between the recognition of revenues and expenses. This approximation threatens our credulity even more when a company uses accelerated depreciation, since the main reason for using it is to defer taxes (and not to better match revenues and expenses).

If we were not to use depreciation at all, we would be forced to charge all assets to expense as soon as we buy them. This would result in large losses in the months when this purchase transaction occurs, followed by unusually high profitability in those periods when the corresponding amount of revenue is recognized, with no offsetting expense. Thus, a company that does not use depreciation will have front-loaded expenses, and extremely variable financial results.

Depreciation Concepts

There are three factors to consider in the calculation of depreciation, which are:

- *Useful life*. This is the time period over which an asset is expected to be productive, or the number of units of production expected to be generated from it. Past its useful life, it is no longer cost-effective to continue operating the asset, so a business would dispose of it or stop using it. Depreciation is recognized over the useful life of an asset.

Tip: Rather than recording a different useful life for every asset, it is easier to assign each asset to an asset class, where every asset in that asset class has the same useful life. This approach may not work for very high-cost assets, where a greater degree of precision may be needed.

- *Salvage value*. When a company eventually disposes of an asset, it may be able to sell the asset for some reduced amount, which is the salvage value. Depreciation is calculated based on the asset cost, less any estimated salvage value. If salvage value is expected to be quite small, it is generally ignored for the purpose of calculating depreciation. Salvage value is not discounted to its present value.

Tip: If the amount of salvage value associated with an asset is minor, it is easier from a calculation perspective to not reduce the depreciable amount of the asset by the salvage value. Instead, assume that the salvage value is zero.

EXAMPLE

Pensive Corporation buys an asset for $100,000, and estimates that its salvage value will be $10,000 in five years, when it plans to dispose of the asset. This means that Pensive will depreciate $90,000 of the asset cost over five years, leaving $10,000 of the cost remaining at the end of that time. Pensive expects to then sell the asset for $10,000, which will eliminate the asset from Pensive's accounting records.

- *Depreciation method*. Depreciation expense can be calculated using an accelerated depreciation method, or evenly over the useful life of the asset. The advantage of using an accelerated method is that more depreciation can be recognized early in the life of a fixed asset, which defers some income tax expense recognition into a later period. The advantage of using a steady depreciation rate is the ease of calculation. Examples of accelerated depreciation methods are the double declining balance and sum-of-the-years' digits methods. The primary method for steady depreciation is the straight-line method.

The *mid-month convention* states that, no matter when a fixed asset is purchased in a month, you assume that it was purchased in the middle of the month for depreciation purposes. Thus, if a fixed asset was bought on January 5th, assume that it was bought on January 15th; or, if you bought it on January 28, still assume that you bought it on January 15th. By doing so, you can more easily calculate a standard half-month of depreciation for that first month of ownership.

If you choose to use the mid-month convention, this also means that a half-month of depreciation should be recorded for the *last* month of the asset's useful life. By doing so, the two-half month depreciation calculations equal one full month of depreciation.

Many companies prefer to use full-month depreciation in the first month of ownership, irrespective of the actual date of purchase within the month, so that they can slightly accelerate their recognition of depreciation, which in turn reduces their taxable income in the near term.

Accelerated Depreciation

Accelerated depreciation is the depreciation of fixed assets at a very fast rate early in their useful lives. The primary reason for using accelerated depreciation is to reduce the reported amount of taxable income over the first few years of an asset's life, so that a company pays a smaller amount of income taxes during those early years. Later on, when most of the depreciation will have already been recognized, the effect reverses, so there will be less depreciation available to shelter taxable income. The result is that a company pays more income taxes in later years. Thus, the net effect of accelerated depreciation is the deferral of income taxes to later time periods.

A secondary reason for using accelerated depreciation is that it may actually reflect the usage pattern of the underlying assets, where they experience heavy usage early in their useful lives.

There are several calculations available for accelerated depreciation, such as the double declining balance method and the sum of the years' digits method. We will describe these methods later in the chapter.

If a company elects not to use accelerated depreciation, it can instead use the straight-line method, where it depreciates an asset at the same standard rate throughout its useful life. It is customary to use the straight-line method for the amortization of intangible assets, since it is difficult to argue that an intangible asset experiences heavy usage earlier in its useful life, and therefore requires an accelerated method of amortization.

All of the depreciation methods end up recognizing the same amount of depreciation, which is the cost of the fixed asset less any expected salvage value. The only difference between the various methods is the speed with which depreciation is recognized.

Accelerated depreciation requires additional depreciation calculations and record keeping, so some companies avoid it for that reason (though fixed asset software can readily overcome this issue). They may also ignore it if they are not consistently earning taxable income, which takes away the primary reason for using it. Companies may also ignore accelerated depreciation if they have a relatively small amount of fixed assets, so that the tax effect of using accelerated depreciation is minimal. Finally, if a company is publicly held, management may be more interested in reporting the highest possible amount of net income in order to buoy its stock price for the benefit of investors - these companies will likely not be interested in accelerated depreciation, which reduces the reported amount of net income.

Straight-Line Method

Under the straight-line method of depreciation, recognize depreciation expense evenly over the estimated useful life of an asset. The straight-line calculation steps are:

1. Subtract the estimated salvage value of the asset from the amount at which it is recorded on the books.
2. Determine the estimated useful life of the asset. It is easiest to use a standard useful life for each class of assets.
3. Divide the estimated useful life (in years) into 1 to arrive at the straight-line depreciation rate.
4. Multiply the depreciation rate by the asset cost (less salvage value).

EXAMPLE

Pensive Corporation purchases the Procrastinator Deluxe machine for $60,000. It has an estimated salvage value of $10,000 and a useful life of five years. Pensive calculates the annual straight-line depreciation for the machine as:

1. Purchase cost of $60,000 – Estimated salvage value of $10,000 = Depreciable asset cost of $50,000
2. 1 ÷ 5-Year useful life = 20% Depreciation rate per year
3. 20% Depreciation rate × $50,000 Depreciable asset cost = $10,000 Annual depreciation

Sum-of-the-Years' Digits Method

The sum of the years' digits (SYD) method is more appropriate than straight-line depreciation if the asset depreciates more quickly or has greater production capacity in earlier years than it does as it ages. Use the following formula to calculate it:

$$\text{Depreciation percentage} = \frac{\text{Number of estimated years of life as of beginning of the year}}{\text{Sum of the years' digits}}$$

The following table contains examples of the sum of the years' digits noted in the denominator of the preceding formula.

Sum of the Years' Digits Calculation

Total Depreciation Period	Initial Sum of the Years' Digits	Calculation
2 years	3	1 + 2
3 years	6	1 + 2 + 3
4 years	10	1 + 2 + 3 + 4
5 years	15	1 + 2 + 3 + 4 + 5

The concept is most easily illustrated with the following example.

EXAMPLE

Pensive Corporation buys a Procrastinator Elite machine for $100,000. The machine has no estimated salvage value, and a useful life of five years. Pensive calculates the annual sum of the years' digits depreciation for this machine as:

Year	Number of estimated years of life as of beginning of the year	SYD Calculation	Depreciation Percentage	Annual Depreciation
1	5	5/15	33.33%	$33,333
2	4	4/15	26.67%	26,667
3	3	3/15	20.00%	20,000
4	2	2/15	13.33%	13,333
5	1	1/15	6.67%	6,667
Totals	15		100.00%	$100,000

The sum of the years' digits method is clearly more complex than the straight-line method, which tends to limit its use unless software is employed to automatically track the calculations for each asset.

Double-Declining Balance Method

The double declining balance (DDB) method is a form of accelerated depreciation. It may be more appropriate than the straight-line method if an asset experiences an inordinately high level of usage during the first few years of its useful life.

To calculate the double-declining balance depreciation rate, divide the number of years of useful life of an asset into 100 percent, and multiply the result by two. The formula is:

$$(100\%/\text{Years of useful life}) \times 2$$

The DDB calculation proceeds until the asset's salvage value is reached, after which depreciation ends.

EXAMPLE

Pensive Corporation purchases a machine for $50,000. It has an estimated salvage value of $5,000 and a useful life of five years. The calculation of the double declining balance depreciation rate is:

$$(100\%/\text{Years of useful life}) \times 2 = 40\%$$

By applying the 40% rate, Pensive arrives at the following table of depreciation charges per year:

Year	Book Value at Beginning of Year	Depreciation Percentage	DDB Depreciation	Book Value Net of Depreciation
1	$50,000	40%	$20,000	$30,000
2	30,000	40%	12,000	18,000
3	18,000	40%	7,200	10,800
4	10,800	40%	4,320	6,480
5	6,480	40%	1,480	5,000
Total			$45,000	

Note that the depreciation in the fifth and final year is only for $1,480, rather than the $3,240 that would be indicated by the 40% depreciation rate. The reason for the smaller depreciation charge is that Pensive stops any further depreciation once the remaining book value declines to the amount of the estimated salvage value.

An alternative form of double declining balance depreciation is 150% declining balance depreciation. It is a less aggressive form of depreciation, since it is calculated as 1.5 times the straight-line rate, rather than the 2x multiple that is used for the double declining balance method. Thus, if you were to use it, the formula would be:

$$(100\%/\text{Years of useful life}) \times 1.5$$

81

EXAMPLE

[Note: We are repeating the preceding example, but using 150% declining balance depreciation instead of double declining balance depreciation]

Pensive Corporation purchases a machine for $50,000. It has an estimated salvage value of $5,000 and a useful life of five years. The calculation of the 150% declining balance depreciation rate is:

$$(100\%/\text{Years of useful life}) \times 1.5 = 30\%$$

By applying the 30% rate, Pensive arrives at the following table of depreciation charges per year:

Year	Book Value at Beginning of Year	Depreciation Percentage	DDB Depreciation	Book Value Net of Depreciation
1	$50,000	30%	$15,000	$35,000
2	35,000	30%	10,500	24,500
3	24,500	30%	7,350	17,150
4	17,150	30%	5,145	12,005
5	12,005	30%	7,005	5,000
Total			$45,000	

In this case, the depreciation expense in the fifth and final year of $3,602 ($12,005 × 30%) results in a net book value that is somewhat higher than the estimated salvage value of $5,000, so Pensive instead records $7,005 of depreciation in order to arrive at a net book value that equals the estimated salvage value.

Depletion Method

Depletion is a periodic charge to expense for the use of natural resources. Thus, it is used in situations where a company has recorded an asset for such items as oil reserves, coal deposits, or gravel pits. The calculation of depletion involves these steps:

1. Compute a depletion base.
2. Compute a unit depletion rate.
3. Charge depletion based on units of usage.

The depletion base is the asset that is to be depleted. It is comprised of the following four types of costs:

- *Acquisition costs.* The cost to either buy or lease property.
- *Exploration costs.* The cost to locate assets that may then be depleted. In most cases, these costs are charged to expense as incurred.

- *Development costs*. The cost to prepare the property for asset extraction, which includes the cost of such items as tunnels and wells.
- *Restoration costs*. The cost to restore property to its original condition after depletion activities have been concluded.

To compute a unit depletion rate, subtract the salvage value of the asset from the depletion base and divide it by the total number of measurement units that you expect to recover. The formula for the unit depletion rate is:

$$\text{Unit depletion rate} = \frac{\text{Depletion base} - \text{Salvage value}}{\text{Total units to be recovered}}$$

Then create the depletion charge based on actual units of usage. Thus, if you extract 500 barrels of oil and the unit depletion rate is \$5.00 per barrel, the charge is \$2,500 to depletion expense.

The estimated amount of a natural resource that can be recovered will change constantly as you gradually extract assets from a property. As you revise the estimates of the remaining amount of extractable natural resource, incorporate these estimates into the unit depletion rate for the remaining amount to be extracted. This is not a retrospective calculation.

EXAMPLE

Pensive Corporation's subsidiary Pensive Oil drills a well with the intention of extracting oil from a known reservoir. It incurs the following costs related to the acquisition of property and development of the site:

Land purchase	\$280,000
Road construction	23,000
Drill pad construction	48,000
Drilling fees	192,000
Total	\$543,000

In addition, Pensive Oil estimates that it will incur a site restoration cost of \$57,000 once extraction is complete, so the total depletion base of the property is \$600,000.

Pensive's geologists estimate that the proven oil reserves that are accessed by the well are 400,000 barrels, so the unit depletion charge will be \$1.50 per barrel of oil extracted (\$600,000 depletion base ÷ 400,000 barrels).

In the first year, Pensive Oil extracts 100,000 barrels of oil from the well, which results in a depletion charge of \$150,000 (100,000 barrels × \$1.50 unit depletion charge).

At the beginning of the second year of operations, Pensive's geologists issue a revised estimate of the remaining amount of proven reserves, with the new estimate of 280,000 barrels being 20,000 barrels lower than the original estimate (less extractions already completed). This means that the unit depletion charge will increase to $1.61 ($450,000 remaining depletion base ÷ 280,000 barrels).

During the second year, Pensive Oil extracts 80,000 barrels of oil from the well, which results in a depletion charge of $128,800 (80,000 barrels × $1.61 unit depletion charge).

At the end of the second year, there is still a depletion base of $321,200 that must be charged to expense in proportion to the amount of any remaining extractions.

Units of Production Method

Under the units of production method, the amount of depreciation that you charge to expense varies in direct proportion to the amount of asset usage. Thus, you charge more depreciation in periods when there is more asset usage, and less depreciation in periods when there is less asset usage. It is the most accurate method for charging depreciation, since it links closely to the wear and tear on assets. However, it also requires that you track asset usage, which means that its use is generally limited to more expensive assets. Also, you need to be able to estimate total usage over the life of the asset.

Tip: Do not use the units of production method if there is not a significant difference in asset usage from period to period. Otherwise, you will spend a great deal of time tracking asset usage, and will be rewarded with a depreciation expense that varies little from the results that you would have seen with the straight-line method (which is far easier to calculate).

Follow these steps to calculate depreciation under the units of production method:
1. Estimate the total number of hours of usage of the asset, or the total number of units to be produced by it over its useful life.
2. Subtract any estimated salvage value from the capitalized cost of the asset, and divide the total estimated usage or production from this net depreciable cost. This yields the depreciation cost per hour of usage or unit of production.
3. Multiply the number of hours of usage or units of actual production by the depreciation cost per hour or unit, which results in the total depreciation expense for the accounting period.

If the estimated number of hours of usage or units of production changes over time, incorporate these changes into the calculation of the depreciation cost per hour or unit of production. This will alter the depreciation expense on a go-forward basis.

EXAMPLE

Pensive Corporation's gravel pit operation, Pensive Dirt, builds a conveyor system to extract gravel from a gravel pit at a cost of $400,000. Pensive expects to use the conveyor to extract 1,000,000 tons of gravel, which results in a depreciation rate of $0.40 per ton (1,000,000 tons ÷ $400,000 cost). During the first quarter of activity, Pensive Dirt extracts 10,000 tons of gravel, which results in the following depreciation expense:

= $0.40 depreciation cost per ton × 10,000 tons of gravel

= $4,000 depreciation expense

MACRS Depreciation

MACRS depreciation is the tax depreciation system used in the United States. MACRS is an acronym for Modified Accelerated Cost Recovery System. Under MACRS, fixed assets are assigned to a specific asset class. The Internal Revenue Service has published a complete set of depreciation tables for each of these classes. The classes are noted in the following exhibit.

MACRS Classes and Depreciation Periods

Class	Depreciation Period	Description
3-year property	3 years	Tractor units for over-the-road use, race horses over 2 years old when placed in service, any other horse over 12 years old when placed in service, qualified rent-to-own property
5-year property	5 years	Automobiles, taxis, buses, trucks, computers and peripheral equipment, office equipment, any property used in research and experimentation, breeding cattle and dairy cattle, appliances and etc. used in residential rental real estate activity, certain green energy property
7-year property	7 years	Office furniture and fixtures, agricultural machinery and equipment, any property not designated as being in another class, natural gas gathering lines
10-year property	10 years	Vessels, barges, tugs, single-purpose agricultural or horticultural structures, trees/vines bearing fruits or nuts, qualified small electric meter and smart electric grid systems
15-year property	15 years	Certain land improvements (such as shrubbery, fences, roads, sidewalks and bridges), retail motor fuel outlets, municipal wastewater treatment plants, clearing and grading land improvements for gas utility property, electric transmission property, natural gas distribution lines
20-year property	20 years	Farm buildings (other than those noted under 10-year property), municipal sewers not categorized as 25-year property, the initial clearing and grading of land for electric utility transmission and distribution plants
25-year property	25 years	Property that is an integral part of the water distribution facilities, municipal sewers
Residential rental property	27.5 years	Any building or structure where 80% or more of its gross rental income is from dwelling units
Nonresidential real property	39 years	An office building, store, or warehouse that is not residential property or has a class life of less than 27.5 years

The depreciation rates associated with the more common asset classes are noted in the following table.

Asset Class Depreciation Rates

Recovery Year	3-Year Property	5-Year Property	7-Year Property	10-Year Property	15-Year Property	20-Year Property
1	33.33%	20.00%	14.29%	10.00%	5.00%	3.750%
2	44.45%	32.00%	24.49%	18.00%	9.50%	7.219%
3	14.81%	19.20%	17.49%	14.40%	8.55%	6.677%
4	7.41%	11.52%	12.49%	11.52%	7.70%	6.177%
5		11.52%	8.93%	9.22%	6.93%	5.713%
6		5.76%	8.92%	7.37%	6.23%	5.285%
7			8.93%	6.55%	5.90%	4.888%
8			4.46%	6.55%	5.90%	4.522%
9				6.56%	5.91%	4.462%
10				6.55%	5.90%	4.461%
11				3.28%	5.91%	4.462%
12					5.90%	4.461%
13					5.91%	4.462%
14					5.90%	4.461%
15					5.91%	4.462%
16					2.95%	4.461%
17						4.462%
18						4.461%
19						4.462%
20						4.461%
21						2.231%

Depreciation for tax reporting purposes is calculated by aggregating assets into the various classes noted in the preceding table, and using the depreciation rates for each class. MACRS ignores salvage value.

The MACRS depreciation rates are used to determine the depreciation expense for taxable income, and the other methods described earlier to arrive at the depreciation expense for net income. Since these depreciation methods have differing results, there will be a temporary difference between the book values of fixed assets under the two methods, which will gradually be resolved over their useful lives. Report the difference between depreciation used for calculating taxable income and for the financial statements as a reconciling item in a company's federal income tax return.

The Depreciation of Land

Nearly all fixed assets have a useful life, after which they no longer contribute to the operations of a company or they stop generating revenue. During this useful life, they are depreciated, which reduces their cost to what they are supposed to be worth at the end of their useful lives. Land, however, has no definitive useful life, so there is no way to depreciate it.

The one exception is when some aspect of the land is actually used up, such as when a mine is emptied of its ore reserves. In this case, depreciate the natural resources in the land using the depletion method, as described earlier in this chapter.

The Depreciation of Land Improvements

Land improvements are enhancements to a plot of land to make it more usable. If these improvements have a useful life, depreciate them. If there is no way to estimate a useful life, do not depreciate the cost of the improvements.

If you are preparing land for its intended purpose, include these costs in the cost of the land asset. They are not depreciated. Examples of such costs are:

- Demolishing an existing building
- Clearing and leveling the land

If you are adding functionality to the land and the expenditures have a useful life, record them in a separate Land Improvements account. Examples of land improvements are:

- Drainage and irrigation systems
- Fencing
- Landscaping
- Parking lots and walkways

A special item is the ongoing cost of landscaping. This is a period cost, not a fixed asset, and so should be charged to expense as incurred.

EXAMPLE

Pensive Corporation buys a parcel of land for $1,000,000. Since it is a purchase of land, Pensive cannot depreciate the cost. Pensive then razes a building that was located on the property at a cost of $25,000, fills in the old foundation for $5,000, and levels the land for $50,000. All of these costs are to prepare the land for its intended purpose, so they are all added to the cost of the land. It cannot depreciate these costs.

Pensive intends to use the land as a parking lot, so it spends $400,000 to pave the land, and add walkways and fences. It estimates that the parking lot has a useful life of 20 years. It should record this cost in the Land Improvements account, and depreciate it over 20 years.

Group Depreciation

Group depreciation is the practice of assembling several similar fixed assets into a single group, which is used in aggregate as the cost base for depreciation calculations. Assets should only be assembled into a group if they share similar characteristics and have approximately the same useful lives. Examples of group depreciation are "group of desks" and "group of trucks" that are treated as single assets.

Group depreciation should be on the straight-line basis. When an asset recorded as part of a group is retired, the related asset cost and accumulated depreciation are removed from the group's asset balance and related accumulated depreciation, respectively.

The use of group depreciation can reduce the time required to calculate depreciation, especially when large numbers of assets are aggregated into a single group. However, the practice is not recommended for the following reasons:

- *Computerized depreciation.* If accounting software is used to automate the calculation of depreciation, no labor is saved by using group depreciation.
- *Capitalization limit.* A large number of small-expenditure items can be clustered into a group and treated as a fixed asset, even though they would have been charged to expense if treated as individual units that fall below the corporate capitalization limit.
- *Asset tracking.* It can be difficult to physically track every asset comprising an asset group.
- *Disposal.* The disposal accounting for an asset within an asset group can be confusing, especially when it is not certain which group an asset was assigned to.
- *Group characteristics.* An asset may be fraudulently inserted into the wrong asset group in order to take advantage of the longer useful life or larger salvage value assumptions used for that group (which would effectively delay expense recognition for the asset).

Composite Depreciation

Composite depreciation is the application of a single straight-line depreciation rate and average useful life to a group of disparate fixed assets. The depreciation steps are:

1. Aggregate the total depreciable cost of all assets in the group.
2. Assign a single useful life to the asset group.
3. Divide the useful life figure by the total depreciable cost to arrive at the total depreciation per year under the straight-line method.
4. Record the depreciation for the entire asset group.

In short, composite depreciation involves the use of a weighted average of the depreciation rates for all of the fixed assets in a group.

If an asset that is being accounted for under this system is sold, the related accounting entry is a debit to cash for the amount received and a credit to the fixed asset account for the historical cost of the asset. If there is a difference between the two, record it against the accumulated depreciation account. This accounting treatment means that no gain or loss is recognized at the point of asset sale or disposal.

The method is most commonly used to calculate depreciation for an entire asset class, such as office supplies or production equipment. Composite depreciation can also be used when there are a number of assets comprising a single larger asset; for example, the roof, air conditioning unit, and frame of a building may all have different useful lives, but can be aggregated for depreciation through the composite method. Another situation where composite depreciation can be used is for the depreciation of all the assets in an entire facility.

Given the ease with which fixed asset accounting software can track the depreciation for individual assets, it is not really necessary to use composite depreciation, which may explain its rare usage. The system may have had greater applicability when manual record keeping was needed for fixed assets.

Depreciation Accounting Entries

The basic depreciation entry is to debit the depreciation expense account (which appears in the income statement) and credit the accumulated depreciation account (which appears in the balance sheet as a contra account that reduces the amount of fixed assets). Over time, the accumulated depreciation balance will continue to increase as more depreciation is added to it, until such time as it equals the original cost of the asset. At that time, stop recording any depreciation expense, since the cost of the asset has now been reduced to zero.

The journal entry for depreciation can be a simple two-line entry designed to accommodate all types of fixed assets, or it may be subdivided into separate entries for each type of fixed asset.

EXAMPLE

Pensive Corporation calculates that it should have $25,000 of depreciation expense in the current month. The entry is:

	Debit	Credit
Depreciation expense	25,000	
Accumulated depreciation		25,000

In the following month, Pensive's controller decides to show a higher level of precision at the expense account level, and instead elects to apportion the $25,000 of depreciation among different expense accounts, so that each class of asset has a separate depreciation charge. The entry is:

	Debit	Credit
Depreciation expense - Automobiles	4,000	
Depreciation expense – Computer equipment	8,000	
Depreciation expense – Furniture and fixtures	6,000	
Depreciation expense – Office equipment	5,000	
Depreciation expense – Software	2,000	
Accumulated depreciation		25,000

The journal entry to record the amortization of intangible assets is fundamentally the same as the entry for depreciation, except that the accounts used substitute the word "amortization" for depreciation.

EXAMPLE

Pensive Corporation calculates that it should have $4,000 of amortization expense in the current month that is related to intangible assets. The entry is:

	Debit	Credit
Amortization expense	4,000	
Accumulated amortization		4,000

Accumulated Depreciation

When you sell or otherwise dispose of an asset, remove all related accumulated depreciation from the accounting records at the same time. Otherwise, an unusually large amount of accumulated depreciation will build up on the balance sheet.

EXAMPLE

Pensive Corporate has $1,000,000 of fixed assets, for which it has charged $380,000 of accumulated depreciation. This results in the following presentation on Pensive's balance sheet:

Fixed assets	$1,000,000
Less: Accumulated depreciation	(380,000)
Net fixed assets	$620,000

Pensive then sells a machine for $80,000 that had an original cost of $140,000, and for which it had already recorded accumulated depreciation of $50,000. It records the sale with this journal entry:

	Debit	Credit
Cash	80,000	
Accumulated depreciation	50,000	
Loss on asset sale	10,000	
Fixed assets		140,000

As a result of this entry, Pensive's balance sheet presentation of fixed assets has changed, so that fixed assets before accumulated depreciation have declined to $860,000, and accumulated depreciation has declined to $330,000. The new presentation is:

Fixed assets	$860,000
Less: Accumulated depreciation	(330,000)
Net fixed assets	$530,000

The amount of net fixed assets declined by $90,000 as a result of the asset sale, which is the sum of the $80,000 cash proceeds and the $10,000 loss resulting from the asset sale.

Depreciation under IFRS

Depreciation under International Financial Reporting Standards is addressed in IAS 16, *Property, Plant, and Equipment*. The IFRS rules are essentially the same as those required by GAAP. The key features of the IFRS rules related to depreciation are:

- Separately depreciate any part of a fixed asset whose cost is significant in relation to the cost of the entire asset.
- Charge depreciation to expense in the period incurred, unless you are rolling it into another asset (as occurs when you add the depreciation on manufacturing equipment into an overhead pool, from which it is allocated to inventory).

- Depreciate a fixed asset on a systematic basis over its useful life (i.e., do not vary the depreciation charge for an unjustifiable reason).
- Review the salvage value and useful life of each asset at least once a year, and make adjustments to the depreciation calculations accordingly on a go-forward basis.
- Select a depreciation method that matches the timing of the future economic benefits of the asset (which argues in favor of usage-based depreciation methods, such as the units of production method, rather than time-based depreciation methods).
- Review the depreciation method at least once a year, and change the method if usage of the benefits provided by the asset has changed significantly.

Other Depreciation Topics

Depreciation has a notable impact on a company's cash flow projections, since it is one of the few expenses that does not involve a cash outflow. Also, the accountant is sometimes asked if depreciation is designed to match a reduction in an asset's market value. Both topics are addressed next.

Impact on Cash Flow Analysis

Depreciation is a major issue in the calculation of a company's cash flows, because it is included in the calculation of net income, but does not involve any ongoing cash outflow. This is because a company only has a net cash outflow in the entire amount of the asset when the asset was originally purchased. Thus, a cash flow analysis should call for the inclusion of net income, with an add-back for any depreciation recognized as expense during the period.

The one exception is a capital lease, where you record it as an asset when acquired, but it is paid for over time, under the terms of the associated lease agreement. In this case, add back the amount of depreciation in the cash flow analysis, but include the amount of any ongoing lease payments. It is possible that the amounts of depreciation and lease payments will roughly offset each other in the analysis.

Depreciation and Market Value

Depreciation is not intended to reduce the cost of a fixed asset to its market value. Market value may be substantially different from net book value, and may even increase over time. Instead, depreciation is merely intended to gradually charge the cost of a fixed asset to expense over its useful life.

Summary

Depreciation is one of the central concerns of the accountant, since the broad range of available methods can result in significant differences in the amount of depreciation expense recorded in each period. Generally, adopt the straight-line depreciation method to minimize the amount of depreciation calculations, unless the usage rate of the assets involved more closely match a different depreciation method. Companies concerned with reducing their tax liabilities will be more likely to use the MACRS depreciation rates when calculating their taxable income.

Tip: Use the straight-line depreciation method whenever possible, because it is easier for outside auditors to verify these calculations. This may lead to a small reduction in your audit fees.

Chapter 7
Subsequent Fixed Asset Measurement

Introduction

In the Initial Fixed Asset Recognition chapter, we addressed which costs to capitalize into a fixed asset during its initial construction or purchase. But what about events later in its life? There are a number of subsequent events, including additional expenditures, depreciation, impairment testing, revaluation, and derecognition. Depreciation is addressed in detail in the Depreciation and Amortization chapter, while asset impairment is covered in the Asset Impairment chapter and derecognition is addressed in the Asset Disposal chapter. However, this still leaves the topics of subsequent expenditure capitalization, as well as the revaluation of fixed assets. These two topics are discussed in the following sections.

Generally Accepted Accounting Principles (GAAP) are largely silent about how to account for the subsequent measurement of fixed assets, other than their impairment or eventual derecognition. Fortunately, there is considerably more guidance in the International Financial Reporting Standards (IFRS), which form the basis for nearly all of the discussion in this chapter.

The Capitalization of Additional Expenditures

Most of the expenditures that a company incurs in relation to a fixed asset on a day-to-day basis should be charged to expense as incurred, because they only relate to the servicing of the asset. Such costs usually involve supplies and labor, and are typically recorded in a repairs and maintenance expense account.

Portions of a fixed asset may require replacement from time to time. Examples of such items are motors that burn out or pipes that corrode. If the cost of these replacements is less than the corporate capitalization limit, charge them to expense as incurred. However, if they exceed the capitalization limit, capitalize and depreciate them over their useful lives (which may vary from the useful life of the machine of which they are a part), subject to the following two rules:

- There are probable future economic benefits associated with the expenditure that will flow to the entity; and
- You can reliably measure the cost of the item.

The capitalization limit is the amount paid for an asset, above which an entity records it as a long-term asset. If an entity pays less than the capitalization limit for an asset, it charges the asset to expense in the period incurred.

When you capitalize the cost of a major replacement to a fixed asset, also derecognize the component being replaced. Otherwise, you would continue to depreciate a component that has already been removed from the asset and is no longer in use. If you cannot separately identify the cost of the component being replaced, estimate its cost and remove both the estimated cost and any related depreciation from the fixed asset of which it is a part.

EXAMPLE

Nautilus Tours owns several submarines, which it uses for shallow-water tourist visits to local reefs. The electric motors used in these submarines have a rated life of five years (versus 15 years for the pressure hulls). One of the motors fails and must be replaced, at a cost of $300,000. The submarine in which the motor is housed was originally purchased in used condition for $6 million, and was recorded as a single asset.

Nautilus must record the cost of the engine replacement as a fixed asset, at a cost of $300,000. However, it must also derecognize that portion of the original cost of the submarine that would have related to the engine, as well as any related depreciation. Nautilus estimates that the original motor had a cost similar to that of the replacement unit, but that only one-third of its depreciation has been recognized (calculated as five years of depreciation completed, out of the 15 years estimated useful life of the submarine). Consequently, Nautilus must derecognize the estimated cost of the original motor with this entry:

	Debit	Credit
Depreciation	100,000	
Loss on derecognition of motor	200,000	
Submarine (motor component)		300,000

Nautilus then records a separate asset for the motor with the following entry:

	Debit	Credit
Motor	300,000	
Cash		300,000

It may be necessary to perform a periodic major inspection of a fixed asset, as a condition of continuing to operate it. For example, a train may require periodic inspections to mitigate the risk of a catastrophic accident. When a company performs such an inspection, capitalize the cost of the inspection into the cost of the asset, and depreciate it until the next inspection is required. When you capitalize such a cost, also derecognize the cost of any inspection performed in a prior period; if no such inspection was performed, you must still derecognize an amount equivalent to what such an inspection would have cost.

EXAMPLE

The submarines owned by Nautilus Tours must undergo a major inspection after every 1,000 hours of operation, or else they will no longer be certified for operation by the insurer. One submarine has reached its 1,000-hour limit, and undergoes a major inspection at a cost of $50,000. Nautilus purchased the submarine in used condition three years before, and has not previously recognized the separate cost of an inspection. It has been depreciating the submarine over 15 years.

Nautilus must record the cost of the major inspection as a fixed asset, at a cost of $50,000. It must also derecognize that portion of the original cost of the submarine that would have related to the immediately preceding inspection (which it estimates to be in the same amount). Since only 20 percent of the depreciation period of the submarine has been recognized (calculated as three years of depreciation completed out of the 15 years estimated useful life of the submarine), the company must now recognize a loss on the remaining amount of depreciation at the time of derecognition. Consequently, Nautilus creates the following derecognition journal entry for the presumed existing inspection asset:

	Debit	Credit
Depreciation	10,000	
Loss on derecognition of inspection	40,000	
Major inspection (inspection date)		50,000

Nautilus then records a separate asset for the new inspection with the following entry:

	Debit	Credit
Major inspection (inspection date)	50,000	
Cash		50,000

Tip: The preceding examples show that component replacements and major inspections are usually depreciated over shorter periods than those used for the asset of which they are a part, resulting in the accelerated recognition of depreciation (in the form of a loss) when they are replaced. To prevent these sudden spikes in expense, consider separately recording these items upon the initial acquisition of an asset; this may include the use of shorter useful lives for them in the depreciation calculations.

The accounting guidelines noted thus far are taken from IFRS. There is little information to reference in GAAP on this topic, though the general leaning of the available information is for the cost of major fixed asset overhauls and inspections to be charged to expense in the period incurred, rather than be capitalized.

One cost that *can* be capitalized under GAAP is the cost incurred to reinstall or rearrangement production equipment, if you expect that these changes will create future benefits from either enhanced production efficiencies or reduced production costs. However, if there is no indication that the changes will extend an asset's useful life, enhance production efficiencies, or increase its productive capacity, charge these costs to expense as incurred.

Asset Revaluation for Tangible Assets

A company that is using the IFRS framework can elect to measure its fixed assets under either the *cost model* or the *revaluation model*. Under the cost model, carry the cost of a fixed asset at its cost, less any accumulated depreciation (see the Depreciation and Amortization chapter) and accumulated impairment losses (see the Fixed Asset Impairment chapter). Under the revaluation model, carry a fixed asset at its fair value, less any subsequent accumulated depreciation and accumulated impairment losses. You cannot selectively apply these models to individual fixed assets. Instead, apply them to entire asset classes (though you can use a different model for a different asset class).

The revaluation method is unique to IFRS. You can only use it if it is possible to reliably measure the fair value of an asset. You must also make revaluations with sufficient regularity to ensure that the amount at which an asset is carried in the company's records does not vary materially from its fair value. Further, if you revalue any fixed asset item, also revalue all other assets in the same fixed asset class; this rule keeps a company from selectively revaluing its fixed assets.

> **Tip:** Though you are required to revalue all of the assets in an asset class at the same time, you can stretch the requirement and revalue them on a rolling basis, as long as you complete the revaluation within a short period of time, and subsequently keep the revaluation analysis up to date.

Use a market-based appraisal by a qualified valuation specialist to determine the fair value of a fixed asset. If a fixed asset is of such a specialized nature that you cannot obtain a market-based fair value, use an alternative method to arrive an estimated fair value. Examples of such methods are using discounted future cash flows or an estimate of the replacement cost of an asset.

> **Tip:** Hiring an appraiser to conduct ongoing revaluations can be expensive, so unless fair values are volatile, limit appraisals to somewhere in the range of every three to five years. For volatile fair values, consider using an appraisal once a year, and only if you estimate that the resulting change in fair value will be significant.

If you revalue fixed assets, you also need to adjust any accumulated depreciation as of the revaluation date. Your options are:

- Force the carrying amount of the asset to equal its newly-revalued amount by proportionally restating the amount of the accumulated depreciation; or

- Eliminate the accumulated depreciation against the gross carrying amount of the newly-revalued asset. This method is the simpler of the two alternatives, and is included in the example at the end of this section.

If you elect to use the revaluation model and a revaluation results in an increase in the carrying amount of a fixed asset, recognize the increase in other comprehensive income, as well as accumulate it in equity in an account entitled "revaluation surplus." However, if the increase reverses a revaluation decrease for the same asset that had been previously recognized in profit or loss, recognize the revaluation gain in profit or loss to the extent of the previous loss (thereby erasing the loss).

If a revaluation results in a decrease in the carrying amount of a fixed asset, recognize the decrease in profit or loss. However, if there is a credit balance in the revaluation surplus for that asset, recognize the decrease in other comprehensive income to offset the credit balance. The decrease that you recognize in other comprehensive income decreases the amount of any revaluation surplus that you may have already recorded in equity.

The following table summarizes the proper recognition of revaluation changes just described.

Asset Revaluation Recognition Rules

Asset Revaluation Change	Recognition
Value increases	Recognize in other comprehensive income and in the "revaluation surplus" equity account
Value increases, and reverses a prior revaluation decrease	Recognize gain in profit or loss to the extent of the previous loss, with the remainder in other comprehensive income
Value decreases	Recognize in profit or loss
Value decreases, but there is a credit in the revaluation surplus	Recognize in other comprehensive income to the extent of the credit, with the remainder in profit or loss

In essence, IFRS is forcing you to prominently display any revaluation losses, and gives less reporting stature to any revaluation gains.

If you derecognize a fixed asset, transfer any associated revaluation surplus to retained earnings. The amount of this surplus that you transfer to retained earnings is the difference between the depreciation based on the original cost of the asset and the depreciation based on the revalued carrying amount of the asset.

EXAMPLE

Nautilus Tours elects to revalue one of its tourism submarines, which originally cost $12 million and has since accumulated $3 million of depreciation. It is unlikely that the fair value of the submarine will vary substantially over time, so Nautilus adopts a policy to conduct revaluations for all of its submarines once every three years. An appraiser assigns a value of $9.2 million to the submarine. Nautilus creates the following entry to eliminate all accumulated depreciation associated with the submarine:

	Debit	Credit
Accumulated depreciation	3,000,000	
Submarines		3,000,000

At this point, the net cost of the submarine in Nautilus' accounting records is $9 million. Nautilus also creates the following entry to increase the carrying amount of the submarine to its fair value of $9.2 million:

	Debit	Credit
Submarines	200,000	
Other comprehensive income – gain on revaluation		200,000

Three years later, on the next scheduled revaluation date, the appraiser reviews the fair value of the submarine, and determines that its fair value has declined by $350,000. Nautilus uses the following journal entry to record the change:

	Debit	Credit
Other comprehensive income – gain on revaluation	200,000	
Loss on revaluation	150,000	
Submarines		350,000

This final entry eliminates all of the revaluation gain that had been recorded in other comprehensive income, and also recognizes a loss on the residual portion of the revaluation loss.

You cannot use the revaluation model under GAAP. Instead, you can only use the cost model.

Asset Revaluation for Intangible Assets

Under IFRS, you are allowed to adopt either the cost model or the revaluation model for intangible assets, as was just described for tangible assets. Here are several variations from the accounting for tangible assets that you must apply to intangible assets:

- Apply the revaluation model to an intangible asset that was received through a government grant. Since the grant may mean that it was initially recognized at a minor amount, the revaluation could result in the recognition of a substantial gain.
- Only determine the fair value of an intangible asset by reference to an active market. Since active markets are relatively rare for intangible assets (other than for transferable licenses), this limits the extent to which you can revalue intangible assets.
- If there is no active market for a specific intangible asset within a class of intangible assets that have all been revalued, carry that asset at its cost, less any accumulated depreciation and accumulated impairment.
- If there is no longer an active market for an intangible asset, retain the carrying amount of the asset at its last revalued amount, less any subsequent accumulated depreciation and accumulated impairment losses. If an active market reappears at a later date, you can then reactivate the revaluation model.

The key issue with revaluing intangible assets is that you can only do so if there is an active market. This is quite rare for intangible assets, so the cost model is effectively the only choice in most situations.

EXAMPLE

The Red Herring Fish Company owns a fishing license for herring, which it purchased for $100,000. The term of the license is ten years, after which the fisheries department of the federal government will auction it again to the highest bidder. There is an active resale market for fishing licenses, since boat operators are constantly entering and departing the market for herring fishing.

After two years, Red Herring has amortized $20,000 of the carrying amount of the fishing license. At that time, the fisheries department announces that it will begin to reduce the number of licenses sold at auction, with the intent of eventually having 30% fewer fishing licenses outstanding. This prospective restriction in supply triggers an immediate jump in the resale market for the price of fishing licenses, to $130,000. Red Herring revalues its fishing license asset based on this jump in price by eliminating all accumulated amortization associated with the asset and then increasing the carrying amount of the asset. The entries are:

	Debit	Credit
Accumulated amortization	20,000	
Intangible assets - licenses		20,000

To eliminate accumulated depreciation

	Debit	Credit
Intangible assets - licenses	50,000	
Revaluation reserve		50,000

To match carrying amount to revalued amount

Red Herring must now amortize the new $130,000 carrying amount of the fishing license over its remaining eight-year term. If the company uses the straight-line method to do so, the annual amortization will be $16,250.

As was the case for tangible assets, you cannot use the revaluation model under GAAP for intangible assets. Instead, you can only use the cost model.

Summary

This chapter has highlighted two of the most important differences between the GAAP and IFRS frameworks in regard to fixed asset accounting. IFRS not only allows the capitalization of subsequent expenditures, but is moderately insistent in forcing you to do so. Conversely, GAAP is generally content to require these expenditures to be charged to expense. Further, IFRS allows for the subsequent revaluation of fixed assets, which is not allowed at all under GAAP. As the world gradually transitions toward IFRS, these two areas will represent key changes that the users of the GAAP framework must keep in mind.

Chapter 8
Fixed Asset Impairment

Introduction

There are rules under both GAAP and IFRS for periodically testing fixed assets to see if they are still as valuable as the costs at which they were recorded in the accounting records. If not, reduce the recorded cost of these assets by recognizing a loss. Also, under some circumstances, you are allowed to recover the amount of these losses, depending upon whether you are using GAAP or IFRS rules. Unfortunately, there are differences between the rules imposed by GAAP and IFRS, which can yield different reporting results. There are two large sections in this chapter that are devoted to the impairment rules under GAAP and IFRS, with numerous subheadings within each section.

Asset Impairment under GAAP

Asset impairment under GAAP is addressed in ASC 360, *Property, Plant, and Equipment*. The GAAP rules are somewhat different from those required under IFRS. This section describes the key features of the GAAP rules related to asset impairment. There are a number of sub-headings listed, since this is a significant topic that covers a large number of areas related to impairment. The most important differences between the GAAP and IFRS treatments of asset impairment are noted in the summary at the end of the chapter.

GAAP: Measurement of Asset Impairment

Recognize an impairment loss on a fixed asset if its carrying amount is not recoverable and exceeds its fair value. This loss is recognized within income from continuing operations on the income statement.

The carrying amount of an asset is not recoverable if it exceeds the sum of the undiscounted cash flows expected to result from the use of the asset over its remaining useful life and the final disposition of the asset. These cash flow estimates should incorporate assumptions that are reasonable in relation to the assumptions the entity uses for its budgets, forecasts, and so forth. If there are a range of possible cash flow outcomes, consider using a probability-weighted cash flow analysis.

> **Tip:** Base the impairment analysis on the cash flows to be expected over the remaining useful life of the asset. If you are measuring impairment for a group of assets (as discussed below), the remaining useful life is based on the useful life of the primary asset in the group. You cannot skew the results by including in the group an asset with a theoretically unlimited life, such as land or an intangible asset that is not being amortized.

The amount of an impairment loss is the difference between an asset's carrying amount and its fair value. Once you recognize an impairment loss, this reduces the carrying amount of the asset, so you may need to alter the amount of periodic depreciation being charged against the asset to adjust for this lower carrying amount (otherwise, you will incur an excessively large depreciation expense over the remaining useful life of the asset).

GAAP: Impairment Testing Exemption for Intangible Assets

GAAP requires that intangible assets having an indefinite life be tested for impairment from time to time. It can be quite difficult to determine the fair values of these assets. In an effort to reduce the cost and complexity of the impairment analysis for this type of asset, GAAP allows a business to first assess a variety of qualitative factors to see if it is more likely than not that such an asset is impaired. If not, there is no need to proceed with a more formal (and time-consuming) impairment test. The "more likely than not" threshold is considered to be the case when the likelihood of impairment exceeds 50 percent.

If the conclusion is reached that it is more likely than not that an intangible asset has been impaired, formal impairment testing must be conducted. You also have the option of bypassing this testing exemption and proceeding straight to an impairment test for these types of assets. If you elect to bypass the option in one reporting period, you can still use the option again in a future period.

In general, the qualitative assessment of an intangible asset having an indefinite life requires that you assess all relevant events and circumstances that could affect the fair value of the asset. Examples of these events and circumstances are:

- Increases in costs that reduce the expectation for future earnings derived from the asset.
- A trend of declining performance, either in terms of revenue, profits, or cash flows.
- Legal or regulatory issues that may constrict future earnings derived from the asset.
- Events within the company that may impact asset performance, such as the departure of key personnel or business partners.

- A decline in the business environment, such as increased competition, declines in demand, and adverse changes in technology.
- A decline in general economic conditions, a constriction in the supply of available capital, adverse changes in foreign exchange rates, and similar issues.

The preceding negative factors should be offset against any positive or mitigating events or circumstances in order to arrive at a broad-based judgment regarding when an intangible asset has been impaired.

GAAP: The Impact of Asset Retirement Obligations

When making the asset impairment determination, include in the carrying amount of the fixed asset any capitalized asset retirement obligations. However, the future cash flows associated with an asset retirement obligation should be excluded from the undiscounted cash flows used to test an asset for recoverability, as well as from the discounted cash flows used to measure its fair value.

For more information about asset retirement obligations, see the Asset Retirement Obligations chapter.

GAAP: Measurement of Disposal Losses on Assets Held for Sale

If an asset has been designated as held for sale, periodically test it for a possible loss on the expected disposal of the asset. Recognize a loss in the amount by which the fair value less costs to sell of the asset is lower than its carrying amount.

Held for sale is a designation given to assets that an entity intends to sell to a third party within one year. Do not depreciate a fixed asset that is designated as held for sale. See the Asset Disposal chapter for more information.

Recognize a disposal loss within income from continuing operations on the income statement.

GAAP: The Asset to be Tested

Test assets for impairment at the lowest level at which there are identifiable cash flows that are largely independent of the cash flows of other assets. In cases where there are no identifiable cash flows at all (as is common with corporate-level assets), place these assets in an asset group that encompasses the entire entity, and test for impairment at the entity level.

Only add goodwill to an asset group for impairment testing when the asset group is a reporting unit, or includes a reporting unit. Thus, do not include goodwill in any asset groups below the reporting unit level.

A reporting unit is an operating segment or one level below an operating segment. An operating segment is a component of a public entity that engages in business activities and whose results are reviewed by the chief operating decision maker, and for which discrete financial information is available.

GAAP: Timing of the Impairment Test

Test for the recoverability of an asset whenever the circumstances indicate that its carrying amount may not be recoverable. Examples of such situations are:

- *Cash flow.* There are historical and projected operating or cash flow losses associated with the asset.
- *Costs.* There are excessive costs incurred to acquire or construct the asset.
- *Disposal.* The asset is more than 50% likely to be sold or otherwise disposed of significantly before the end of its previously estimated useful life.
- *Legal.* There is a significant adverse change in legal factors or the business climate that could affect the asset's value.
- *Market price.* There is a significant decrease in the asset's market price.
- *Usage.* There is a significant adverse change in the asset's manner of use, or in its physical condition.

GAAP: Accounting for the Impairment of an Asset Group

If there is an impairment at the level of an asset group, allocate the impairment among the assets in the group on a pro rata basis, based on the carrying amounts of the assets in the group. However, the impairment loss cannot reduce the carrying amount of an asset below its fair value.

Tip: The accounting standard goes on to state that you only have to determine the fair value of an asset for this test if it is "determinable without undue cost and effort." Thus, if an outside appraisal would be required to determine fair value, you can likely dispense with this requirement and simply allocate the impairment loss to all of the assets in the group.

EXAMPLE

Luminescence Corporation operates a small floodlight manufacturing facility. Luminescence considers the entire facility to be a reporting unit, so it conducts an impairment test on the entire operation. The test reveals that a continuing decline in the market for floodlights (caused by the surge in LED lights in the market) has caused a $2 million impairment charge. Luminescence allocates the charge to the four assets in the facility as follows:

Asset	Carrying Amount	Proportion of Carrying Amounts	Impairment Allocation	Revised Carrying Amount
Ribbon machine	$8,000,000	67%	$1,340,000	$6,660,000
Conveyors	1,500,000	13%	260,000	1,240,000
Gas injector	2,000,000	16%	320,000	1,680,000
Filament inserter	500,000	4%	80,000	420,000
Totals	$12,000,000	100%	$2,000,000	$10,000,000

GAAP: Reversing an Impairment Loss

Under no circumstances are you allowed to reverse an impairment loss under GAAP.

> **Tip:** Unlike IFRS, GAAP does not allow the reversal of a fixed asset impairment loss. Consequently, it may be useful to obtain a second opinion (e.g., your outside auditors) before recognizing such an impairment in the first place.

GAAP: Reversing a Disposal Loss

It is allowable under GAAP to recognize a gain on any increase in the fair value less costs to sell of a fixed asset that is designated as held for sale. The amount of this gain is capped at the amount of any cumulative disposal loss already recognized for the asset. This gain will increase the carrying amount of the asset.

EXAMPLE

Luminescence Corporation has designated one of its fluorescent bulb factories as held for sale. The asset group comprising the factory has a carrying amount of $18 million. After six months, Luminescence determines that the fair value less costs to sell for the factory is $16 million, due to falling prices for similar factories, so it recognizes a disposal loss of $2 million. A few months later, the market for such factories rebounds, and the company finds that the factory now has a fair value less costs to sell of $19 million, which is an increase of $3 million.

Luminescence can only recognize a $2 million gain, which reverses the prior disposal loss.

Asset Impairment under IFRS

Asset impairment under IFRS is addressed in IAS 36, *Asset Impairment*. The IFRS rules are somewhat different from those required by GAAP, and are much lengthier. This section describes the key features of the IFRS rules related to asset impairment. There are a number of sub-headings listed, since the IAS is a comprehensive document that covers a large number of areas related to impairment. The most important differences between the IFRS and GAAP treatment of asset impairment are noted in the summary at the end of the chapter.

IFRS: The Impairment Test

An asset is impaired when its carrying amount is greater than its recoverable amount. The recoverable amount of an asset or cash-generating unit is the higher of its fair value less any costs to sell, and its value in use. *Value in use* is the present value of any future cash flows you expect to derive from an asset or cash-generating unit.

In some cases, there is no way to determine the fair value of an asset less costs to sell, since there is no active market for the asset. If so, just use the value in use as the recoverable amount of an asset.

> **Tip:** If either an asset's fair value less costs to sell or its value in use is higher than its carrying amount, there is no impairment. Thus, you do not need to calculate both figures as part of an impairment test.

When a fixed asset approaches the end of its useful life, it may be sufficient to use the fair value less costs to sell as the foundation for an impairment test, and ignore its value in use. The reason is that the value of an asset at this point in its life is mostly comprised of any proceeds from its disposal, rather than from future cash flows (which are likely to be minor).

> **Tip:** The instructions in IAS 36 imply that a significant investigation of fair values and discount rate calculations for cash flows is needed to conduct an impairment test. However, the standard also states that "estimates, averages, and computational short cuts may provide reasonable approximations" of these requirements. Consequently, use short cuts whenever you have a reasonable basis for doing so.

IFRS: The Asset to be Tested

Conduct an impairment test for an individual asset, unless the asset does not generate cash inflows that are mostly independent of those from other assets. If an asset does not generate such cash inflows, instead conduct the test at the level of the cash-generating unit of which the asset is a part. All subsequent testing of and accounting for an impairment at the level of a cash-generating unit is identical to its treatment as if it had been an individual asset.

A cash-generating unit is the smallest identifiable group of assets that generates cash inflows independently from the cash inflows of other assets. Examples of cash-generating units are product lines, businesses, individual store locations, and operating regions. It is allowable for a cash-generating unit to have all of its cash inflows derive from internal transfer pricing, as long as the unit could sell its output on an active market. Once a group of assets is clustered into a cash-generating unit, continue to define the same assets as being part of the unit for future impairment testing (unless there is a justifiable reason for a change).

An impairment test should remain at the level of the individual asset, rather than for a cash-generating unit, in either of the following cases:

- The fair value less costs to sell of the asset is higher than its carrying amount.
- The value in use (i.e., discounted cash flows) of the asset is estimated to be close to its fair value less costs to sell.

EXAMPLE

Rio Shipping owns a rail line that extends from its private shipping terminal on Baffin Island to a warehousing area two miles inland, where it stores ore shipped to it from several mines further inland. The rail line exists only to support deliveries of ore, and it has no way of creating cash flows independent of Rio's other operations on Baffin Island. Since it is impossible to determine the recoverable amount of the rail line, Rio aggregates it into a cash-generating unit, which is its entire shipping operation on Baffin Island.

EXAMPLE

Rio Shipping enters into a contract with the Port of New York to provide point-to-point ferry service on several routes across the Hudson River. The Port requires service for 18 hours a day on four routes. One of the four routes has minimal passenger traffic, and so is operating at a significant loss. Rio can identify the ferry asset associated with this specific ferry route.

Rio cannot test for impairment at the individual asset level for the ferry operating the loss-generating route, because it does not have the ability to eliminate that route under its contract with the Port. Instead, it must test for impairment at the cash-generating unit level, which is all of the ferry routes together.

IFRS: Goodwill and Impairment Testing

If a company has acquired assets as part of a business combination, allocate the goodwill associated with that combination to any cash-generating units, but only if those units are expected to benefit from the synergies of the combination.

Tip: You can safely ignore this rule in many cases, because the standard also states that the goodwill allocation only extends down to the point at which management monitors goodwill for its own internal purposes. In most cases, goodwill monitoring only extends down to the business unit level; thus, as long as a cash-generating unit is smaller than a business unit, the requirements of this standard do not apply.

If you *do* allocate goodwill to a cash-generating unit and the company then sells that unit, include the allocated goodwill in the carrying amount of the unit; this will impact the amount of any gain or loss that you recognize on disposal of the unit.

If a company sells assets from a cash-generating unit to which goodwill has been allocated, assign a portion of the goodwill to the assets being sold, based on the relative values of the assets being sold and that portion of the unit being retained.

EXAMPLE

Rio Shipping had previously acquired a container ship unloading dock in the Port of Los Angeles for $50 million, of which $10 million was accounted for as goodwill. Rio accounts for the overhead cranes in the dock as a cash-generating unit, to which it allocates $6 million of the goodwill associated with the acquisition.

Two years later, Rio sells one of the cranes for $5 million. Management estimates that the value of the remainder of the cash-generating unit is $15 million. Based on this information, Rio's accounting staff allocates $1.5 million of the goodwill to the crane, based on the following calculation:

$6 million goodwill × ($5 million crane value ÷ ($5 million crane value + $15 million cash-generating unit value))

= $6 million goodwill × 25% of the combined value of the crane asset and cash-generating unit

= $1.5 million goodwill allocation

IFRS: Corporate Assets and Impairment Testing

Assets that are recognized at the corporate level are ones that do not generate cash inflows independently of other assets, and you cannot fully attribute their carrying amounts to other cash-generating units. An example of a corporate asset is a research facility. It is not usually possible to allocate the cost of these assets to any cash-generating units, unless there is a direct relationship between them.

IFRS: Timing of the Impairment Test

IFRS states that you should assess whether there is any indication of impairment at the end of each reporting period, so this is an extremely frequent test.

Even if there is no indication of impairment, test an intangible asset for impairment if the asset has an indefinite useful life or if it is not yet available for use (e.g., intangible assets that are not yet being amortized). Perform this test at least once a year, and do so at the same time each year. If you have multiple intangible assets, test each one at a different time of the year. If you initially recognized an intangible asset during the current fiscal year, test it for impairment by the end of the current fiscal year.

The reason why the standard requires this annual analysis of intangible assets that are not yet available for sale is that there is more uncertainty surrounding the ability of these assets to generate sufficient future economic benefits. Given the higher level of uncertainty, there is more ongoing risk that they will be impaired.

IFRS: Indications of Impairment

The following are indicators of impairment to consider:

- *Adverse effects*. There have been, or are about to be, significant changes that adversely affect the operating environment of the business.
- *Damage or obsolescence*. There is evidence of damage to the asset, or of obsolescence.
- *Discount rate change*. Interest rates have increased, and this will materially impact the value in use of an asset, based on a reduction in the discounted present value of its cash flows. This is only the case if changes in market interest rates will actually alter the discount rate used to calculate the value in use.

Value in use is the present value of any future cash flows you expect to derive from an asset or cash-generating unit.

EXAMPLE

Rio Shipping acquired a freighter three years ago for $20 million, and routinely conducts an impairment analysis that is based on the discounted cash flows to be expected from the ship over the next ten years. The discount rate that Rio uses for the analysis is 6%, which is based on the current long-term interest rates that a similar company could obtain in the market place.

Short-term interest rates have recently spiked to 9%. If Rio were to use this rate as the discount rate, it would greatly reduce the present value of future cash flows, and likely create an impairment issue. However, since short-term rates fluctuate considerably, and the freighter still has a long useful life, management judges that this is the wrong interest rate to use as a basis for the discount rate, and elects to ignore it. Their decision is bolstered by the fact that long-term interest rates are holding steady at 6%.

- *Economic performance*. The economic performance of an asset has declined, or is expected to decline. This can include higher than expected maintenance costs, actual net cash flows that are worse than the budgeted amount, or a significant decline in net cash flows or operating profits.

- *Market capitalization change.* The carrying amount (i.e., book value) of all the assets in the company is more than the entity's market capitalization.
- *Market value decline.* An asset's market value declines significantly more than would be indicated by the passage of time or normal use.
- *Usage change.* There have been or are about to be significant changes in the usage of an asset, such as being rendered idle, plans for discontinuance or restructuring, plans for an early asset sale, or assessing an intangible asset from having an indefinite life to having a finite one.

Any of the preceding indicators or other factors may reveal that there is a possibility of asset impairment; if subsequent investigation reveals that there will be no impairment charge, the mere existence of one or more of these indicators may be grounds for adjusting the useful life, depreciation method, or salvage value associated with an asset.

EXAMPLE

Rio Shipping finds that a worldwide glut in the market for supertankers has reduced the usage level of its Rio Sunrise supertanker by 10 percent. This does not translate into a sufficient drop in the cash flows or market value of the ship to warrant an impairment charge. Nonetheless, Rio's management is concerned that the glut could continue for many years to come, and so it alters the depreciation method for the supertanker from the straight-line method to the 150% declining balance method, in order to accelerate depreciation and reduce the carrying amount of the asset more quickly.

IFRS: Intangible Asset Measurement

Test any intangible asset that has an indefinite useful life for impairment on an annual basis. To save time in performing this annual test, use the most recent detailed calculation of such an asset's recoverable amount that was made in a preceding period, but only if the situation meets *all* of the following criteria:

- *Related assets and liabilities are unchanged.* The assets and liabilities of the cash-generating unit of which the intangible asset is a part have not changed significantly (if the intangible asset is part of a cash-generating unit at all);
- *Remote likelihood of change.* The events and circumstances since the last calculation indicate only a remote likelihood that the current recoverable amount would be less than the asset's carrying amount; and
- *Substantial difference.* The most recent calculation of the recoverable amount yielded an amount substantially greater than the asset's carrying amount.

IFRS: Determining Value in Use

Value in use is one of the two components of the calculation of an asset's recoverable value (which must be higher than an asset's carrying amount in order to avoid an asset impairment). Value in use is essentially the discounted cash flows associated with an asset or cash-generating unit. Consider the following issues when deriving an asset's value in use:

- Possible variations in the amount or timing of cash flows related to an asset
- The current market risk-free rate of interest
- Such other factors as illiquidity and risk related to holding the asset

If you feel that these considerations warrant a change in the value in use of an asset, build adjustments into either the cash flows or discount rate used to derive the value in use. Adjustments to the cash flows can include a weighted average of all possible cash flow outcomes.

The cash flow estimates used to derive the value in use should be based on the following:

- Management's best estimate of the economic conditions likely to exist over the remaining useful life of the asset. These estimates should be based on reasonable and supportable assumptions, with a greater weighting given to external evidence.
- The most recent budget or forecast that has been approved by management, covering a maximum of five years (unless you can justify a longer period by having already shown the ability to forecast accurately over a longer period). Do not include any changes in cash flows expected to arise from future restructurings or from the presumed future enhancement of an asset's performance.

> **Tip:** Include in a cash flow analysis those changes arising from a future restructuring, once management has committed to the plan. Thus, if you know that cash flows will improve as a result of such a plan, gaining management approval of the plan may be crucial to avoiding an impairment charge.

- Projections beyond the period covered by the most recent budget or forecast that are extrapolations using a steady or declining growth rate for subsequent years (unless you can justify an increasing rate). Do not use a growth rate that exceeds the long-term average growth rate for the product, market, industry, or country where the company operates (unless the higher rate can be justified).

Tip: One of the reasons given in the standard for using a steady or declining growth rate in projections is that more favorable conditions will attract more competitors, who will keep the cash flow growth rate from increasing. Thus, if you want to use an increasing cash flow growth rate in your forecasts, you need to justify what will keep competitors from driving the rate down, such as the existence of significant barriers to entry, or such legal protection as a patent.

Also, ensure that the assumptions on which the cash flow projections are based are consistent with the results the company has experienced in the past, which thereby establishes another evidence trail which supports the veracity of the cash flow projections.

Tip: This accounting standard makes it quite clear that inordinately high cash flow projections are frowned upon, so expect to run afoul of the auditors if you attempt to insert unjustifiable cash flow increases in the value in use calculations. Do not try to avoid an impending impairment charge with alterations to cash flows, since you are merely pushing off the inevitable until somewhat later in the useful life of the asset, when it is impossible to hide the issue over the few remaining years of the life of the asset.

When constructing the cash flow projections for the value in use analysis, be sure to include these three categories of cash flow:

- *Cash inflows*. This arises from continuing use of the asset.
- *Cash outflows*. This is from the expenditures needed to operate the asset at a level sufficient to generate the projected cash inflows, and should include all expenditures that can be reasonably allocated to the asset. If this figure is derived for a cash-generating unit where some of the assets have shorter useful lives, the replacement of these assets over time should be considered part of the cash outflows.
- *Cash from disposal*. This is the net cash proceeds expected from the eventual sale of the asset following the end of its useful life.

Do not include in the cash flow projections any cash flows related to financing activities or income taxes.

Tip: As just noted, you are supposed to include in the cash flow projections the cash outflows connected to overhead that is applied to an asset. Since a larger amount of overhead application will reduce the value in use of the asset and make an impairment charge more likely, establish an overhead application procedure that justifiably allocates the smallest amount of overhead possible to any assets that are subject to impairment tests. Only include those overhead costs for which there is a direct linkage to the asset.

Once you have compiled the cash flows related to an asset, establish a discount rate for use in deriving the net present value of the cash flows. This discount rate should reflect the current assessment of:

- The time value of money by the market for an investment similar to the asset under analysis. This means that the risk profile, cash flow timing, and cash flow amounts of the asset should be reflected in the investment for which you are using a market-derived interest rate.
- The risks specific to the asset for which you have not already incorporated adjustments into the cash flow projections.

IFRS: Determining the Fair Value less Costs to Sell

The fair value less costs to sell is one of the two components of the calculation of an asset's recoverable amount (which must be higher than an asset's carrying amount in order to avoid an asset impairment). There are several ways to determine the fair value less costs to sell, as outlined here.

The best source of information for the fair value less costs to sell is a price in a binding sales agreement in an arm's length transaction, which is adjusted for any incremental costs to sell. It can be difficult to find such a situation that dovetails so perfectly with an in-house asset, so expect to use one of the following approaches that do not yield such perfect information (listed in declining order of preference):

1. *Pricing in an active market.* If an asset trades in an active market, assume that its market price is a reasonable representation of its fair value, from which you would then subtract any costs of disposal to arrive at the fair value less costs to sell. In such a market, assume that the bid price is the market price. If there are no bid prices, use the price of the most recent transaction instead (as long as there has been no significant change in the economic circumstances since the date of the transaction).
2. *Best information available.* In the absence of an active market or a binding sale agreement, use the best information available to estimate the amount that you could obtain by disposing of the asset in an arm's length transaction between knowledgeable and willing parties. Consider the result of the recent sales of similar assets elsewhere in the industry as "best information."

> **Tip:** The best information used to derive fair value less costs to sell should not include a forced sale, except if management believes that it will be compelled to sell an asset in this manner.

When deriving fair value less costs to sell, what is involved in "costs to sell"? Examples of costs to sell are:

- Asset removal costs
- Costs to bring the asset into condition for sale
- Legal costs
- Taxes on the sale transaction

These are only examples of costs to sell; if you have similar types of costs that relate to a sale transaction, consider them to be costs to sell.

IFRS: Accounting for the Impairment of an Asset

Recognize an impairment loss when the recoverable amount of an asset is less than its carrying amount. The amount of the loss is the difference between the recoverable amount and the carrying amount. Recognize this loss immediately in the income statement.

If you have revalued the asset already, recognize the impairment loss in other comprehensive income to the extent of the prior revaluation, with any additional impairment being recognized as a normal expense.

After you recognize an impairment loss, also adjust the depreciation on the asset in future periods to account for the reduced carrying amount of the asset.

EXAMPLE

Rio Shipping owns a small coastal freighter with an original cost of $14 million and estimated salvage value of $4 million, and which it has been depreciating on the straight-line basis for five years. The freighter now has a carrying amount of $9 million.

Rio conducts an impairment test of the freighter asset, and concludes that the fair value less cost to sell of the asset is much lower than original estimates, resulting in a recoverable amount of $7 million. Rio takes a $2 million impairment charge to reduce the carrying amount of the freighter from $9 million to $7 million.

The freighter still has five years remaining on its useful life, so Rio revises the straight-line depreciation for the asset to be $600,000 per year. This is calculated as the revised $7 million carrying amount minus the $4 million salvage value, divided by the five remaining years of the freighter's useful life.

IFRS: Accounting for the Impairment of a Cash-Generating Unit

Recognize an impairment loss when the recoverable amount of a cash-generating unit is less than its carrying amount. You cannot reduce the carrying amount of the cash-generating unit as a whole, since it is not recorded in the company's records as such – it is recorded as a group of individual assets. To record the loss, you must allocate it in the following order:

1. Reduce the amount of any goodwill assigned to the cash-generated unit. If there is any loss still remaining, proceed to the next step.
2. Assign the remaining loss to the assets within the cash-generating unit on the basis of the carrying amount of each asset. When doing so, you cannot reduce the carrying amount of an asset below the highest of its:
   - Value in use (i.e., discounted cash flows)

- Fair value less costs to sell
- Zero

If you are unable to assign all of the pro rata portion of a loss to an asset based on the preceding rule, allocate it to the other assets in the cash-generated unit based on the carrying amounts of the other assets.

EXAMPLE

Rio Shipping owns Rio Bay, which is a container ship that it acquired as part of an acquisition. Rio Shipping has allocated $2 million of goodwill from the acquisition to the Rio Bay for the purposes of its annual impairment test. The ship is designated as a cash-generating unit that is comprised of three assets, which are:

- Hull – Carrying amount of $20 million
- Engines – Carrying amount of $7 million
- Crane hoists – Carrying amount of $3 million

Thus, the total carrying amount of the Rio Bay is $32,000,000, including the allocated goodwill.

Rio determines that the recoverable amount of the Rio Bay is $28,000,000, which represents an impairment loss of $4 million. To allocate the loss to the assets comprising the cash-generating unit, the company first allocates the loss to the outstanding amount of goodwill. This eliminates the goodwill, leaving $2 million to be allocated to the three assets comprising the unit. The allocation is conducted using the following table:

Asset	Carrying Amount	Proportion of Carrying Amounts	Impairment Allocation	Revised Carrying Amount
Hull	$20,000,000	67%	$1,340,000	$18,660,000
Engines	7,000,000	23%	460,000	6,540,000
Crane hoists	3,000,000	10%	200,000	2,800,000
Totals	$30,000,000	100%	$2,000,000	$28,000,000

IFRS: Reversing an Impairment Loss

At the end of each reporting period, assess whether any prior impairment loss has declined. The following are all indicators of such an impairment decline:

- *Economic performance.* The economic performance of the asset is better than expected.
- *Entity performance.* There have been significant favorable changes in the company to enhance the asset's performance or restructure the operations of which it is a part.

- *Environment.* The business environment in which the company operates has significantly improved.
- *Interest rates.* Interest rates have declined, which may reduce the discount rate used to calculate discounted cash flows, thereby increasing the recoverable amount of the asset.
- *Market value.* The asset's market value has increased.

If this analysis concludes that the amount of impairment has declined or been eliminated, estimate the new recoverable amount of the asset and increase the carrying amount of the asset to match its recoverable amount. This adjustment is treated as a reversal of the original impairment loss. You must also document what change in estimates caused the impairment recovery.

If you are reversing an impairment charge, only increase the carrying amount of an asset back to where that carrying amount would have been without the prior impairment charge, and net of any amortization or depreciation that would have been recognized in the absence of an impairment charge. Also, once the reversal is recorded, revise the periodic depreciation charge so that it properly reduces the new carrying amount over the remaining life of the asset.

EXAMPLE

Rio Shipping has almost fully automated the operations of its Rio Giorgio container ship, so that it can cruise the oceans with a crew of just three people (one per shift). Rio Shipping has also installed an advanced impeller propulsion system that cuts the ship's fuel requirements in half. These changes vastly reduce the cash outflows normally needed to operate the ship.

Rio had previously recognized a $4 million impairment loss on Rio Giorgio. The new cash flow situation results in a recoverable amount that matches the carrying amount of the ship prior to its original impairment charge. However, there would have been an additional $200,000 of depreciation during the period between the original impairment loss and the reversal of the impairment charge, so Rio Shipping can only reverse $3.8 million of the original impairment amount.

If you reverse an impairment charge for a cash-generating unit, allocate the reversal to all of the assets comprising that unit on a pro rata basis, using the carrying amounts of those assets as the basis for the allocation. This is the same concept already described for the allocation of an impairment loss – only now it is in reverse. When you calculate this allocation back to individual assets, the resulting asset carrying amount cannot go above the lower of:

- The recoverable amount of the asset, or
- The carrying amount of the asset, net of depreciation or amortization, as if the initial impairment had never been recognized.

If there is an allocation limitation caused by either of these items, allocate the remaining impairment reversal among the other assets in the unit.

EXAMPLE

Rio Shipping conducts a re-examination of the recoverable amount of its Rio Bay container ship, which was described in an earlier example for the initial recognition of impairment losses. Various changes to the propulsion system of the ship have reduced its operating costs to the point where Rio Shipping can justifiably increase its estimate of the ship's recoverable amount by $1 million. The revised carrying amounts of the assets comprising the cash-generating unit are carried forward from the prior example, and are noted below:

Asset	Revised Carrying Amount
Hull	$18,660,000
Engines	6,540,000
Crane Hoist	2,800,000
Total	$28,000,000

The following table shows the adjusted carrying amounts of the three assets following the allocation of the impairment reversal back to them.

Asset	Carrying Amount	Proportion of Carrying Amounts	Initial Reversal Allocation	Adjusted Carrying Amount
Hull	$18,660,000	67%	$670,000	$19,330,000
Engines	6,540,000	23%	230,000	6,770,000
Crane Hoist	2,800,000	10%	100,000	2,900,000
Totals	$28,000,000	100%	$1,000,000	$29,000,000

* Calculation not shown here

However, to properly allocate the impairment reversal back to these assets, Rio Shipping must determine the carrying amount of each asset, net of depreciation, as if the initial impairment had never occurred. This causes a problem, because the hull and crane hoist both have a longer estimated useful life than the engines, which are expected to be replaced midway through the life of the other assets. Consequently, the engines have been depreciated at a quicker rate than the other assets, and so cannot accept the full amount of the impairment allocation.

This results in the following additional allocation of the impairment reversal, where only a portion of the allocation can go to the engines, while the remaining impairment reversal is then allocated among the other two assets.

Asset	Adjusted Carrying Amount	Carrying Amount as if Impairment Never Occurred*	Impairment Reversal Still to Allocate**	Proportion of Adjusted Carrying Amounts	Second Stage Reversal Allocation
Hull	$19,330,000	$20,500,000		87%	$148,000
Engines	6,770,000	6,600,000	$170,000		
Crane Hoist	2,900,000	3,400,000		13%	$22,000
Totals	$29,000,000	---	$170,000	100%	$170,000

*   Calculation not shown here
**   Calculated as the adjusted carrying amount of $6,770,000 minus the carrying amount as if the initial impairment had never occurred, of $6,600,000.

Recognize any impairment reversal in the income statement as soon as it occurs. There is a variation on this rule that involves revalued assets. See the Asset Revaluation chapter for more information.

Even if the analysis to reverse an impairment does not actually result in an impairment reversal, it may provide sufficient cause to adjust the remaining useful life of the asset, as well as the depreciation method used or its estimated salvage value.

The preceding discussion of how to reverse an impairment loss applies equally to individual assets and cash-generating units.

> **Tip:** This discussion of impairment reversals does not include goodwill, which cannot be reversed. This is because IAS 38, *Intangible Assets*, prohibits the recognition of internally generated goodwill, which such an increase is construed to be.

Summary

The IFRS treatment of fixed asset impairment is much more detailed than the treatment given it under GAAP (which is unusual, given the usual prolixity of GAAP in comparison to IFRS). Despite this difference in verbiage, there are only a small number of significant differences between GAAP and IFRS, which are noted in the following table.

Differences Between GAAP and IFRS

Item	GAAP Treatment	IFRS Treatment
Cash flow forecasts	Shall cover the remaining useful life of the asset	Numerous restrictions on the forecast period; generally limited to five years
Comparison to carrying amount	GAAP compares the carrying amount to an asset's fair value	IFRS compares the carrying amount to an asset's recoverable amount, which is the higher of the asset's fair value less costs to sell or its value in use
Impairment loss reversal	Prohibited for impairment losses, but allowed to reverse prior disposal losses on held for sale assets	Allowed up to the amount of the original impairment

Chapter 9
Fixed Asset Disposal

Introduction

There are a number of issues related to the disposal of an asset. You may need to designate an asset as held-for-sale before even selling it, which requires some knowledge of the circumstances under which this designation is required. There are also different designations for discontinued operations. Further, you need to know how to remove an asset from the accounting records. Finally, there are slight differences between the GAAP and IFRS accounting for disposals. We will address all of these issues in the following sections.

Related Podcast Episode: Episode 122 of the Accounting Best Practices Podcast discusses the disposal of fixed assets. It is available at: **accounting-tools.com/podcasts** or **iTunes**

Asset Derecognition

An asset is derecognized upon its disposal, or when no future economic benefits can be expected from its use or disposal. Derecognition can arise from a variety of events, such as an asset's sale, scrapping, or donation.

The net effect of asset derecognition is to remove an asset and its associated accumulated depreciation from the balance sheet, as well as to recognize any related gain or loss. You cannot record a gain on derecognition as revenue. The gain or loss on derecognition is calculated as the net disposal proceeds, minus the asset's carrying amount.

The Held-for-Sale Classification

There is a special asset classification under GAAP that is called *held-for-sale*. This classification is important for two reasons:

- All assets classified as held for sale are presented separately on the balance sheet.
- Do not depreciate or amortize assets classified as held for sale.

Under GAAP, classify a fixed asset or a disposal group as held for sale if all of the following criteria are met:

- Management commits to a plan to sell the assets.
- The asset is available for sale immediately in its present condition.
- There is an active program to sell the asset.

- It is unlikely that the plan to sell the asset will be changed or withdrawn.
- Sale of the asset is likely to occur, and should be completed within one year.
- The asset is being marketed at a price that is considered reasonable in comparison to its current fair value.

EXAMPLE

Ambivalence Corporation plans to sell its existing headquarters facility and build a new corporate headquarters building. It will remain in its existing quarters until the new facility is complete, and will transfer ownership of the building to a buyer only after it has moved out. Since the company's continuing presence in the existing building means that it cannot be available for sale immediately, the situation fails the held-for-sale criteria, and Ambivalence should not reclassify its existing headquarters building as held-for-sale. This would be the case even if Ambivalence had a firm purchase commitment to buy the building, since the actual transfer of ownership will still be delayed.

A disposal group is a group of assets that you expect to dispose of in a single transaction, along with any liabilities that might be transferred to another entity along with the assets (such as debts, obligations under a warranty agreement, and so forth). If you remove an asset from a disposal group, re-evaluate the assets remaining in the group to see if they still meet the six held-for-sale criteria just noted.

The one-year limitation noted in the preceding criteria can be circumvented in any of the following situations:

- *Expected conditions imposed.* An entity other than the buyer is likely to impose conditions that will extend the sale period beyond one year, and the seller cannot respond to those conditions until after it receives a firm purchase commitment, and it expects that commitment within one year.

EXAMPLE

Ambivalence Corporation has a geothermal electricity-generating plant on the site of its Brew Master production facility. It plans to sell the geothermal plant to a local electric utility. The sale is subject to the approval of the state regulatory commission, which will likely require more than one year to issue its opinion. Ambivalence cannot begin to obtain the commission's approval until after it has obtained a firm purchase commitment from the local utility, but expects to receive the commitment within one year. The situation meets the criteria for maintaining an asset in the held-for-sale classification for more than one year.

- *Unexpected conditions imposed.* The seller obtains a firm purchase commitment, but the buyer or others then impose conditions on the sale that are not expected, and the seller is responding to these conditions, and the seller expects a favorable resolution of the conditions.

EXAMPLE

Ambivalence Corporation enters into a firm purchase commitment to sell its potions plant, but the buyer's inspection team finds that some potions have leaked into the local water table. The buyer demands that Ambivalence mitigate this environmental damage before the sale is concluded, which will require more than one year to complete. Ambivalence initiates these activities, and expects to mitigate the damage. The situation meets the criteria for maintaining an asset in the held-for-sale classification for more than one year.

- *Unlikely circumstances.* An unlikely situation arises that delays the sale, and the seller is responding to the change in circumstances, and is continuing to market the asset at a price that is reasonable in relation to its current fair value.

EXAMPLE

Ambivalence Corporation is attempting to sell its charm bracelet manufacturing line, but market conditions deteriorate, and it is unable to sell the line at the price point that it wants. Management believes that the market will rebound, so it leaves the same price in place, even though the market price is probably 20% lower. Given that the price now exceeds the current fair value of the manufacturing line, the company is no longer marketing it at a reasonable price, and so should no longer list the asset in the held-for-sale classification.

If a company acquires an asset as part of a business combination and wants to immediately classify it as held for sale, the asset must meet these requirements:

- Sale of the asset is likely to occur, and should be completed within one year.
- If any of the other criteria noted above are not met as of the acquisition date, it is probable that they will be met shortly after the acquisition has been completed.

Tip: The Accounting Standards Codification states in ASC 360-10-45-12 that three months is "usually" the amount of time allowed for the buyer to meet the held-for-sale criteria. Given the wording of this pronouncement, there is probably some leeway in the actual amount of time allowed.

If you classify assets as held-for-sale, measure them at the lower of their carrying amount or their fair value minus any cost to sell. If you must write down the carrying amount of an asset to its fair value minus any cost to sell, then recognize a loss in the amount of the write down. You may also recognize a gain on an increase in the fair value minus any cost to sell, but only up to the amount of any cumulative losses that were previously recognized.

The cost to sell is the costs incurred in a sale transaction that would not have been incurred if there had been no sale. Examples of costs to sell are title transfer fees and brokerage commissions. If a sale is expected to be more than one year in the future, discount the cost to sell to its present value.

When you classify an asset as held-for-sale, do not also accrue any expected future losses associated with operating it while it is so classified. Instead, recognize these costs only as incurred.

EXAMPLE

Ambivalence Corporation sells its Brew Master product line in 20X1, recognizing a gain of $100,000 prior to applicable taxes of $35,000. During the final year of operations of the Brew Master line, Ambivalence lost $50,000 on its operation of the line; it lost $80,000 during the preceding year. The applicable amount of tax reductions related to these losses were -$17,000 and -$28,000, respectively. It reports these results in the income statement as follows:

	20X0	20X1
Discontinued operations:		
Loss from operation of the Brew Master product line (net of applicable taxes of $28,000 and $17,000)	$(52,000)	$(33,000)
Gain on disposal of Brew Master product line (net of applicable taxes of $35,000)	--	$65,000

Part of the sale agreement requires that Ambivalence reimburse the buyer for any outstanding warranty claims. In the following year, the amount of these claims is $31,000, prior to an applicable tax reduction of -$11,000. Ambivalence reports this update to the discontinued operation in the following year with this disclosure in the income statement:

	20X0	20X1	20X2
Discontinued operations:			
Loss from operation of the Brew Master product line (net of applicable taxes of $28,000 and $17,000)	$(52,000)	$(33,000)	--
Gain on disposal of Brew Master product line (net of applicable taxes of $35,000)	--	$65,000	--
Adjust to gain on disposal of Brew Master product line (net of applicable taxes of $11,000)	--	--	$(20,000)

When you itemize the assets and liabilities of discontinued operations in the balance sheet, do not present them as a combined net figure. Instead, present them separately as assets and liabilities.

Reclassification from Held for Sale

What if, despite initial expectations, an asset that has been classified as held for sale is not sold? If an asset no longer meets any one of the six criteria for classification noted in the preceding section, remove it from the held-for-sale classification. At the time of reclassification, measure it at the lower of:

- The carrying amount of the asset prior to its classification as held-for-sale, minus any depreciation or amortization that would have been charged to it during the period when it was classified as held-for-sale, or
- The fair value of the asset when the decision was made not to sell it.

This measurement requirement effectively keeps a company from shifting assets into the held for sale classification in order to fraudulently avoid incurring any related depreciation expense.

Note: The FASB Accounting Standards Codification states in ASC 360-35-44 that an asset being reclassified *from* the held-for-sale designation should now be classified as held and used. Since there does not appear to be any distinction between the held and used classification and the normal accounting for fixed assets that are in use, we will assume that these assets are actually returned to their normal fixed asset accounting designations.

When you adjust the accounting records for this measurement, record the transaction as an expense that is included in income from continuing operations, and record the entry in the period when you make the decision not to sell the asset. Charge the expense to the income statement classification to which you would normally charge depreciation for the asset in question. Thus, the adjustment for a production machine would likely be charged to the cost of goods sold, while the adjustment for office equipment would likely be charged to general and administrative expense.

EXAMPLE

Ambivalence Corporation intends to sell its potion brewing factory, and so classifies the related assets into a disposal group and reports the group as held for sale, in the amount of $1,000,000. The journal entry is:

	Debit	Credit
Equipment held-for-sale	1,000,000	
Production machinery		1,000,000

After six months, the controller determines that the fair value of the disposal group has declined to $950,000, and so writes down the equipment cost with this entry:

	Debit	Credit
Loss on decline of fair value of held-for-sale equipment	50,000	
Equipment held-for-sale		50,000

The carrying value of the disposal group is now $950,000. After three more months, an independent appraiser determines that the fair value of the disposal group has now increased to $1,010,000. The controller can only record a gain up to the amount of any previously recorded losses, so he records the gain with this entry:

	Debit	Credit
Equipment held-for-sale	50,000	
Recovery of fair value of held-for-sale equipment		50,000

The carrying value of the disposal group is now $1,000,000.

After one full year has passed, management concludes that it cannot sell the disposal group, and decides to continue operating the potion brewing factory. The controller reclassifies the disposal group out of the held-for-sale classification with this entry:

	Debit	Credit
Production machinery	1,000,000	
Equipment held-for-sale		1,000,000

During the period when Ambivalence classified the disposal group as held for sale, it would have incurred a depreciation expense on the group of $50,000. The fair value of the group has now been re-appraised at $975,000. Since the carrying amount less depreciation of $950,000 is lower than the fair value of $975,000, Ambivalence records a charge of $50,000 to reduce the carrying amount of the group to $950,000 with the following entry:

	Debit	Credit
Depreciation – Production machinery	50,000	
Accumulated depreciation – Production machinery		50,000

Tip: The reclassification of assets into and out of the held-for-sale classification requires additional accounting effort to track. To minimize this effort, maintain a high capitalization limit, so that most assets are charged to expense when purchased. Also, if you expect that an asset will be sold within a very short time period, it is easier to not shift the asset into the held-for-sale classification and then almost immediately sell it; instead, depreciate the asset up until the point of sale. Clearly, some judgment is needed to follow the intent of the held-for-sale rules without engaging in an excessive amount of unnecessary accounting work.

Discontinued Operations

If a business reports a component of the entity as held-for-sale and disposes of it, the business should report the results of that component of the entity within the discontinued operations section of its income statement. The business should only do so if both of the following conditions are met:

- The disposal has resulted in the operations and cash flows of the component having been removed from the business, and
- The business no longer has a significant continuing involvement in the component.

There may be indirect cash flows associated with the disposal of a component that do not interfere with the first of the preceding criteria. These indirect cash flows may include:

- Interest income from seller financing of the sale transaction
- Contingent consideration that may be received from the buyer at a later date
- Royalties received from the buyer

A business is considered to still have a significant continuing interest in a component when it has the ability to influence the operating or financial policies of the component that it has disposed of. This can be a difficult determination to make, since it involves the aggregate impact of a company's continuing ownership interest in a component and any contractual arrangements with it. A company may be considered to have a significant continuing interest in a component if a contractual arrangement has a major impact on the component's overall operations, or gives the company a large involvement in the component's operations.

The following scenarios do *not* result in continuing cash flows or involvement by the selling business in a component:

- *Payments related to the sale price.* Contingent payments related to the purchase price of the component may go on for some time after the transaction closes.
- *Payments related to contingencies.* The parties may settle obligations related to such contingencies as product warranty obligations well after the sale date.
- *Payments related to employee benefits.* The parties may settle obligations related to employee terminations, pension plans, and other obligations after the sale date.

If you determine that the classification of a component has changed, either into or out of the discontinued operations classification, reclassify these operations into the new category designation for all periods presented in the company's comparative financial statements.

Tip: The requirement to reclassify prior periods either into or out of the discontinued operations classification is inordinately burdensome, since a business may not have detailed records for a component for prior years. Consequently, only change classifications if there is strong evidence in favor of doing so.

If there are adjustments to the sale price of a discontinued operation in later accounting periods, classify them separately within the discontinued operations section of the income statement, and describe them in the notes accompanying the financial statements.

Abandoned Assets

If a company abandons an asset, consider the asset to be disposed of, and account for it as such (even if it remains on the premises). However, if the asset is only temporarily idle, do not consider it to be abandoned, and continue to depreciate it in a normal manner.

If you have abandoned an asset, reduce its carrying amount down to any remaining salvage value on the date when the decision is made to abandon the asset.

Idle Assets

Some fixed assets will be idle from time to time. There is no specific consideration of idle assets in GAAP, so continue to depreciate them in a normal manner. However, here are additional considerations regarding what an idle asset may indicate:

- *Asset impairment.* If an asset is idle, it may be an indicator that the value of the asset has declined, which may call for an impairment review.
- *Disclosure.* Identify idle assets separately on the balance sheet, and disclose why they are idle.
- *Useful life.* If an asset is idle, this may indicate that its useful life is shorter than the amount currently used to calculate its depreciation. This may call for a re-evaluation of its useful life.

Asset Disposal Accounting

There are two scenarios under which you may dispose of a fixed asset. The first situation arises when you are eliminating a fixed asset without receiving any payment in return. This is a common situation when a fixed asset is being scrapped because it is obsolete or no longer in use, and there is no resale market for it. In this case, reverse any accumulated depreciation and reverse the original asset cost. If the asset is fully depreciated, that is the extent of the entry.

EXAMPLE

Ambivalence Corporation buys a machine for $100,000 and recognizes $10,000 of depreciation per year over the following ten years. At that time, the machine is not only fully depreciated, but also ready for the scrap heap. Ambivalence gives away the machine for free, and records the following entry.

	Debit	Credit
Accumulated depreciation	100,000	
Machine asset		100,000

A variation on this situation is to write off a fixed asset that has not yet been completely depreciated. In this case, write off the remaining undepreciated amount of the asset to a loss account.

Fixed Asset Disposal

EXAMPLE

To use the same example, Ambivalence Corporation gives away the machine after eight years, when it has not yet depreciated $20,000 of the asset's original $100,000 cost. In this case, Ambivalence records the following entry:

	Debit	Credit
Loss on asset disposal	20,000	
Accumulated depreciation	80,000	
Machine asset		100,000

The second scenario arises when you sell an asset, so that you receive cash (or some other asset) in exchange for the fixed asset being sold. Depending upon the price paid and the remaining amount of depreciation that has not yet been charged to expense, this can result in either a gain or a loss on sale of the asset.

EXAMPLE

Ambivalence Corporation still disposes of its $100,000 machine, but does so after seven years, and sells it for $35,000 in cash. In this case, it has already recorded $70,000 of depreciation expense. The entry is:

	Debit	Credit
Cash	35,000	
Accumulated depreciation	70,000	
Gain on asset disposal		5,000
Machine asset		100,000

What if Ambivalence had sold the machine for $25,000 instead of $35,000? Then there would be a loss of $5,000 on the sale. The entry would be:

	Debit	Credit
Cash	25,000	
Accumulated depreciation	70,000	
Loss on asset disposal	5,000	
Machine asset		100,000

The "loss on asset disposal" or "gain on asset disposal" accounts noted in the preceding sample entries are called disposal accounts. They may be combined into a single account or used separately to store gains and losses resulting from the disposal of fixed assets.

It is also possible to accumulate the offsetting debits and credits associated with the elimination of an asset and related accumulated depreciation, as well as any cash received, in a temporary disposal account, and then transfer the net balance in this account to a "gain/loss on asset disposal" account. However, this is a lengthier approach that is not appreciably more transparent and somewhat less efficient than treating the disposal account as a gain or loss account itself, and so is not recommended.

An unusual disposal scenario forwarded by a reader is what to do when a supplier buys back an asset under the terms of a warranty agreement that guarantees replacement of defective goods. In this case, the supplier is unable to remedy the situation, and so buys back the asset. The buyer has already recorded a fixed asset and begun depreciating it. The refund is essentially a sale of the asset, with the proceeds from the refund treated as though it were a payment for the asset by a third party. This means there is a debit to cash in the amount of the refund, a credit to the fixed asset account for the original purchase price, and a debit to accumulated depreciation. There may also be a gain or loss, depending on the amount of depreciation already charged to expense and the exact amount refunded by the supplier.

Asset Disposal under IFRS

Asset disposal under International Financial Reporting Standards is addressed in IAS 16, *Property, Plant, and Equipment*. The IFRS rules are essentially the same as those required by GAAP. The key features of the IFRS rules related to asset disposal are:

- Derecognize an asset when it is disposed of or when you expect no future economic benefits from its use.
- Do not classify a gain on the sale of an asset as revenue (unless it is classified as an inventory item and held-for-sale).
- Include any gain or loss on asset derecognition in the same period when you derecognize it. This gain or loss is calculated as the difference between the net disposal proceeds and the carrying amount of the asset.

One item of note is that, if you replace part of a fixed asset, derecognize the carrying amount of the replaced part, even if the replaced part has not been depreciated as a separate item. If you cannot determine the carrying amount of the replaced part, use the cost of the part that is replacing it as a reasonable indication of what the replaced part cost when it was originally acquired.

Tip: It may be useful to adopt a relatively high capitalization limit (the dollar amount paid for an asset, above which an entity records it as a long-term asset) in order to charge the cost of many of these replacement parts to expense as incurred. This avoids the extra time needed to investigate and derecognize the parts being replaced.

Summary

The disposal of an asset is a relatively simple matter, as long as there is adequate documentation of what is being derecognized. If not, you will likely have a large number of fully-depreciated assets and their offsetting accumulated depreciation in the accounting records, relating to assets that have long since departed the premises.

The held-for-sale classification introduces additional complexity to the reporting of fixed assets, and also impacts the recordation of depreciation. Be aware of the held-for-sale criteria and properly report assets in this classification; otherwise, the company's auditors may require that you do so as part of their year-end audit recommendations, and alter the depreciation calculations for the impacted assets, resulting in an adjustment to the preliminary financial results for the year.

Chapter 10
Fixed Asset Disclosures

Introduction

This chapter contains an itemization of the various disclosures required under both Generally Accepted Accounting Principles (GAAP) and International Financial Reporting Standards (IFRS). Within the general categories of GAAP and IFRS, there are numerous subheadings related to the disclosures for specific topics within the general fixed assets category.

In this chapter, we state that a company's financial statements should contain a variety of disclosures. This means that the disclosures are to be located either within the body of the financial statements themselves, or within the accompanying notes. In most cases, the appropriate place will be the accompanying notes.

GAAP Disclosures

This section contains the disclosures for various aspects of fixed assets that are required under GAAP. At the end of each set of requirements is a sample disclosure containing the more common elements of the requirements.

GAAP: General Fixed Asset Disclosures

The financial statements should disclose the following information about a company's fixed assets:

- *Accumulated depreciation.* The balances in each of the major classes of fixed assets as of the end of the reporting period.
- *Asset aggregation.* The balances in each of the major classes of fixed assets as of the end of the reporting period.
- *Depreciation expense.* The amount of depreciation charged to expense in the reporting period.
- *Depreciation methods.* A description of the methods used to depreciate assets in the major asset classifications.

EXAMPLE

Suture Corporation gives a general description of its fixed asset recordation and depreciation as follows:

> The company states its fixed assets at cost. For all fixed assets, the company calculates depreciation utilizing the straight-line method over the estimated useful lives for owned assets or, where appropriate, over the related lease terms for leasehold improvements. Useful lives range from 1 to 7 years.

Our fixed assets include the following approximate amounts:

	December 31,	
	20X2	20X1
Computer equipment	$9,770,000	$8,410,000
Computer software	2,800,000	1,950,000
Furniture and fixtures	860,000	780,000
Intangible assets	1,750,000	4,500,000
Leasehold improvements	400,000	360,000
Less: Accumulated depreciation and amortization	(5,400,000)	(4,800,000)
Totals	$10,180,000	$11,200,000

GAAP: Asset Retirement Obligations

If a company's assets are subject to asset retirement obligations, disclose the following information:

- *Description.* Describe any asset retirement obligations, as well as fixed assets with which they are associated.
- *Fair values.* Disclose the fair values of any assets that are legally restricted for purposes of setting asset retirement obligations. If you cannot reasonably estimate the fair value of an asset retirement obligation, state the reasons for this estimation difficulty.
- *Reconciliation.* Present a reconciliation of the beginning and ending carrying amounts of all asset retirement obligations, in aggregate, showing the changes attributable to the following items:
  - Accretion expense
  - Liabilities incurred in the reporting period
  - Liabilities settled in the reporting period
  - Revisions to estimated cash flows

EXAMPLE

Suture Corporation discloses the following information about its asset retirement obligations:

> The company records the fair value of a liability for an asset retirement obligation (ARO) that is recorded when there is a legal obligation associated with the retirement of a tangible long-lived asset and the liability can be reasonably estimated. The recording of ARO primarily affects the company's accounting for its mining of properties in Nevada for various substances used in its medical research. The company performs periodic reviews of its assets for any changes in the facts and circumstances that might require recognition of a retirement obligation.
>
> The following table indicates the changes to the company's before-tax asset retirement obligations in 20X3, 20X2, and 20X1:

(000s)	20X3	20X2	20X1
Balance at January 1	$5,350	$4,450	$2,900
Liabilities assumed in ABC acquisition	--	--	1,200
Liabilities incurred	200	250	100
Liabilities settled	(1,000)	(400)	(200)
Accretion expense	270	250	300
Revisions in estimated cash flows	1,320	800	150
Balance at December 31	$6,140	$5,350	$4,450

> In the table above, the amounts for 20X2 and 20X3 associated with "Revisions in estimated cash flows" reflect increased cost estimates to abandon the Harkness Mine in Nevada, due to increased regulatory requirements.

GAAP: Capitalized Interest Disclosures

If a company has capitalized any of its interest expense, disclose the total amount of interest cost it incurred during the period, as well as the portion of it that has been capitalized.

EXAMPLE

Suture Corporation discloses the following information about the interest cost it has capitalized as part of the construction of a laboratory facility:

> The company incurred interest cost of $800,000 during the year. Of that amount, it charged $650,000 to expense and included the remaining $150,000 in the capitalized cost of its Dumont laboratory facility.

GAAP: Change in Estimate Disclosures

It is relatively common to have changes in estimates related to fixed assets, since there are a variety of situations in which you may conclude that it is necessary to alter an asset's useful life, salvage value, or depreciation method – all of which are considered changes in estimate. If so, disclose the effect of a change in estimate on income from continuing operations, net income, and any per-share amounts for the reporting period. This disclosure is required only if the change is material.

EXAMPLE

Suture Corporation reports the following change in estimate within the notes accompanying its financial statements:

> During 20X4, management assessed its estimates of the residual values and useful lives of the company's fixed assets. Management revised its original estimates and now estimates that the medical production equipment that it had acquired in 20X1 and initially estimated to have a useful life of 8 years and salvage value of $100,000 will instead have a useful life of 12 years and salvage value of $80,000. The effects of this change in accounting estimate on the company's 20X4 financial statements are:
>
> Increase in:
>
> | | |
> |---|---|
> | Income from continuing operations and net income | $250,000 |
> | Earnings per share | $0.03 |

GAAP: Intangible Asset Impairment Disclosures

If you have recognized an impairment loss for an intangible asset, disclose the following information for each such impairment:

- *Amount*. Note the amount of the impairment loss and the method used to determine fair value.
- *Description*. Describe the asset and the circumstances causing the impairment.
- *Location*. Note the line item in the income statement in which the loss is reported.
- *Segment*. State the segment in which the impaired asset is reported.

EXAMPLE

Suture Corporation determines that the values of several acquired patents have declined, which it discloses as follows:

> The company has written down the value of its patents related to the electronic remediation of cancer, on the grounds that subsequent testing of this equipment has not resulted in the levels of cancer remission that management had anticipated. The company employed an appraiser to derive a new value that was based on anticipated cash flows. The resulting loss of $4.5 million was charged to the cancer treatment segment of the company, and is contained within the "Other Gains and Losses" line item on the income statement. The remaining value ascribed to these intangible assets as of the balance sheet date is $1.75 million. Management does not plan to sell the patents.

GAAP: Intangible Asset Disclosures

If you have acquired individual intangible assets or such assets that are part of a group, disclose the following information about them:

For Assets Subject to Amortization

- *Amortization expense.* Disclose the amortization charged to expense in the reporting period, as well as the estimated aggregate amortization expense for each of the next five fiscal years.
- *Amortization period.* Note the weighted-average amortization period, both for all intangible assets and by major intangible asset class.
- *Carrying amount.* Disclose the total amount of intangible assets, as well as the amount assigned to any major class of intangible asset. Also disclose accumulated amortization, both in total and by class of intangible asset.
- *Residual value.* If there is any significant residual value, disclose it in total and by major intangible asset class.

For Assets Not Subject to Amortization

- *Carrying amount.* Disclose the total amount of intangible assets, as well as the amount assigned to any major class of intangible asset.
- *Policy.* Describe the company's accounting policy for the treatment of any costs incurred in the renewal of an intangible asset's term.
- *Renewal costs.* If you capitalize renewal costs, disclose by major intangible asset class the total costs incurred during the reporting period to renew the term of an intangible asset.
- *Renewal Period.* If these assets have renewal terms, state the weighted-average period before the next renewal for each major class of intangible asset.

EXAMPLE

Suture Corporation discloses the following information about its intangible assets:

	As of December 31, 20X1	
	Gross Carrying Amount	Accumulated Amortization
Amortized intangible assets		
Patents	$4,000,000	$1,450,000
Trademarks	1,200,000	400,000
Unpatented technology	800,000	650,000
Total	$6,000,000	$2,500,000
Unamortized intangible assets		
Distribution license	$500,000	
Trademark	450,000	
Total	$950,000	

Aggregate amortization expense:	
For the year ended 12/31/X1	$560,000
Estimated amortization expense:	
For the year ended 12/31/X2	$560,000
For the year ended 12/31/X3	420,000
For the year ended 12/31/X4	420,000
For the year ended 12/31/X5	380,000
For the year ended 12/31/X6	380,000

IFRS Disclosures

This section contains the disclosures for various aspects of fixed assets that are required under IFRS. At the end of each set of requirements is a sample disclosure containing the more common elements of the requirements.

IFRS: General Fixed Asset Disclosures

The financial statements should disclose the following information about a company's fixed assets for each class of asset:

- *Base*. The measurement base used to determine the gross carrying amount.
- *Commitments*. The amount of any contractual obligations to acquire fixed assets.
- *Construction expenditures*. The amount of expenditures recognized to date in the carrying amount of an asset during its construction.
- *Depreciation*. The depreciation methods used.
- *Disposition compensation*. The amount paid to the company by third parties for fixed assets that were impaired, lost, or given up, and which are included in profit or loss.
- *Reconciliation*. Show a reconciliation in the following format of the carrying amount at the beginning and end of the reporting period:
  - Asset additions
  - Assets or disposal groups classified as held for sale
  - Assets acquired through business combinations
  - Changes resulting from revaluations
  - Impairment losses recognized or reversed in other comprehensive income
  - Impairment losses recognized in profit or loss
  - Impairment losses reversed in profit or loss
  - Depreciation
  - Net exchange differences caused by the translation of the financial statements from the company's functional currency to a different presentation currency
  - Other changes
- *Restrictions*. The descriptions and amounts of any restrictions on the title to assets, as well as on assets pledged as security for liabilities.
- *Summary totals*. The gross carrying amount and accumulated depreciation (which includes any accumulated impairment losses) at the beginning and end of the reporting period.
- *Useful life*. The useful lives or depreciation rates used.

EXAMPLE

Franklin Drilling discloses the following information about its oil and gas operations:

The company states its fixed assets at cost, less accumulated depreciation and accumulated impairment losses. The initial cost of an asset comprises its purchase price or construction costs, any costs attributable to bringing the asset into operation, the initial estimate of any decommissioning obligation, and borrowing costs. Exchanges of assets are measured at fair value unless the exchange transaction lacks commercial substance or the fair values of either asset is not reliably measurable. The company recognizes the gain or loss on derecognition of an asset in profit or loss.

The company measures its oil and gas properties, as well as related pipelines, using the unit-of-production method. Amortization of the cost of producing wells is over the amount of proved developed reserves. The company depreciates the remainder of its fixed assets on a straight line basis over its expected useful life, which ranges from 3-7 years for furniture and fixtures to 20-30 years for refineries.

The company's investment in and depreciation of fixed assets is as follows:

(000s)	Buildings	Oil and Gas Properties	Furniture and Fixtures	Total
At January 1, 20X1	$14,000	$182,000	$9,000	$205,000
Asset additions	3,000	43,000	1,000	47,000
Assets acquired	5,000	70,000	4,000	79,000
Revaluation changes	--	10,000	--	10,000
Impairment losses	--	(18,000)	--	(18,000)
Exchange adjustments	1,000	11,000	--	12,000
Depreciation	(8,000)	(98,000)	(5,000)	(111,000)
Totals	$15,000	$200,000	$9,000	$224,000

IFRS: Capitalized Interest Disclosures

If you have capitalized the cost of interest into any fixed assets, disclose the following information:

- *Capitalized amount.* The amount of interest cost capitalized during the reporting period.
- *Capitalization rate.* The capitalization rate used to calculate the amount of borrowing costs eligible for capitalization.

EXAMPLE

Franklin Drilling discloses the following information about its capitalization of interest:

> The company incurred $13 million of interest costs during the year ended 12/31/X1, of which it charged $2 million to expense and capitalized $11 million. The capitalized amounts were related to the development of various oilfield production facilities. The capitalization rate that the company used to calculate the amount of borrowing costs eligible for capitalization was 6.5%, which was based on long-term market interest rates for loans associated with development projects of similar duration and risk.

IFRS: Change in Estimate Disclosures

During the life of a fixed asset, it is possible that you may evaluate it and conclude that there has been a change in accounting estimate, resulting in changes in the current period or future periods. If so, you may need to disclose changes for such items as:

- Depreciation methods
- Estimated costs to dismantle, remove or restore fixed assets
- Residual values
- Useful lives

> **Tip:** Only make disclosures about changes in estimate if the changes are *material* to the results of the entity. The carrying amounts of most assets are not large enough to result in a material change in the financial statements, no matter how large the change in estimate may be.

EXAMPLE

Franklin Drilling reports the following change in estimate within the notes accompanying its financial statements:

> During 20X1, management assessed the depreciation methods, removal costs, residual values, and useful lives of its fixed assets. Management has adjusted its estimates and now concludes that the pipeline from its Braithwaite Field is corroding faster than anticipated, and so has adjusted its remaining useful life from 15 years to 10 years. The effect of this change in accounting estimate on the company's 20X1 financial statements is a reduction of its income from continuing operations of $2 million.

IFRS: Estimates of Recoverable Amounts

A company may have cash-generating units that contain allocations of goodwill or intangible assets with indefinite useful lives.

If the amount of goodwill or these intangible assets is a significant proportion of the company's total carrying amount of goodwill or intangible assets with indefinite useful lives, disclose the following information:

- *Basis of measurement.* Whether value in use or fair value less costs to sell has been used to determine the unit's recoverable amount. The following disclosures also apply, depending on the basis of measurement:
  - o *Fair value basis.* Describe the methodology used to determine fair value less costs to sell. If the methodology does not include the use of an observable market price, also disclose key assumptions used, and describe how management determined the values assigned to each key assumption, and whether they are based on past experience or are consistent with externally-based information; if not, describe how they differ from past experience or externally-based information. If the fair value less costs to sell is based on discounted cash flow estimates, disclose the period and growth rate of the projections, as well as the discount rate applied to them.
  - o *Value in use basis.* Describe the key assumptions used as the basis for cash flow projections. Also, note how management determined the values assigned to each key assumption, and whether they are based on past experience or are consistent with externally-based information; if not, describe how they differ from past experience or externally-based information. Also note the cash flow projection period, and include a justification if this period exceeds five years. Further, describe the growth rate used to extrapolate cash flow projections, and justify the rate if it exceeds the long-term average growth rate for the product, market, or country. Finally, note the discount rate applied to the cash flow projections.
- *Goodwill allocation.* The carrying amount of the goodwill allocated to the unit.
- *Intangible allocation.* The carrying amount of the intangible assets with indefinite useful lives allocated to the unit.
- *Sensitivity test.* If a reasonably possible change in a key assumption used to determine the recoverable amount would result in the carrying amount exceeding the recoverable amount, disclose:
  - o *Amount at risk.* The amount by which the unit's recoverable amount exceeds its carrying amount.
  - o *Assumption value.* The value assigned to the key assumption causing the disclosure.
  - o *Sensitivity.* The amount by which the value must change for the recoverable amount to equal the unit's carrying amount.

If the amount of goodwill or intangible assets with indefinite useful lives is allocated among several cash-generating units, and the amount so allocated is not significant in comparison to a company's total carrying amount of goodwill or intangible assets with indefinite useful lives, make the following disclosures:

- *Quantification*. State the aggregate amount of goodwill or intangible assets with indefinite useful lives that have been allocated to units.
- *Significance*. State that the amount of the allocation is not significant.

EXAMPLE

Franklin Drilling discloses the following information about the recoverable amounts of its assets:

The recoverable amount of the Brickel Oil Field cash-generating unit has been determined based on a value in use calculation. That calculation uses cash flow projections based on financial budgets approved by management and covering a five-year period, using a discount rate of 7.9 percent. Cash flows beyond that five-year period have been extrapolated using a steady 5.6 percent growth rate. This growth rate does not exceed the long-term average growth rate for the market in which Franklin operates. Management believes that any reasonably possible change in the key assumptions on which the recoverable amount of the Brickel cash-generating unit is based would not cause its carrying amount to exceed its recoverable amount.

IFRS: Held for Sale Disclosures

If you have designated any assets as held for sale, make the following disclosures:

- *Classification*. Separately present a fixed asset classified as held for sale in the balance sheet. If there are liabilities associated with the asset, also separately present them in the balance sheet. You must also separately present in other comprehensive income the income or expense related to an asset that is classified as held for sale.

Tip: You cannot combine the assets and liabilities associated with an asset designated as held for sale and present them on a net basis. They must be presented separately.

- *Description*. Describe the asset that has been classified as held for sale.
- *Impairment gains and losses*. State the amount of any impairment losses or loss reversals associated with the asset that is held for sale.
- *Plan changes*. Describe the circumstances leading to a decision to change the held for sale status of an asset, as well as the impact of this decision on the results of operations for all reporting periods presented.
- *Prior periods*. If you have separately classified the amounts for a fixed asset as held for sale in the current period, you do not have to do so for the same

asset in any prior periods that may be presented alongside the results of the current reporting period.

- *Sale terms.* Describe the circumstances of the projected asset sale, and the manner and timing of the sale.
- *Segment.* The segment of which the asset is a part.

EXAMPLE

Franklin Drilling makes the following disclosure about its assets classified as held for sale as of the end of the current period:

> Franklin Drilling has an active program to identify and dispose of any fixed assets that are either non-strategic or underutilized. Under the dictates of this program, the company has identified its Baikal pipeline as non-strategic, and classified it as held for sale. The Baikal pipeline has a carrying amount of $80 million. The company recorded an impairment loss on the pipeline of $20 million in 20X1, and of an additional $25 million in 20X3. The company has identified a buyer for the pipeline, and expects to sell the asset for an amount approximating its current carrying amount within the next year. The pipeline is recorded as held for sale within the company's Transportation segment.

IFRS: Impairment Disclosures

If you have reduced the carrying amount of any fixed assets due to impairment, make the disclosures noted below. These disclosures are to be aggregated at the asset class level, not for individual assets.

- *Impairment recognized.* The amount of any impairment losses recognized in profit or loss during the reporting period, and the line items in which the losses are included.
- *Impairment reversals.* The amount of impairment reversals recognized in profit or loss during the reporting period, and the line items in which the losses are included.
- *Revalued asset impairments.* The amount of impairment losses on revalued assets recognized in other comprehensive income during the reporting period.
- *Revalued asset impairment reversals.* The amount of impairment reversals recognized in other comprehensive income during the reporting period.

If you are reporting on the results of a company's segments, you will also have to report the amount of impairment losses and impairment reversals in profit or loss and other comprehensive income for the reporting period for each segment.

If there is a material impairment loss or reversal for an individual asset or cash-generating unit, disclose the following information:

- *Circumstances.* The circumstances that led to either the recognition or reversal of the impairment.
- *Description.* A description of the asset or cash-generating unit. In either case, also note the reportable segment to which it belongs, if any. If the subject is a cash-generating unit and the method of aggregating the unit has changed, describe the change in aggregation method and the company's reasons for doing so.
- *Quantification.* The amount of the impairment loss or loss reversal.
- *Recoverable basis.* State whether the recoverable amount of the asset or cash-generating unit is its value in use or its fair value less costs to sell.
  - *Fair value basis.* If the recoverable amount is based on its fair value less costs to sell, describe the basis for the determination (such as by referring to prices in an active market).
  - *Value in use basis.* If the recoverable amount is based on its value in use, note the discount rate used in the current calculation, as well as any previous estimate of the value in use.

If, on the other hand, the amount of an impairment or impairment reversal is not material at the level of an individual asset or cash-generating unit, instead disclose aggregate impairment losses and reversals, as well as the following information:

- *Circumstances.* The circumstances that led to the recognition of the impairment losses or reversals.
- *Classes impacted.* The classes of assets affected by impairment losses or reversals.

EXAMPLE

Franklin Drilling discloses the following information about the impairment of its fixed assets:

During 20X1, the company recognized impairment losses of $9 million. The main elements of the write-down were $7 million related to our Medina oil field development, and $2 million for the Pablo Montez pipeline project. Both impairments were triggered by our decision not to proceed with project completion, due to excessive political risk and increased completion costs. These losses are recognized in the Other Gains and Losses line item in our income statement. The impairment loss on the Medina oil field development is recognized in our Exploration segment, while the impairment loss on the Pablo Montez pipeline project is recognized in our Transportation segment.

IFRS: Intangible Asset Disclosures

Disclose the following information about intangible assets in the notes accompanying the financial statements for each class of assets, and further subdivided by internally-generated intangible assets and other intangible assets:

- *Amortization expense.* Where the amortization expense appears in the statement of comprehensive income.
- *Amortization methods.* The amortization methods used, if the assets have finite useful lives.
- *Gross amounts.* The beginning and ending balances of gross carrying amounts and the combined amount of accumulated amortization and accumulated impairments.
- *Reconciliation.* A reconciliation of the beginning and ending carrying amounts, including additions from internal development, additions from business combinations, additions acquired separately, assets classified as held for sale, revaluation changes, impairment changes, amortization, foreign currency exchange differences, and other items.
- *Useful life determination.* Whether the useful lives are considered finite or indefinite. If the former, disclose the duration of the useful lives.

If any intangible assets are accounted for under the revaluation model, disclose by asset class the effective date of revaluation, the aggregate carrying amount of revalued items, the carrying amount that would have been recognized if the cost model had been used, and a reconciliation of the revaluation surplus (if any), as well as any restrictions on the distribution of the revaluation surplus to shareholders.

In addition, disclose the following more general information as necessary:

- *Committed purchases.* Any amounts contractually committed for the acquisition of intangible assets.
- *Government grants.* If assets were acquired through a government grant and recognized at fair value, disclose their initial fair values, carrying amounts, and whether they are now measured under the cost model or the revaluation model.
- *Indefinite useful lives.* The carrying amounts of assets with indefinite useful lives, and the reasons for assigning them indefinite status.
- *Material changes.* If there have been material changes in accounting estimate, such as useful lives, amortization methods, and/or residual amounts, disclose the nature and amount of these changes.
- *Material items.* The carrying amount, remaining amortization period, and description of any specific intangible assets that are material to the financial statements.
- *Pledged as security.* The carrying amounts of any intangible assets pledged as security for liabilities.

- *Research and development*. The aggregate amount of research and development expense recognized during the period.
- *Restricted title*. The amount and name of any intangible assets with restricted titles.

IFRS also encourages, but does not require, the disclosure of any fully amortized intangible assets that are still in use, as well as a description of any intangible assets that do not meet the criteria for asset recognition, but which the company controls.

The cost model and the revaluation model are described in the Subsequent Asset Measurement chapter.

IFRS: Revaluation Disclosures

If the business has fixed assets that have been revalued, disclose the following information:

- *Appraiser*. Whether an independent valuation entity was involved.
- *Assumptions*. The methods and assumptions used to estimate fair value.
- *Carrying amount*. The carrying amount for each asset class that would have been recognized under the cost model.
- *Date*. Effective date of the revaluation.
- *Surplus*. The revaluation surplus, including the change in its balance during the period and restrictions imposed on the distribution of this surplus to shareholders.
- *Valuation method*. Whether valuations were derived from observable prices in an active market, or from recent market transactions on arms' length terms, or other methods.

EXAMPLE

Franklin Drilling discloses the following information about the revaluation of a cash-generating unit:

> The company has conducted an appraisal of the value of its Brickel Oil Field cash-generating unit, using the services of an independent valuation firm. This appraiser independently estimated cash flows to be generated by the cash-generating unit, which formed the basis for its opinion of fair value. The result of this appraisal was a revaluation that increased the unit's carrying amount by $25 million as of June 1, 20X1.

> Following the revaluation, the unit has a cumulative revaluation surplus of $37 million. It is unlikely that this revaluation can be distributed to shareholders, due to restrictions on cash flows out of the country where the unit is located.

> If the company had recognized the carrying amount of the unit under the cost model, it would have had a carrying amount of $172 million as of 12/31/20X1.

IFRS: Optional Disclosures

The following disclosures are not required, but may provide useful information to the recipients of a company's financial statements:

- *Fair value.* The fair value of fixed assets when it differs materially from their carrying amount.
- *Fully depreciated assets.* The gross carrying amount of any fully depreciated fixed assets that the company is still using.
- *Idle equipment.* The carrying amount of any temporarily idle fixed assets.
- *Retired assets.* The carrying amount of any fixed assets that have been retired from active use, but which are not classified as held for sale.

Summary

In nearly all areas of accounting, the sheer volume of GAAP pronouncements greatly exceeds IFRS, but this is not the case for disclosures related to fixed assets. IFRS consistently requires more disclosure that GAAP on a variety of topics, particularly for estimates of recoverable amounts, impairments, intangible assets, and revaluations. Consequently, if you are reporting under IFRS, you may need to collect and aggregate additional information in order to meet disclosure requirements.

Chapter 11
Not-for-Profit Fixed Asset Accounting

Introduction

A not-for-profit entity is defined under Generally Accepted Accounting Principles (GAAP) as one possessing the following characteristics to some degree:

- *Contributions.* It receives significant contributions from other parties who do not expect any return compensation.
- *Purpose.* It does not exist primarily to earn a profit.
- *Ownership.* It does not have the ownership structure common in a business enterprise.

Thus, a not-for-profit entity is not one that is owned by investors, or which provides special benefits to its owners, members, or participants. Examples of not-for-profit organizations are associations, libraries, museums, and universities.

The accounting for fixed assets in a not-for-profit organization can be different from the accounting normally used by for-profit entities, *if the assets are donated.* In this chapter, we will review when to capitalize a contributed asset, what value to assign to it, and whether to depreciate it.

Initial Recognition of Fixed Assets

When a not-for-profit entity receives a contribution of any kind (not just a fixed asset), it records the asset with an offsetting entry to a revenue or gain account. Record a contribution as revenue if it is part of the entity's ongoing major activities, or record it as a gain if the contribution is part of peripheral or incidental activity.

If the contributor places a restriction on the use of a fixed asset, this does not impact the underlying value of the donation, so you would record the same amount for such a contributed asset as you would for one without a restriction, with no change in the timing of recognition.

If a not-for-profit entity receives a contributed asset for which there is a major uncertainty about its value, you do not have to recognize it in the accounting records. Examples of such assets are those of historical value, photographs, or items that may be of use solely for scientific research.

Conversely, record an asset that has a future economic benefit or service potential (usually by exchanging it for cash or using it to generate goods or services).

EXAMPLE

Newton Enterprises provides free science classes to high school students. It receives the following contributions:

- A philosopher's stone. The stone is of historical significance, but probably does not transmute lead into gold. Since there is considerable uncertainty about its value, Newton does not record the asset.
- A used lawn mower. The lawn mower is of no direct use to Newton's primary operations, and will be sold. Newton accordingly records the lawn mower as a gain.
- An electron microscope. The microscope is of direct use in Newton's primary operations, so Newton records it as revenue.

As an example of the journal entries to be used for a donated asset, if the microscope in the preceding example were to be valued at $50,000, the journal entry might be:

	Debit	Credit
Scientific devices	50,000	
Revenue		50,000

If the lawn mower in the preceding example were to be valued at $1,000, the journal entry might be:

	Debit	Credit
Maintenance equipment	1,000	
Gain on contributed assets		1,000

Restrictions on Contributed Assets

If a donor makes a contribution that is an *unconditional promise to give*, recognize the contribution when received. This calls for sufficient verifiable documentation that the promise was both made and received. The promise should be legally enforceable. If a contributor is able to rescind the promise to give, do not recognize the asset being contributed.

If a contributor makes a contribution that is a conditional promise to give, only recognize the asset when the underlying conditions have been substantially met (e.g., at the point when the promise becomes unconditional).

EXAMPLE

Newton Enterprises receives an offer from a contributor to pay $2 million for a new classroom building, but only if Newton can raise matching funds from other contributors within one year. Given the conditional nature of this offer, Newton cannot record the asset until the matching funds have been raised within the specified time period.

You may consider a conditional promise to give to be essentially unconditional if there is only a remote possibility that the condition will not be met.

EXAMPLE

Newton Enterprises receives a promise of multi-year funding for new schools, but only if Newton supplies its financial statements to the contributor at the end of each fiscal year. There is only a remote possibility that Newton will not comply with this requirement, so Newton can treat the contribution as an unconditional promise to give.

What if a donor contributes a fixed asset, but attaches a conditional promise to the contribution? You now have the fixed asset on your premises, but can you record it as a fixed asset? No. Until the condition has been met or the donor has waived it, record the received asset as a refundable advance from the donor.

Valuation of Contributed Assets

Recognize a donated asset at its fair value as of the receipt date. The following techniques are available for deriving fair value:

- *Market approach.* Use information from actual market transactions to arrive at an estimated fair value. Ideally, this information is based on quoted prices in an active market for identical items, but may also use information from transactions for similar items, or just the best available information.
- *Income approach.* Use discounted cash flows to derive the present value of an asset.
- *Cost approach.* Use an asset's current replacement cost. This is essentially the cost of acquiring or building a substitute asset that has comparable utility.

If you elect to use the income approach, and the asset being contributed will not be received for at least a year, use the projected fair value of the asset as of the date when you expect to receive it, discounted back to its present value. Where it is impossible to determine fair value as of a future date, use the fair value of the asset at the initial recognition date, though without any discounting to present value.

EXAMPLE

Newton Enterprises is given an office building for use as a training center by a city government that has no use for the building. The city is suffering through a severe downturn, and the government was unable to find a buyer for the building. In general, there is very little market information available for the valuation of similar buildings, given the paucity of sale transactions. Newton also has trouble using the income approach to derive a value for the building, since it gives science classes for free. Thus, it elects to use the cost approach to value the building, under which it determines that the cost to create a substitute building of comparable utility would be $700,000.

Valuation of Contributed Services

What if volunteers donate their time to construct a fixed asset? Record the value of these services in either of the following situations:

- The services create or enhance non-financial assets; or
- The services require specialized skills, are provided by persons with those skills, and would otherwise need to be purchased.

Value these services at either their fair value or at the fair value of the fixed asset created or the change in value of the fixed asset being improved.

EXAMPLE

Newton Enterprises constructs a science school, using the services of a large group of volunteers, which include architects, carpenters, electricians, and plumbers. Newton spends $800,000 on materials for the building project. Once the asset is placed in service, a third-party appraiser estimates that the fair value of the building is now $1.2 million. Newton can therefore record the building asset at a cost of $1.2 million, of which $400,000 is the value of contributed services.

Valuation of Art, Historical Treasures, and Similar Items

If a donor contributes works of art, historical treasures, or similar items, you can recognize them as assets, with offsetting revenue or gains. This only applies if the items contributed are not part of a collection. If such contributions are part of a collection, use any of the following alternatives for reporting them:

- Record them as fixed assets.; or
- Record as fixed assets only those items received after a specific date; or
- Do not record them.

You are not allowed to record only *selected* collections or items as fixed assets; instead, you must consistently apply any recordation policy selected for *all* collections or items.

Capitalize the cost of major preservation or restoration projects, and assign them useful lives that extend until the next expected preservation or restoration project for the same asset.

EXAMPLE

Newton Enterprises maintains a small science museum, to which a donor contributes an original quadruplex telegraph built by Thomas Edison. An independent appraisal establishes that the device has a fair value of $150,000. Newton adds the telegraph to its Edison collection and records it as a fixed asset. This results in revenue of $150,000, as well as a new fixed asset.

Depreciation of Fixed Assets

A not-for-profit entity should depreciate any contributed assets that it has recorded as fixed assets, if they have a useful life. If an asset's useful life is extremely long (as would be the case for a work of art), you do not have to recognize depreciation for it. Only avoid depreciation in this manner if both of the following conditions exist:

- The asset should be preserved perpetually, due to its cultural, aesthetic, or historical value; and
- The entity has the ability to preserve the asset (such as by preserving it in a protected environment), and is currently doing so.

Depreciate art collections, on the grounds that they experience wear and tear during their intended uses that requires periodic major restoration efforts.

If you have capitalized the cost of a major restoration project, depreciate this cost over the expected period before the next restoration project is expected. Do this even if the asset being restored or preserved is not depreciated.

Recordation of Fixed Assets

Use the same record keeping standards for donated fixed assets as stated in the Fixed Asset Record Keeping chapter. In addition, maintain information about the following two items:

- *Donor*. Identify the person or entity that contributed the asset, along with contact information.
- *Restrictions*. Note any restrictions placed on use of the asset by the donor.

These two additional items may interact. For example, you may no longer have a need for an asset, and wish to sell it to create space for another asset. If so, you may need to contact the donor to have a restriction lifted, or to have the asset returned to the donor.

It is also useful to maintain a report that itemizes the restrictions on fixed assets, so that the entity does not deal with an asset in a manner that will violate a restriction. This report should be periodically updated and issued to the management team for review.

Fixed Asset Controls in a Not-for-Profit Entity

A key reason to designate an asset as a fixed asset is that an entity's system of controls for fixed assets will then apply to it. These controls should be well-documented, monitored by management, and reviewed by auditors. However, a not-for-profit may not record a contribution as a fixed asset at all, as may be the case with historical or research objects. To afford these contributions the same protections offered by the traditional control system to designated fixed assets, it would be helpful to record them in a manner similar to "normal" fixed assets. For example, record them as line items in the fixed asset register, but with a zero cost, or in a separate manual journal that is kept separate from the formal accounting records. The key point here is that a contribution that is *not* recorded in the accounting records will likely find its way out of the entity sooner or later, whether or not that is the intent of management.

Similarly, it is useful to set a low capitalization limit in a not-for-profit entity, just so that there is a record available of the existence of fixed assets and their locations. This is of particular importance in an entity that relies in large part on the services of volunteers. There may be significant turnover among volunteers, so there is no institutional memory of where fixed assets are located. Setting a low capitalization limit is an inexpensive way to supplement what little institutional memory of fixed assets there may be.

Summary

A not-for-profit entity must deal with several fixed asset decisions that a for-profit business never encounters – whether to record a contributed asset, at what value to record it, and whether to depreciate it at all. These decisions are only for *contributed* assets. For fixed assets that are purchased in the normal manner, the accounting found in all other chapters of this book will apply.

Chapter 12
Fixed Asset Record Keeping

Introduction

A fundamental part of fixed asset accounting is to properly record the information associated with each asset, as well as to aggregate this information into reports that managers can use. This chapter addresses the accounts normally used to record fixed assets in the general ledger, as well as the forms used to record key information about several types of fixed assets. Finally, it goes into considerable detail regarding several types of fixed asset reports.

Related Podcast Episode: Episode 139 of the Accounting Best Practices Podcast discusses a lean system for fixed assets. It is available at: **accounting-tools.com/podcasts** or **iTunes**

Tip: You may need to assemble a large amount of documentation, depending upon the fixed asset to which it relates. To avoid the cost of doing so, consider as high a capitalization limit as possible. This means that only the more expensive items are recorded as assets, while all other expenditures are charged to expense in the period incurred. This approach will accelerate the recognition of expenses, but reduces the total cost of record keeping.

Fixed Asset Accounts

When you are recording fixed assets in the general ledger, you need some accounts in which to record them. The standard approach is to create a set of general ledger accounts that correspond to the asset classes into which you plan to aggregate fixed assets. Typical asset classes to consider are:

- Buildings
- Computer equipment
- Computer software
- Furniture and fixtures
- Intangible assets
- Land
- Land improvements
- Leasehold improvements
- Machinery
- Office equipment
- Vehicles

There should be a separate asset class for any group of assets that has similar characteristics, usage patterns, and useful lives.

If a company has specialized assets, you can certainly create a new asset class for them. For example, if a company builds pipelines, it can aggregate them into a pipelines asset class.

> **Tip:** Do not create an account if you have no assets to record in it. If you eventually acquire new types of assets, you can always create accounts for them at a later date.

You may want to create an offsetting accumulated depreciation account for each fixed asset account, though it is acceptable to have a single accumulated depreciation account for all tangible assets and a single amortization account for all intangible assets.

> **Tip:** Use a single accumulated depreciation account for all fixed assets, unless there is a clear reporting need to have separate accumulated depreciation accounts for each class of fixed asset. When you have multiple accumulated depreciation accounts, there is an increased risk that entries will be made to the wrong accounts, so that the total accumulated depreciation is correct, but you must spend time investigating why individual account balances are wrong.

The exact account codes assigned to the general ledger fixed asset accounts will depend upon the number of digits used in the chart of accounts, and the presence of other asset accounts in the chart. The chart of accounts is a listing of all accounts used in the general ledger, usually sorted in order by account number. Accounts are usually listed in order of their appearance in the financial statements, starting with the balance sheet and continuing with the income statement.

Asset accounts typically begin with the numeral "1", and fixed assets appear on the chart of accounts after cash, investments, accounts receivable, and inventory, so let us assume that the second digit is a "5", to place the fixed assets after the items just noted. We could then assign them the account numbers noted in the following table.

Four-Digit Account Numbering System

Account Number	Account Name
1505	Buildings
1510	Computer equipment
1515	Computer software
1520	Furniture and fixtures
1525	Intangible assets
1530	Land
1535	Land improvements
1540	Leasehold improvements
1545	Machinery
1550	Office equipment
1555	Vehicles
1605	Accumulated depreciation – Buildings
1610	Accumulated depreciation – Computer equipment
1615	Accumulated depreciation – Computer software
1620	Accumulated depreciation – Furniture and fixtures
1625	Accumulated amortization – Intangible assets
1630	Accumulated depreciation – Land
1635	Accumulated depreciation – Land improvements
1640	Accumulated depreciation – Leasehold improvements
1645	Accumulated depreciation – Machinery
1650	Accumulated depreciation – Office equipment
1655	Accumulated depreciation – Vehicles

Note that there are gaps in the numbering between each account. This leaves room to add additional accounts in the future.

These sample account numbers include a complete set of accumulated depreciation accounts, just to show how this more comprehensive treatment would be categorized.

Tip: If you elect to set up a separate accumulated depreciation account to offset each fixed asset account, mirror the numbering of the fixed asset account in its offsetting accumulated depreciation account. Thus, the 1505 building account number noted above has an accumulated depreciation account of 1605. This makes it easier to create mistake-free depreciation journal entries.

What about the accounts to which you charge depreciation expense? You can have a single account each for depreciation expense and amortization expense, if you only want to charge these expenses to the company as a whole. However, if you want to charge these expenses to individual departments, create a depreciation expense account for each department. Again, the precise layout and numbering will depend upon the chart of accounts, but the basic concept is to use the same depreciation expense account number for all departments, with a department code either preceding or following the depreciation account code. An example of the account numbering that might be used is noted in the following table.

Five-Digit Account Numbering System

Account Number	Account Name
10-850	Accounting department – Depreciation expense
20-850	Engineering department – Depreciation expense
30-850	Production department – Depreciation expense
40-850	Sales department – Depreciation expense

This format shows a department-specific code at the front of the depreciation account number (which remains 850 in all cases). An alternative treatment is to reverse the order of the coding, so that the department-specific code is located at the end of the account number, as noted in the following table.

Reversed Account Numbering Format

Account Number	Account Name
850-10	Depreciation expense – Accounting department
850-20	Depreciation expense – Engineering department
850-30	Depreciation expense – Production department
850-40	Depreciation expense – Sales department

Construction Project Record Keeping

If there is a large construction project that will result in a fixed asset, you need to carefully compile and organize the expenditures related to the project, so that the correct amount can be capitalized. This information used to be manually compiled in a project cost sheet that summarized expenditures by such categories as labor, materials, and contractor fees. However, it is much easier to create a general account code for each project, as well as sub-codes to further refine the expenditure categories, and then use the accounts payable module of the accounting software to aggregate the required information.

You will still need to assemble copies of the various invoices and payroll records into a project binder, which provides sufficient source documentation for auditors to verify the amounts of the capitalized expenditures. Further, the in service date should be documented, which is when the project has resulted in an asset that is ready for its intended use – this is the depreciation start date.

An item requiring special documentation is the capitalization of interest related to a construction project. Follow the requirements of GAAP or IFRS in calculating the amount to capitalize (as described in the Interest Capitalization chapter), and document the calculation.

Further documentation of buildings is noted in the following section, which relates to expenditures *after* a building has been placed in service.

Building Record Keeping

One of the most difficult record keeping chores for the accountant is for the expenditures related to a building that has already been constructed and placed in service. There may be invoices arriving from many suppliers, and the accounting staff needs to sort through them and decide which are related to building enhancements that can be capitalized, and which should be charged to expense.

The simplest way to handle these expenditures is to adopt a default position that they should be charged to expense in the period incurred. Not only does this massively reduce the amount of long-term record keeping, but it also reflects reality – very few ongoing expenditures should be capitalized. In addition, require the controller to code any invoices that are higher than a certain expenditure level, and provide the controller with a detailed explanation of which expenditures should be capitalized. This two-step approach shunts aside most supplier invoices into the expense category, and places final authority for capitalization in the hands of an expert who has specific guidelines for what to capitalize.

A record keeping system should be set up for a building at two levels – one set of information for the entire building as it was originally constructed or purchased, and a second set of information for any additions to it that were subsequently capitalized. Thus, the key record keeping items are:

- *Description.* Provide brief description of the building that is sufficient to identify it.
- *Address.* Note the street address of the building.
- *Cost.* This is the initial capitalized cost of the building, which is used for subsequent depreciation, as well as for impairment testing.
- *In service date.* This is the date on which the building is ready for its intended use, and is the traditional trigger date for the start of depreciation.
- *Useful life.* This is the estimated useful life of the building. There may be an asset class for buildings, where you use a standardized useful life for all buildings owned by the company. However, most companies own very few buildings, so it may be acceptable to adopt a different useful life for each building, especially if there are significant differences in the useful lives of the various buildings.
- *Assessed value.* The government will create an assessed value for the property, on which it then charges a tax rate. You may want to track the assessed value over time, as well as compile a record of any requests for review of the assessed value, and the results of the requests.
- *Impairment circumstances.* If there has been a write down in the value of a building due to impairment, note the circumstances of the impairment, and when it occurred. This may require extensive documentation if there have been several impairments or impairment reversals.

- *Land reference.* If the company owns the land on which the building is located, include a cross-reference to the land records (see the Land Record Keeping section below).

If you also capitalize additional expenditures after the building has been put into service, consider adding the following information to the building record:

- *Expenditure documentation.* This may be quite large, if the capitalized item involves multiple expenditures and suppliers. If so, create a summary sheet that lists all of the expenditures included in the capitalized item, with references to the supplier name, invoice number, invoice date, and expenditure amount. The auditors will need this information to verify your capitalization transaction.
- *Justification for capitalization.* Provide an explanation of why the expenditures have been capitalized, referencing the specific provisions of GAAP or IFRS under which you elected to do so. See the Subsequent Fixed Asset Measurement chapter for more information.
- *Depreciation information.* Describe the useful life of the capitalized expenditures and the depreciation method used to derive the ongoing depreciation expense.

EXAMPLE

Gargantuan Corporation's accounting staff creates the following asset record for one of its buildings:

Asset number: 006498

Description: Corporate headquarters building

Address: 543 Big Circle, Munificent, California 90022

Cost: $25,410,000

In service date: March 1, 20X3

Useful life: 30 years

Assessed value: $24,500,000 as of notification on November 30, 20X4

Impairment circumstances: None

Land reference: See asset number 006497

Subsequent capitalizations: Added multi-level parking garage with in-service date of January 15, 20X5, with capitalized cost of $2,800,000. See attached summary sheet for details.

Justifications for subsequent capitalizations: Adds to use of the building and generates separate cash flow from parking fees. See GAAP standards in ASC 360-10.

Depreciation for subsequent capitalizations: Useful life and depreciation method match the remaining life of the building.

161

Equipment Record Keeping

There are typically far more fixed assets in the equipment category (which can include office equipment and furniture and fixtures) than in any other category. Given the volume and generally lower cost of these items in comparison to building or land assets, the record keeping tends to be more minimal, with perhaps just a purchase order stapled to a copy of the supplier invoice. However, the record keeping for equipment should be more extensive, including the following items:

- *Description.* This is a description of the equipment that is sufficient to identify it.
- *Tag number.* This is the identification number of the asset tag that the company affixes to its assets.
- *Serial number.* If no tag numbers are used, instead list the serial number of the asset, as assigned by the manufacturer.
- *Location.* Note the location where the asset resides.
- *Responsible party.* This is the name or position of the person who is responsible for the equipment.
- *In service date.* This is the date on which the equipment is ready for its intended use, and is the traditional trigger date for the start of depreciation.
- *Cost.* The cost may simply be the original purchase price, or it may be a more extensive record of additions to the equipment over time as high-cost items are replaced.
- *Useful life.* This can be the manufacturer's recommended equipment life, or you can supplement it over time if management concludes that the useful life should be changed, with notations regarding the impact on the depreciation rate.
- *Asset class.* Note the class of assets in which the equipment is categorized. Since a standard depreciation method is typically assigned to an asset class, you do not also have to specify the depreciation method. If you use a standard useful life for an asset class, you do not have to separately record an asset's useful life.
- *Warranty period.* This is the period during which the manufacturer will pay for repairs to the equipment. If there is a cost-effective warranty extension option, note it here.
- *Supplier contact information.* This may include several addresses for the supplier, such as for its field servicing, customer service, warranty, and sales departments.
- *Impairment circumstances.* If there has been a write down in the value of the equipment due to impairment, note the circumstances of the impairment, and when it occurred. This may require extensive documentation if there have been several impairments or impairment reversals.

By retaining this additional equipment information, you can more easily track down assets, determine who is responsible for them, and determine if the manufacturer is responsible for any repairs.

It is useful to consolidate this record with any manufacturer's warranty documents, as well as a copy of key maintenance records.

EXAMPLE

Gargantuan Corporation's accounting staff creates the following asset record for one of its equipment fixed assets:

Asset number: 007231

Asset description: Print-on-demand book printer

Tag number: 1049

Serial number: BF-44078

Location: Printing department

Responsible party: Printing department manager

In service date: May 12, 20X5

Cost: $200,000

Useful life: 4 years

Asset class: Office equipment

Warranty period: May 1, 20X5 to April 30, 20X6. Can be extended an additional year with a $20,000 payment prior to April 30, 20X6.

Supplier contact information: PrintTech, 18 Gutenberg Way, Mainz, Minnesota 55046

Impairment circumstances: Carrying cost reduced by $50,000 in July 20X7, caused by the printer being rendered largely idle as the result of most book printing operations being outsourced. There are no immediate plans to sell the asset.

Land Record Keeping

There are several unique aspects to a land asset that call for different record keeping, primarily relating to the government entity that has jurisdiction over it, assessed values, and use restrictions. These issues should be itemized, along with the usual identification information, in a land record. The key items to record are:

- *Description*. This is a general description of the property, and may include notes about the structures erected on it.
- *Cost*: The purchase price of the land.
- *Location*. This may be the surveyor's legal description of the property, as well as its address.
- *County*. This is the county in which the land is located, or the government entity which assesses taxes on the property.

- *Zoning classification.* If a zoning classification has been assigned to the property, note it here, as well as the specific limitations of the zoning. Examples are residential, commercial retail, or heavy industry zoning.
- *Easements.* Note any legally allowed access to the land by others.
- *Restrictions on use.* Note any restrictions other than those already imposed by the zoning.
- *Assessed value.* The government will create an assessed value for the property, on which it then charges a tax rate. You may want to track the assessed value over time, as well as a record of any requests for review of the assessed value, and the results of the requests.
- *Land improvements.* If there have been any depreciable improvements to the land (such as sewer lines or a parking lot), note them here, as well as a cross-reference to the land improvement asset record.
- *Buildings on property.* If there have been any buildings constructed on the land, note them here, as well as a cross-reference to the buildings' asset records.

It may also make sense to consolidate the land record with all land-related documents, such as survey information and assessment notices.

EXAMPLE

Gargantuan Corporation's accounting staff creates the following asset record for one of its land assets:

Asset number: 006497

Description: Land used for corporate headquarter building

Cost: $2,000,000

Location: 543 Big Circle, Munificent, California 90022

County: El Brazo County

Zoning classification: Commercial office

Easements: None

Restrictions on use: Industrial use prohibited

Assessed value: $2,200,000 as of notification on November 30, 20X4

Land improvements: Landscaping of $150,000, added to capitalized cost of land. Sewer lines of $175,000, depreciated separately under asset 006499 as a land improvement.

Buildings on property: Corporate headquarters, see asset number 006498

Lease Record Keeping

In many cases with smaller assets such as copiers, a company will enter into an operating lease where it has the use of an asset for a specific time period, and then returns the asset to the lessor. In cases where a company essentially owns the leased asset, the transaction is known as a capital lease. There are some differences in the record keeping required for each type of lease, as noted below.

Operating Lease Record Keeping

Under an operating lease, the company is obligated to return the asset at the end of the lease period, and may have the option to renew the lease for an additional period. To be cognizant of these issues, record the following information in an operating lease file:

- *Leased asset description.* This is a brief description of the asset, sufficient to identify it.
- *Leased asset location.* Give a sufficiently accurate location that you can find the asset when it is time to return it to the lessor. A location coding system may be sufficient.
- *Serial number.* There may be no asset tag, since the company does not own it, so list its serial number instead in order to uniquely identify the asset.
- *Lease payment terms.* The amount of each payment, when it is due at the lessor, and any differing amounts to be paid for the first and last payments of the lease.
- *Lessor contact information.* There may be multiple addresses for the lessor, such as a contact address, payment address, an address to which you make a lease termination notice, and yet another address to which you return the asset upon the expiration of the lease.
- *Termination notice date.* If a lease contains an automatic renewal, be aware of the notice date by which you have to notify the lessor of termination. This is an important item, so post it prominently.
- *Lease ending date.* Note the date on which the lease ends. This is a critical date, so consider posting it in numerous places. You need to terminate any automated payments to the lessor as of this date.
- *Lease extension terms.* Describe the terms under which you can extend the lease duration.
- *Lease termination terms.* Note the terms under which you can terminate the lease, such as notification to the lessor by a certain date in writing, a lease termination fee, and return of the asset to the lessor by a certain date.

Finance Lease Record Keeping

The information recorded for a finance lease is similar to the information just described for an operating lease. In addition to the information just noted for an operating lease, also record the standard information that you would use for a fixed asset – its useful life, salvage value, asset class, depreciation method, and the circumstances of any asset impairment.

You may think that it is sufficient to simply keep copies of the lease agreements on hand, since most of the information described in this section is contained within the leases. However, it can be difficult to locate key information in a voluminous lease document, so we recommend summarizing the key information in summary form.

EXAMPLE

Gargantuan Corporation's accounting staff creates the following asset record for one of its land assets:

Leased asset description: Automated scanner

Leased asset location: Document retention warehouse

Serial number: A04781

Lease payment terms: $1,000 per month for 60 months, payable at the lessor on the 15th of each month

Lessor contact information: Scanners International, 789 17th Street, Denver Colorado 80222

Termination notice date: August 14, 20X6

Lease ending date: September 15, 20X6

Lease extension terms: $750 per month with maintenance included for five additional years

Lease termination terms: Ship to lessor address, postage paid, to be received within five days following the lease termination date

---

Document Retention

How long should you retain documents related to fixed assets? The exact requirements will vary, depending upon the rules imposed by any government that wishes to audit them. Given that these requirements can be quite long, consider using the following two policies:

- *Do not keep title records on site.* Title records are too valuable to keep on site, where they may be stolen, lost, or destroyed. Instead, keep copies on site for audit purposes, and keep the originals in a secure place, such as a lock box in a bank.
- *Exclude fixed asset records from archiving.* An efficient company likely has an archiving process for shifting its less necessary documents off-site into lower-cost storage areas, and then destroying them at pre-planned intervals. Exclude all fixed asset records from the archiving process, to avoid any risk of destroying the paperwork associated with a fixed asset that may still be on the premises. Instead, have a separate procedure for eliminating these

documents only when the related assets have been disposed of and there is no government requirement for further document retention.

Fixed Asset Reports

There are several reports related to fixed assets that are of use in monitoring their remaining carrying amounts, where they are located, who is responsible for them, and whether they should be replaced. The exact format of these reports will vary depending on a company's individual circumstances; the general layouts shown here are intended to be only a general guideline, likely requiring some modification. Each of the following subheadings deals with a separate report.

Depreciation Report

The depreciation report is usually available as a standard report from your accounting software. If you are calculating depreciation manually, use the format shown in the following exhibit to summarize the key information about depreciation for each asset.

Sample Depreciation Report

Asset Class	Description	Purchase Cost	Periodic Depreciation	Accumulated Depreciation	Carrying Amount
Equipment	Drill press	$50,000	$1,000	$15,000	$35,000
Equipment	Lathe	15,000	300	3,600	11,400
Equipment	Stamper	35,000	700	5,600	29,400
Software	CAD/CAM software	80,000	1,333	33,325	46,675
Software	ERP software	480,000	8,000	152,000	328,000
Software	MRP II software	200,000	3,333	36,663	163,337
Totals		$860,000	$14,666	$246,188	$613,812

The columns in the report are explained as follows:

- *Asset class.* This is the general category of assets with which an asset is associated. This is a useful tool for searching for assets in the report. It is also an easy way to audit the report, for you should only see certain types of assets linked to certain classes. Thus, there should be no buildings listed in the computer equipment class (or being depreciated as computer equipment!).
- *Description.* This is a brief description of the asset, and is probably sufficient identification for companies having few assets. If there are many assets, consider adding a column to the report for asset serial numbers.
- *Purchase cost.* This is the installed cost of the asset, also known as its gross carrying amount. This forms the basis for depreciation calculations.

- *Periodic depreciation.* This is the amount of depreciation recorded for each individual asset in the current accounting period. The total of this column is used for the periodic depreciation journal entry.
- *Accumulated depreciation.* This is the accumulated amount of depreciation for each asset, from its initial purchase to the current date. The total accumulated depreciation for all assets in the report should match the amount of accumulated depreciation listed on the balance sheet.
- *Carrying amount.* This is the net cost of each asset that has not yet been depreciated. The total of this column should match the net fixed asset figure stated in the balance sheet.

Additional columns to consider for the report are:

- *Account number.* It is useful to include the account number, either for each line item or just for a sub-total (if used) for each asset class. You can then reference the account number when constructing the depreciation journal entry for each accounting period.
- *Serial number.* If there are many fixed assets, you may need a serial number to uniquely identify each one, rather than just using a description.
- *Purchase date.* The purchase date of an asset is necessary information for verifying the accuracy of a depreciation calculation.
- *Depreciation method.* The depreciation method should be the same for each asset within an asset class, so stating the method is a useful audit tool for spotting incorrect methods. You can contract the method to save space in the report. For example, list the straight-line method as "SL".
- *Depreciation period.* The period over which an asset is depreciated should be the same for each asset within an asset class, so auditors can use the period stated in the report as evidence that a depreciation period was incorrectly set up.
- *Salvage value.* If you use salvage value (it is generally easier not to if salvage values are minor), list them in the report. This aids in auditing the depreciation calculations shown in the report.
- *Accumulated impairment.* If there has been any impairment charged against an asset, state the accumulated amount in the report. This aids in auditing the depreciation calculations in the report, since the amount of depreciation will likely decline following the impairment.
- *Depreciation completion date.* State the month and year in which depreciation is completed for each asset. This is useful information for the annual budget, which includes depreciation information by month or quarter.

Note that the report is sorted by asset class, so that you can first search it by general category, and then by individual asset. You then have several options for sorting within each asset class, the most common ones being by asset name or purchase date. It can be quite useful to use subtotals for each asset class, which you can then reference when creating depreciation journal entries by asset class (such as for furniture and fixtures, or computer equipment).

Include any intangible assets in this report, if they have a carrying amount. Even intangible assets with no amortization period can be listed, as a reminder to periodically test them to see if amortization is warranted.

An alternative version of this report is to construct it on an electronic spread-sheet, with a separate column for the depreciation in each reporting period (which may amount to *a lot* of columns). You would probably not print the entire report at one time, but it is a useful way to lay out and verify depreciation calculations.

Audit Report

Either internal or external auditors may need to periodically verify the existence of fixed assets, for which they need to verify the location and identification of each asset. The report shown in the following exhibit provides the essential information needed for this task.

Sample Audit Report

Location	Description	Tag Number	Model Number	Serial Number
Cell 13	Deburring machine	03341	LFX-43	A047J4
Cell 13	Drill press	03325	Alpha 17	JJ00752
Cell 08	Grinder	03329	DOM-5A4	KS6730A
Cell 08	Lathe	03350	Merc-88	K721G
Cell 02	Notching machine	03339	Mark 2	0042189
Cell 13	Power shears	03347	Anders 4	KDL5521
Cell 02	Stamper	03352	Zelda 11	082G54

The columns in the report are explained as follows:

- *Location.* The location code can follow a variety of formats, such as building number, or room number, or a more precise bin location. When selecting the location code, be aware that extremely precise ones will likely require more frequent updates, when they are periodically moved. Of course, a greater level of identification precision also means that you can locate assets more easily in an audit.
- *Description.* This is a brief description of the asset, which is supported by the following three items.
- *Tag number.* If the company affixes identification tags to its fixed assets, list the tag number here.
- *Model number.* This is a field for the supplier's model number, which can assist in identifying a machine if there are several machines from the same supplier on the premises.

- *Serial number.* This is a field for the supplier's unique identification code for a machine, which is useful when the company does not apply its own tags to machines, or when there are several identical machines from the same supplier on the premises.

Additional columns to consider for the report are:

- *Serial number location.* Serial numbers may be located in extremely difficult-to-reach parts of a machine, so consider stating where auditors need to look.
- *Responsible employee.* If someone is responsible for an asset, and an auditor cannot find the asset, the next logical step would be to find the person responsible for it and have him locate the asset.
- *Notes field.* If auditors print out the report, they may want to write notes on it as they conduct the audit. If so, include a notes field on the far right side of the report.

Note that the report is sorted alphabetically by description, but a useful alternative sort is by location code (which in the example is machining centers within the factory). By using a location sort, the auditor can more easily cluster fixed assets on the report in a manner that matches the flow of his audit work.

An extremely useful feature of this report is to only print it for those assets above a certain cost, because low-cost assets are not worth the effort to locate. Doing so can strip away a very large percentage of all assets, which leaves auditors with a small subset of assets on which to focus. Other selection options are to only print it for specific locations, or based on the gross carrying amount or net carrying amount of an asset.

Responsibility Report

If a company assigns responsibility for fixed assets to specific individuals, create a report that matches assets with those people. This report should be issued to the responsible parties at regular intervals, so they can verify the existence of the assets assigned to them. This report is quite similar to the audit report, in that most of the information on the report is intended to assist in locating an asset. A sample of the report appears in the following exhibit.

Sample Responsibility Report

Responsible Party	Location	Description	Tag Number
Murchison, A.	Cell 13	Deburring machine	03341
Murchison, A.	Cell 13	Drill press	03325
Barnett, R.	Cell 08	Grinder	03329
Barnett, R.	Cell 08	Lathe	03350
Smith, W.	Cell 02	Notching machine	03339
Murchison, A.	Cell 13	Power shears	03347
Smith, W.	Cell 02	Stamper	03352

The columns in the report are explained as follows:

- *Responsible party.* This is either the name or employee number of the individual who is responsible for the assets listed on the report.
- *Location.* This is a coded description of where each asset is located.
- *Description.* This is the standard equipment description, which should be sufficient to identify a machine.
- *Tag number.* This is the primary identification code for a fixed asset. If tags are not used, substitute a serial number field instead.

Additional columns to consider for the report are:

- *Serial number.* This is a field for the supplier's unique identification code for a machine, which is useful when the company does not apply its own tags to machines, or when there are several identical machines from the same supplier on the premises.
- *Initialing field.* The report can be used as a formal acknowledgment of responsibility, in which case you can include a field on the right side of the report, on which the responsible party initials next to each fixed asset, showing that he has observed the asset.

The report shown in the example is sorted alphabetically by machine, but that is only an efficient report layout if there are very few assets. For higher-volume situations, a better sort sequence is by the name of the responsible party, and then by location code.

Asset Replacement Report

It is useful to have an asset replacement report that spotlights those fixed assets most likely to require replacement in the near future. The report matches indicators of wear and tear with the age and recommended replacement ages of equipment. A sample of the report appears in the following exhibit.

Sample Asset Replacement Report

Description	Tag Number	Asset Age (years)	Recommended Replacement Age (years)	Maintenance Trend		Original Cost
				20X1	20X2	
Deburring machine	03341	8	10	$900	$3,100	$25,000
Drill press	03325	11	15	500	1,500	18,000
Grinder	03329	10	10	850	2,700	40,000
Lathe	03350	5	10	--	200	11,000
Notching machine	03339	9	10	2,000	3,500	12,000
Power shears	03347	6	5	400	800	8,000
Stamper	03352	3	5	200	200	39,000

The columns in the report are explained as follows:

- *Description.* This is the standard equipment description, which should be sufficient to identify a machine.
- *Tag number.* This is the primary identification code for a fixed asset. If tags are not used, substitute a serial number field instead.
- *Asset age.* This is the current date minus the acquisition date, and is an indicator of replacement.
- *Recommended replacement age.* This is the manufacturer's recommended number of years of use before replacement. This can be misleading if equipment is not heavily used during its normal lifespan, since low utilization could greatly prolong its usage period.
- *Maintenance trend (two-year).* This is the cost of maintenance in each of the past two years, as compiled from the records for parts usage and maintenance staff time. This could be expanded to additional years if the information is sufficiently useful.
- *Original cost.* The original cost of the asset is presumed to be its replacement cost, though this may not be correct if prices have since changed significantly, or if there is a need for equipment having a different capacity level.

Additional columns to consider for the report are:

- *Cost of replaced components.* In some larger equipment, it may be possible to replace many components, so that essentially only the housing is original equipment. If so, it may be useful to aggregate the cost of new components within a machine, which may indicate a considerably prolonged asset life.
- *Replacement cost.* This is better than the original cost listed in the basic report format, since it gives the reader a better understanding of what it will cost to replace the asset. However, it also calls for additional research, which may not be a viable undertaking without a formal capital budgeting analysis.

This report is presented with a sort by machine description, but it may also be useful to sort it either by asset age or maintenance trend, with the oldest machines or those with the highest maintenance costs listed at the top of the report.

Maintenance Report

From the perspective of the accountant, there are two primary events in the life of a fixed asset that are worthy of documentation. These are the initial purchase of the asset (as described in the Capital Budgeting Analysis chapter) and the replacement or sale of the asset (as just described in the Asset Replacement Report). But what about the expenses incurred in between? If fixed assets are consuming a large part of a company's potential profits in maintenance costs, management should know about this. The following exhibit shows the division of maintenance costs between scheduled and unscheduled costs, where the primary focus of the report is on large unscheduled maintenance costs. The capacity utilization shown in the report can be used as a leading indicator for unscheduled maintenance, since high utilization levels may be a cause of unplanned equipment breakdowns.

Sample Maintenance Report

Description	Scheduled Maintenance Cost	Unscheduled Maintenance Cost	Capacity Utilization
Deburring machine	$500	$400	70%
Drill press	1,200	--	10%
Grinder	200	1,000	65%
Lathe	100	--	45%
Notching machine	--	--	15%
Power shears	800	$3,000	98%
Stamper	300	--	52%

The columns in the report are explained as follows:

- *Description.* This is the standard equipment description, which should be sufficient to identify a machine.
- *Scheduled maintenance cost.* This is the cost of planned maintenance, which is typically the maintenance required or recommended by the manufacturer at normal maintenance intervals. This cost should vary very little over time, except when there are large overhauls planned at longer intervals than the normal maintenance.
- *Unscheduled maintenance cost.* This is the cost of maintenance that is unplanned, usually because the machine failed. This can be a large expense, especially if overtime or rush delivery charges are involved. It can also be an indicator of a near-term machine replacement.
- *Capacity utilization.* This is the amount of machine usage during the reporting period, as a percentage of the total time available.

Additional columns to consider for the report are:

- *Tag number.* This is the primary identification code for a fixed asset, and may be needed if there are many similar assets in the report.
- *Bottleneck flag.* This is a yes/no flag that indicates whether an asset is considered a bottleneck, and therefore crucial to the operations (and profitability) of the company. The flag serves to focus attention on key assets.
- *Reason code.* Include a reason code next to the unscheduled maintenance cost column, which indicates the reason why the cost was incurred.

It may be useful to run the unscheduled maintenance portion of this report on a trend line, and bring the results to management's attention if there is a sudden or (especially) prolonged increase in costs for a particular machine. This is a prime indicator that the machine is either being operated at its maximum capacity, or that it is approaching failure and requires replacement.

Summary

This chapter has addressed where to record accounting information about fixed assets, as well as other information about them in a set of additional records and reports. The level of record keeping to engage in will be driven by the cost of the organization's fixed assets – a large number of expensive assets that comprise the bulk of the corporate assets should be a warning flag that you should be engaging in a great deal of documentation. If not, the auditors will have a difficult time verifying the existence and cost of the fixed assets. On the other hand, if you have an asset-light corporation (as is common in the services industries), the cost and number of fixed assets may be so minimal that anything more than brief asset descriptions could be a waste of time.

Chapter 13
Fixed Asset Controls

Introduction

The use of an adequate set of controls for fixed assets is mandatory, simply because of the amount of cash tied up in these assets. If even a single fixed asset is improperly acquired, accounted for, or disposed of, it can have a material adverse impact on a company's financial results. Theft is also a major concern for high-value assets that can be easily moved. Further, the ongoing and natural deterioration of fixed assets over time virtually requires that you keep an ongoing watch over this declining valuation, in order to optimize the best time to dispose of them at the best price. This chapter describes a number of controls that can assist with these issues.

> **Related Podcast Episode:** Episode 15 of the Accounting Best Practices Podcast discusses fixed asset controls. It is available at: **accountingtools.com/podcasts** or **iTunes**

Controls for Fixed Asset Acquisition

The key focus of controls for the acquisition of key assets is to ensure that the company needs the assets. This means that controls are designed to require an evaluation of how a proposed acquisition will fit into the company's operations, and what kind of return on investment it will generate. A secondary set of controls are also needed to ensure that all acquisitions are forced to follow this review process. With these goals in mind, consider using the following controls:

- *Require an approval form.* There should be an approval form, such as the one shown in the Capital Budgeting Analysis chapter, that requires an applicant to describe the asset, how it is to be used, and the return on investment that will be generated (if any). This standardizes the information about each fixed asset, and also provides a handy signature form for various approvals.
- *Require independent analysis of the approval form.* Someone who is skilled in asset analysis should review each submitted approval form. This analysis can include a verification that all supporting documents are attached to the form, that all assumptions are reasonable, and that the conclusions reached appear to be valid. The person conducting this analysis does not necessarily render an opinion on whether to acquire the asset, but should point out any flaws in the proposal. This person should *not* report to the person who submitted the proposal, since that would be a conflict of interest.
- *Concentrate asset analyses in an annual review process.* When you review asset purchase requests at varying intervals throughout the year, there is no

basis of comparison against other asset purchase proposals, and so management will be less likely to turn down the requests. A better approach is to have a formal, annual review of these requests, where you can compare and contrast them and see which ones make the most sense. Though it may appear excessively bureaucratic, this approach can prevent a company from a number of unnecessary expenditures.

- *Require multi-level approvals for more expensive assets.* If an asset request is *really* expensive, impose a requirement for a number of approvals by people in positions of increasing levels of authority. Though clearly time-consuming, the intent is to make a number of people aware of the request, so that the organization as a whole will be absolutely sure of its position before allowing a purchase to proceed.

- *Focus more attention on rush requests.* Someone may try to avoid the usual review steps in order to obtain an asset right now on a rush basis. These are precisely the sorts of situations where it may make sense to impose a tighter review, since the rush nature of the purchase may be keeping people from due deliberation of the alternatives available. The exact nature of this control will vary under the circumstances, but the key point is to not eliminate *all* reviews and approvals just because someone says that an asset must be bought at once.

- *Impose a mandatory waiting period.* Though controversial, it can make sense to impose a waiting period before any asset is purchased, on the grounds that due deliberation may reveal that some assets are simply not needed, and so should not be bought. Taken to extremes, such a control can result in an excessively plodding organization, so use it with care.

The controls just noted are all very fine for preventing the wrong assets from being purchased, but how do you keep someone from circumventing them? Here are several prevention controls to consider:

- *Do not issue a purchase order without a signed approval form.* Train the purchasing staff to not order fixed assets unless the requestor has a signed approval form. Better yet, route all such purchase orders to a senior executive, such as the chief financial officer, for approval.

- *Reconcile fixed asset additions to approval forms.* If asset purchases are allowed without an authorizing purchase order, compare all additions listed in the fixed asset general ledger accounts to the signed approval forms, to see if any assets were bought without approval. This is an after-the-fact control, since an asset will have already been bought, but proper education of the responsible party can prevent such purchases from happening again.

- *Use prenumbered approval forms.* Someone may try to forge the signatures on an approval form, so consider using prenumbered forms. Also, store them in a locked cabinet, and keep track of all forms taken from the cabinet. This control may be overkill – after all, the presumed penalties for being caught with a forged approval form would likely deter most people.

A final control that is quite useful for judging the accuracy of asset purchase requests is to conduct a post-completion project analysis. This analysis spots variations between the projections that managers inserted into their original asset purchase proposals and what eventually transpired. There will always be differences between these two sets of information, since no one can forecast results perfectly. However, look for patterns of egregious optimism in the original purchase proposals, to determine which managers are continually overstating their projections in order to have their proposals approved. If you find problems, this may lead to a variety of actions to keep a manager from repeating these actions in the future.

The controls noted here will absolutely slow down the fixed asset acquisition process, and with good reason – part of their intent is to encourage more deliberation of why an asset is being acquired. Nonetheless, these controls will appear onerous to those people trying to obtain assets that are relatively inexpensive, so it is certainly acceptable to adopt a reduced set of controls for such assets, perhaps simply treating them as accounts payable that require a single approval signature on a purchase order.

Similarly, you can consider a more streamlined set of controls for assets that must be acquired at once. However, keep in mind that some managers intent on subverting the system of controls can characterize *everything* as a rush requirement, just to avoid the usual reviews and approvals. Consequently, if you adopt a reduced set of controls for such purchases, at least conduct an after-the-fact review of the circumstances of these purchases, to see if the reduced controls were actually justified.

Controls for Fixed Asset Construction

Most fixed assets arrive in one shipment, are installed, and placed in service in short order – quite possibly within a single accounting period. However, others may require many months or even several years to construct. In these latter cases, you need an additional set of controls to monitor expenditures over the course of the project, which are:

- *Assign a monitoring cost accountant.* For a really large project, there should be a designated person who is responsible for tracking the costs accumulating against the project, and reporting this information to management. The ideal person for this task is a cost accountant, since this position is trained in cost accumulation and analysis.
- *Conduct milestone reviews.* For longer-term asset installations, there should be a series of milestone events at which the management team responsible for the project examines expenditures to date, progress on the project, and any issues relating to the remaining tasks to be completed. Though rare, the team may occasionally use the information obtained in this review to cancel the project entirely. A more common response is a variety of adjustments to improve the odds of successful completion within the cost budget.

Controls for Fixed Asset Theft

Fixed assets may have a significant resale value, which makes the more portable ones subject to theft. Here are several controls that can be of assistance in preventing or at least mitigating asset losses due to theft:

- *Segregate fixed asset responsibilities.* You are making it much easier for an employee to steal an asset if you give that person complete responsibility over all aspects of asset purchasing, recordation, and disposal, since they can alter documents at will. Consequently, the person who receives a fixed asset should not be the same person who records the transaction, while the person who disposes of an asset cannot also record the sale. Further, the person who audits fixed assets should not be involved with fixed assets in any other way.

- *Lock out the fixed asset master file.* Depending on the nature of your accounting systems, there may be a fixed asset master file in which detailed information about every fixed asset is kept. If someone were to steal a fixed asset, they could cover all traces of the act by removing the asset from the master file, or at least altering it. Consequently, require password access to this file.

- *Restrict access to assets.* If some assets are especially valuable and can be easily removed from the premises, restrict access to them with a variety of security card access systems, gates, security guards, and so forth.

- *Assign assets to employees.* If you assign responsibility for specific assets to employees, and tie some portion of their annual performance appraisals to the presence and condition of those assets, that represents a built-in asset monitoring system. This control works best at the department level, where department managers are assigned responsibility for the assets in their areas. Create a system that issues a periodic report to each responsible person, detailing the assets under their control, and reminding them to notify a senior manager if any assets are missing. Also, if you shift responsibility for assets from one person to another, you need a process for doing so, where the newly-responsible person formally evaluates the condition of the asset and takes responsibility for it.

- *Look for duplicate serial numbers.* Though rare, it is possible that employees may be stealing fixed assets and selling them back to the company through a dummy corporation. To detect this, enter the asset serial number in the fixed asset record for each asset, and then run a report that looks for matching serial numbers. If you find a duplicate number, this means that an asset was stolen and sold back to the company.

- *Conduct a fixed asset audit.* Have an internal auditor conduct an annual audit of all fixed assets to verify where they are located, the condition they are in, and whether they are still being used.

Tip: If the auditors search for every fixed asset in a company's accounting records, the audit may be prolonged. To shorten it, they should concentrate on the 20 percent of assets that usually make up about 80 percent of the total cost of all fixed assets, with a spot check of other assets falling outside this key group.

- *Affix an identification plate to all assets.* Solidly affix an identification plate to any fixed asset that can be moved, so that you can clearly identify it. Better yet, engrave an identification number into the asset, which eliminates the risk of someone removing the identification plate. Another alternative is to affix a radio frequency identification (RFID) tag to each asset, so that they can be more easily located with an RFID scanner. If you use any form of identification tag, be sure to record the unique number on each tag in the appropriate asset record, so that the information in the record can be traced back to the actual asset.
- *Link RFID tags to alarm system.* Install an RFID scanner next to every point of exit, which will trigger an alarm if anyone attempts to remove an asset that has an RFID tag attached to it.

Controls for Fixed Asset Valuation

Fixed assets gradually lose their value over time, so you need controls to monitor what they are worth. The results of these controls may lead to further actions. The controls are:

- *Conduct asset impairment reviews.* Generally accepted accounting principles mandate that you write down the book value of a fixed asset if the value of the asset falls below its book value. To do this, have a regularly scheduled valuation review, possibly involving the services of an outside appraisal firm.

Tip: Asset impairment reviews can be quite expensive, both in terms of staff time and the cost of appraisers, so only review the most expensive fixed assets. There is only a small potential valuation decline in lower-cost assets, so there is no point in reviewing them. The cutoff point for conducting an asset impairment review may be much higher than the capitalization limit used to record fixed assets. For example, the capitalization limit might be $5,000, while the impairment review cutoff might be $100,000.

- *Conduct asset disposition reviews.* The goals of this review are to decide whether a company continues to need a fixed asset, and if so, how to obtain the highest price for it. If you do not use this control, assets tend to remain on the premises long after they are no longer needed, and lose value during that time. The best group for conducting this analysis is the industrial engineering staff, since they are responsible for the production layout, and most fixed assets are located in this area.

- *Use appraisers to value dissimilar exchanges.* The accounting standards allow you to record a gain or loss on the difference in value of dissimilar assets if you exchange them with a third party. Since fair value can be a matter of opinion, this can result in the creation of an artificial gain or loss. Consider using the valuation services of an outside appraisal firm to eliminate this problem.

> **Tip:** Outside appraisal firms are expensive, and do not provide actual value to a company that improves its profits. Instead, they simply give an impartial and presumably expert opinion of asset values that can be used to improve the accuracy of accounting records. Consequently, if you have the choice of using an internal or external appraisal, use the internal one for assets that cannot possibly have a large valuation; any difference in value that an outside appraiser would provide would not be worth the cost of their services in these cases.

Controls for Fixed Asset Depreciation

Depreciation calculation errors are extremely common, since there are opportunities to incorrectly enter the asset amount, useful life, salvage value, and depreciation method in whatever calculation spreadsheet or software is being used. Here are several controls that can mitigate this problem:

- *Conduct separate review of master file additions.* Have a second person review any records added to the fixed asset master file. This review should involve a comparison of the amounts paid to the amount listed in the master file, to ensure that the amount being depreciated is correct. Also, verify that the asset classification in which each asset is placed is the correct one, since this usually drives the depreciation method used and the useful life over which it will be depreciated. Further, verify that any salvage value used has been properly substantiated. Finally, verify that the recorded asset location is correct, so that anyone attempting to locate the asset in the future will be able to find it.
- *Audit depreciation calculations.* Have the internal audit staff periodically review a selection of the depreciation calculations, to see if an asset is being depreciated over the correct useful life, with the correct depreciation method, and with a verifiable salvage value. Errors will be more common if this information is being maintained on an electronic spreadsheet, given the greater risk of manual errors in this format.
- *Send copy of disposal form to accounting.* If there is an asset disposal form that must be filled out prior to the disposal of a fixed asset, route a copy of it to the accounting department, so that it can write off the asset and stop recording a periodic depreciation charge for it.

Controls for Fixed Asset Disposal

There tends to be a certain amount of fixed asset "leakage" out of a company, especially for smaller and more mobile assets, such as computers. In many cases, the resale value of these items near the end of their useful lives is so small that a company may very well be justified in giving them away to employees or simply dropping them into the scrap bin. However, there may be a fair amount of residual value remaining in some assets, so consider using the following controls to recapture some of that value:

- *Conduct asset disposition reviews.* The goals of this review are to decide whether a company continues to need a fixed asset, and if so, how to obtain the highest price for it. If you do not use this control, assets tend to remain on the premises long after they are no longer needed, and lose value during that time. The best group for conducting this analysis is the industrial engineering staff, since they are responsible for the production layout, and most fixed assets are located in this area. [this control was also described earlier as a valuation control]
- *Require signed approval of asset dispositions.* Create a form that describes the asset to be disposed of, the method of disposition, and the cash to be received (if any). The person whose authorization is required could be a specialist in asset disposition, or perhaps the purchasing manager, who might have some knowledge of asset values. The point of this control is to require a last look by someone who might know of a better way to gain more value from a disposal.
- *Monitor cash receipts from asset sales.* Most fixed assets are sold for cash, and sometimes for significant amounts of cash. Given the amount of funds involved, it can be quite a temptation for employees to find ways to either not record asset sales or falsify sale documents to record smaller sales, and then pocket the undocumented cash. You can monitor this by requiring that a bill of sale from the purchasing entity accompany the documentation for each asset sale. It is also useful to periodically audit asset sale transactions, if only to show the staff that these transactions are being monitored.

The Control of Laptop Computers

There are millions of laptop computers assigned to employees throughout the world, and they represent a massive tracking problem for any accountant assigned to monitor them. They are moderately expensive, easily damaged, difficult to track, and employees routinely take them home at night. How do you impose controls over them? The routine controls noted in this chapter do not work for laptops, because those controls are primarily designed for literally "fixed" assets.

Laptops require an entirely different controls approach. The key factors in designing a different control system for them are that they have a cost that hovers at or below the normal capitalization limit for most firms, and their values decline to near zero within just a few years. With these points in mind, consider setting the corporate capitalization limit somewhere above the laptop cost, so that your asset records are not burdened with them. Second, assign specific responsibility for each laptop to the employee to whom it was issued, and tell them the corporate policy is to replace all laptops every three years. Finally, give the old laptops to employees at the time of replacement. The laptops very likely have minimal value after three years anyways, so the company loses nothing by giving them away. Also, since the employees know they will soon own these laptops themselves, they will be much more inclined to safeguard them.

This approach makes for a vastly easier control environment for the accountant, probably reduces the likelihood of damage to laptops, and makes employees extremely happy.

Summary

This chapter has outlined a large number of fixed asset controls. It requires judgment to decide how many of them to use, since an excessive level of control is burdensome, while minimal controls lead to profligate spending and lost assets. The answer to this conundrum usually lies in the nature of the assets themselves. For example, a hydroelectric company is incredible unlikely to lose its turbines, and so can dispense with most of the controls related to asset theft for those items. On the other hand, given the massive cost of turbines, it needs an exceptional level of control over its purchases. Conversely, a company whose only fixed assets are laptop computers should seriously consider treating them as office supplies, given how difficult it would otherwise be to keep track of them, and how inexpensive they are to replace. Thus, you must tailor controls to the circumstances.

> **Tip:** This chapter has made it clear that you can implement quite a large number of controls over fixed assets. If you were to apply the same controls over all fixed assets, the administrative burden would be considerable. To reduce it, consider increasing the capitalization limit (the cost at which you begin recording an expenditure as an asset, rather than an expense) to the highest possible point. While this will result in more expenditures being charged to expense in the short term, it also reduces the administrative burden imposed by the control system.

Chapter 14
Fixed Asset Policies and Procedures

Introduction

There are a number of possible transactions that can potentially be generated over the useful life of a fixed asset, ranging from the initial budgeting for it to its eventual disposal. Given the significant cost of fixed assets, you should adhere to a carefully-defined set of policies and procedures for these transactions, so that you only acquire those assets really needed, account for them correctly, and eliminate them only when it makes economic sense to do so. Without the policies and procedures listed in this chapter, there is a heightened risk of investing in assets that you do not need, or of accounting for them incorrectly.

Capital Budgeting Policies and Procedures

There is a significant need for policies and procedures in the area of capital budgeting, since this is a major control point over fixed assets into which all purchase requests must be funneled. If you do not impose policies and procedures here, there is a heightened risk of unauthorized fixed asset purchases being made. There are two key policies to enforce, one requiring the use of a review process, and the other establishing a capitalization limit, which defines the minimum asset cost that must undergo the review. They are:

> **Policy:** Employees must submit a capital budgeting request for any asset purchase exceeding the corporate capitalization limit.

> **Policy:** The corporate capitalization limit is $____. Any expenditure above this amount where the asset has a useful life of at least one year is to be classified as a fixed asset, while all other expenditures are to be charged to expense in the period incurred.

Once a fixed asset is approved through the capital budgeting process, you may still elect to add a specific approval limit for a purchase transaction, thereby adding another layer of control to the system of acquisition. Such a policy might be:

> **Policy:** An asset that has been approved through the capital budget can be authorized for purchase by the responsible manager if it is equal to or less than $____, and by the chief financial officer if it is greater than this amount.

In addition to these baseline policies, consider using the following policy, which requires senior management to periodically review the size of the capitalization limit. Ideally, you want to set a level that balances the volume of fixed asset record keeping with charging an excessive amount to expense.

Policy: The corporate capitalization limit shall be reviewed at intervals of __ year(s).

It is highly advisable to have a strong system in place for reviewing the results of fixed asset purchases, so that senior management can review and act upon any flaws in the capital budgeting process that are causing inappropriate purchases to be made, or to spotlight those managers who consistently overestimate projected results in their capital budgeting proposals. The following policy is designed to trigger such reviews.

Policy: The results of all capital purchases in excess of $_____ shall be reviewed and reported to management within __ months of final installation.

There should be two procedures for users of the capital budgeting process. One procedure contains instructions for how to complete the capital budgeting application form, and is highly recommended if the application process is complex. A sample procedure is:

1. Obtain a capital budgeting application form from the budget analyst. See the next section for a sample capital budgeting form.
2. Complete the project name and description in the header fields of the form. Leave the submission date and project number fields blank (the budget analyst will complete these fields for you).
3. Itemize both the initial cash flows required for the project and any subsequent cash flow changes resulting from it, aggregated by year. Include expenditures for the purchase of the requested asset, as well as the cash flow impact of any changes in working capital (particularly inventory), incremental changes in gross profits, and the impact of any changes in depreciation on income taxes.
4. Fully document any legal or risk mitigation reasons for acquiring the asset, as well as the date by which the company will be out of compliance if it does not make the investment.
5. Note the change in throughput at the bottleneck operation and any change in operating costs that is tied to the proposed investment.
6. Note the net present value associated with the proposed investment, and attach a detailed derivation of the net present value. Contact the budget analyst for the discount rate and tax rate to use in the net present value calculation.
7. Attach to the proposal a detailed itemization of all cash flow estimates related to the asset, as well as your assumptions regarding changes in revenues, profit margins, tax rates, and other business conditions that may alter the outcome of owning the asset.

8. Obtain the approval signature of the department manager who will be responsible for the asset.
9. Forward the completed form to the budget analyst.

The other procedure for the capital budgeting process is oriented toward the analyst who reviews completed capital budgeting application forms. It is more general in nature, and is designed to give the analyst guidelines for how to review an application, as well as specific issues to address. A sample procedure is:

1. Upon receipt of a completed capital budgeting application form, assign a project number to it and fill in the project number and submission date fields in the header section of the form.
2. Review the form to see if any fields have not been completed, or have been insufficiently completed. If there are issues, contact the submitter and go over the information that is missing. Hold any further review until the application has been re-submitted.
3. Review the calculations that accompany the application to verify that they are correct, and verify that the totals in the supporting documentation are used in the lead page of the application.
4. Review all assumptions noted in the supporting documentation to see how they compare to the assumptions used in other applications, both currently and in the recent past. If the assumptions vary significantly from those used elsewhere, contact the submitter for justification.
5. Review all cash flow projections with the submitter, as well as the purchasing, engineering, and sales departments to see if the amount and timing of the projected cash flows are reasonable.
6. Review the post implementation reviews of projects that were previously submitted by the same person, and note in the application if this person has a history of projecting results that cannot be realized, as well as the extent of these variances.
7. If the project appears to have a high degree of risk, note this issue in the application, and discuss with the controller whether to apply a higher discount rate to the net present value calculation to incorporate risk more fully into the cash flows associated with the application.
8. Following your review, and any adjustments by the submitter, evaluate whether you believe the application should be approved, and state your recommendation in the application, along with your reasons.
9. Copy the application and store the copy.
10. Forward the original of the application to the next person on the approval list, and request that it be returned to you following that person's review.
11. Monitor the progress of the approvals through the company, and shift the document to the next approver as needed.
12. If the application is rejected, communicate this information to the submitter, as well as the reasons why it was rejected.
13. If the application is approved, communicate this information to the submitter, and forward the approval to the accounting and purchasing departments.

It is highly advisable to conduct a post installation review to see if an approved project has generated the results predicted in the original capital budgeting application. This procedure is intended for the budget analyst, and so can be quite specialized, with references to specific types of analysis to conduct. You may find that the following procedure will require significant alterations to meet the needs of your business:

1. Once a fixed asset has been installed for at least _____ months, schedule a post implementation review.
2. Compare the business assumptions detailed in the application to actual business conditions, and quantify how these changes impacted the result of the project.
3. Compare the forecasted expenditures in the application to actual expenditures, and investigate why any additional expenditures were needed.
4. Compare the forecasted positive cash flows in the application to actual positive cash flows, and investigate any significant variances.
5. Compare the forecasted changes in throughput with actual results, and investigate any significant variances.
6. Validate with corporate counsel any legal reasons given for an asset purchase, and whether that legal basis for the decision has since changed.
7. Validate with the corporate risk manager any risk-related reasons given for an asset purchase, and whether this basis for the decision has since changed.
8. Route a preliminary copy of your findings to the project sponsor for comments, and add his comments to your findings.
9. Forward a summary of your findings to the senior management team, along with any recommendations regarding how to improve the capital budgeting process in the future.
10. If necessary, conduct another analysis at a longer interval, such as annually, to see if the project results have changed.

The Capital Request Form

The capital request form is intended to provide a summary that identifies a proposed fixed asset, why it is needed, and its impact on the business. The following sample shows how the form could be structured, though it may need to be modified to meet the specific needs of a business. This form is typically treated as a cover page, with additional analyses attached that may cover a number of additional pages.

Sample Capital Request Application

Capital Request Form

Project Name	Project Number

Project Sponsor	Sponsor Contact Information		Submission Date

Project Type

☐ Constraint improvement   ☐ Risk reduction

☐ Cost reduction   ☐ Scheduled equipment replacement

☐ Environmental/legal requirement ☐ Other

Project Description

Description Block

Financial Summary

Year 1 Revenue	-	Year 1 Expenses	=	Year 1 Cash Flow
Year 2 Revenue	-	Year 2 Expenses	=	Year 2 Cash Flow
Year 3 Revenue	-	Year 3 Expenses	=	Year 3 Cash Flow

Net Present Value	Internal Rate of Return	Payback Period

Constraint Summary

Throughput Impact
Operating Expenses Impact
ROI Impact

Approvals

All proposals	Financial analyst signature	Attorney signature
< $25,000	Department manager signature	
$25,000+	CEO signature	

Asset Recognition Procedures

One of the areas in which a procedure can be quite useful is for the initial recognition of a fixed asset in your accounting system. This involves not just capitalizing the cost of the asset, but also creating a permanent record for each asset.

We address these issues with several procedures. The first is for the initial recognition of the cost of the asset in your accounting system, as follows:

1. Determine the base unit for the asset. This determination is based upon a number of factors, such as whether the useful lives of various components of the asset are significantly different, at what level you prefer to physically track the asset, and the cost-effectiveness of tracking assets at various levels of detail. Reviewing the base units used for other assets may assist in this determination. Consult with the controller as needed. (see the Initial Fixed Asset Recognition chapter for more information about base units)
2. Compile the total cost of the base unit. This is any cost incurred to acquire the base unit and bring it to the condition and location intended for its use. These activities may include the construction of the base unit and related administrative and technical activities.
3. Determine whether the total cost of the base unit exceeds the corporate capitalization limit. If it does not, charge the expenditure to expense. Otherwise, continue to the next step.
4. Assign the base unit to the most appropriate asset class for which there is a general ledger category (such as furniture and fixtures, office equipment, or vehicles).
5. Record a journal entry that debits the asset account for the appropriate asset class and credits the expenditure account in which the cost of the base unit had originally been stored.

If you always purchase and install fixed assets quickly, you do not need a procedure for interest capitalization. However, if there are situations where you are constructing an asset over a prolonged period of time, consider adding the following procedure:

1. Construct a table that includes the amounts of expenditures made during a construction period and the dates when the expenditures were made.
2. Determine the date on which interest capitalization ends, which should be the date on which the asset has been brought to the condition and location intended for its use.
3. Calculate the capitalization period for each expenditure, which is the number of days from the expenditure to the end of the interest capitalization period.
4. Calculate the capitalization rate, which is the interest rate applicable to the company's borrowings during the construction period. If you have incurred a specific borrowing to finance the asset, use the interest rate on that borrowing.
5. Multiply the capitalization rate by each expenditure, and multiply the result by the fraction of a year represented by the capitalization period for each expenditure, to arrive at the interest to be capitalized for that expenditure.

6. If the total calculated interest capitalization is more than the total interest cost incurred by the company during the calculation period, only capitalize the total interest cost incurred by the company during the calculation period.
7. Record the interest capitalization as a debit to the project's fixed asset account and a credit to the interest expense account.

The next procedure addresses the creation of an asset record. The record format used may be similar to one of the formats listed in the Fixed Asset Record Keeping chapter, or there may be a more customized format that more closely matches the needs of the company. The exact information listed in this procedure will vary, depending on the information that you want to record. The following procedure is designed to create a record for a manufacturing asset:

1. Create a new record for the _____ asset and assign the next sequential record number to this document.
2. Describe the asset in one sentence. If this asset is similar to other company assets, use the same description format. Otherwise consider using a manu-facturer-provided description.
3. List the number on the company-provided tag (if any) affixed to the equipment. If no tag was used, enter "No Tag."
4. Enter the manufacturer-provided serial number on the equipment. If you cannot find the serial number, contact the manufacturer to find out where it should be located. If there is no serial number, enter "No Serial Number."
5. Note the location of the asset. Where possible, specify the location at least by building, and preferably by room. If it is located in the production area, specify the work center in which it is located.
6. State the name or at least the position title of the person who is responsible for the asset.
7. State the month and year on which the asset was ready for its intended use, whether or not it was actually used as of that date.
8. Note the total initial capitalized cost of the asset. This should match the amount recorded in the general ledger or fixed asset journal for the asset. Do not use the amount listed on the supplier invoice, since other costs may also have been added.
9. Assign the asset to an asset class by comparing its characteristics to the standard asset classes used by the company. If in doubt, review related as-sets to determine the classes to which they were assigned.
10. State the useful life of the asset. Use the designated useful life for the asset class into which the asset has been categorized. If the manufacturer recom-mends a substantially different useful life, discuss with the controller wheth-er to create a new asset class for the asset, or depart from the standard useful life used for the asset class to which you have assigned the asset.
11. State the warranty period. This may be a standard warranty provided by the manufacturer, or an extended warranty that the company purchased.

12. List the manufacturer's contact information. This may include the e-mail, telephone, and address for the supplier's field servicing, customer service, warranty, and sales departments.
13. Present the record to the controller, who should review and approve it. Correct any issues noted by the controller.
14. Following approval, print the asset record and store it by asset class and then by record number in the fixed asset record binder.

Use the preceding procedure for equipment record keeping as the basis for a procedure for a variety of other types of fixed asset records.

Asset Revaluation Policies and Procedures

Under IFRS, you are allowed to revalue fixed assets, but only for entire asset classes – you cannot selectively revalue some assets and not others within the same asset class. If you intend to use revaluation, consider using the following policy, which specifies which classes are to be revalued:

> **Policy:** The company will use the revaluation model to adjust the carrying amount of its fixed assets in the ____, ____, and ____ asset classes. It will use the cost model for the carrying amount of all other fixed asset classes.

Use the following procedure to revalue fixed assets:

1. Consult the asset class revaluation schedule to determine when the next revaluation is to be completed.
2. Run a detailed schedule of the fixed assets within the asset classes to be revalued.
3. Hire an independent appraiser to conduct the revaluations, and forward the detailed schedule to the appraiser.
4. In cases where the appraiser is unable to derive a market valuation, use estimates of future cash flows associated with the assets in question, discounted to their present values. Use the company's incremental cost of capital as the discount rate.
5. If there is an upward revaluation adjustment, debit the fixed asset account for the amount of the incremental increase and credit a gain in other comprehensive income. If the increase reverses a revaluation decrease for the same asset, recognize the gain in profit or loss to the extent of the previous loss, and record any remaining gain in other comprehensive income.
6. If there is a downward revaluation adjustment, recognize the loss in profit or loss with a debit, and credit the fixed asset account. If the decrease reverses a previous revaluation increase for the same asset, recognize the loss in other comprehensive income to the extent of the previous gain, and record any remaining loss in profit or loss.

7. If there is a revaluation adjustment, eliminate all existing accumulated depreciation by debiting the accumulated depreciation account and crediting the offsetting amount to the fixed asset account.
8. If there is a revaluation adjustment, examine the depreciation schedule being used for the asset to see if its useful life, depreciation method, or salvage value should be changed. Because of the change in the carrying amount of the asset caused by the revaluation, the amount of prospective depreciation expense recognized per period should change, even in the absence of any other changes in assumptions.

Asset Exchange Policies and Procedures

The exchange of assets between entities is relatively rare, so companies tend to address them on an ad hoc basis, rather than formulating specific policies and procedures. If there is any expectation of even an occasional asset exchange, consider formal documentation of the process, to account for them consistently.

A good starting point for a formalized asset exchange system is a policy that requires an outside appraisal of every received asset over a certain estimated value. Set the minimum level in order to avoid wasting money on too many appraisals. The first of the two policies shown below sets a minimum estimated value, but this can admittedly be difficult when the whole point of the appraisal is to determine that value. Accordingly, you could consider the second policy, which instead restricts the appraisal to certain asset classes. The assumption in this later case is that the asset values in certain asset classes are significantly higher, and so should be appraised.

> **Policy:** An independent appraiser shall determine the value of assets received as part of a non-monetary exchange, if the estimated value of the assets received exceeds $____.

> **Policy:** An independent appraiser shall determine the value of assets received as part of a non-monetary exchange if the assets received are to be aggregated into either the buildings, land, production equipment, or vehicles asset classifications.

If you acquire a fixed asset through a non-monetary exchange, use the next procedure to arrive at the proper recorded cost for it:

1. The cost of the asset received is the fair value of the asset surrendered to the other party. Recognize a gain or loss on the difference between the recorded cost of the asset surrendered and the asset received.
2. If you cannot determine the fair value of the asset surrendered, instead use the fair value of the asset received. Recognize a gain or loss on the difference between the recorded cost of the asset surrendered and the asset received.
3. If you cannot determine the fair value of either asset, record the cost of the asset received at the cost of the asset surrendered.

4. If the asset exchange involves the payment of cash that is 25 percent or more of the fair value of the exchange, recognize the transaction at its fair value, using either steps 1 or 2 in this procedure.

5. If the asset exchange involves the payment of cash that is less than 25 percent of the fair value of the exchange, then (if you are the recipient of the cash) record a gain to the extent that the amount of cash received exceeds a proportionate share of the cost of the surrendered asset. If the transaction results in a loss, record the entire loss at once. If you are paying the cash, record the asset received at the sum of the cash paid plus the cost of the asset surrendered.

Depreciation Policies and Procedures

If the accounting staff is pressured to report altered earnings (either up or down), one way to do so is to alter the useful lives, salvage values, and depreciation methods used to derive the depreciation expense. To keep this from happening, there are a variety of policies that restrict the use of several techniques that can alter reported earnings. For example:

> **Policy:** Salvage value shall be set at zero for all depreciation calculations, unless the expected amount of salvage value is at least $____ .

The preceding policy keeps the accounting staff from deferring depreciation by assuming that assets will have salvage values.

> **Policy:** All fixed assets shall be assigned to one of the following asset classes, and their useful lives and depreciation methods shall conform to the classes to which they are assigned.

Asset Class	Useful Life	Depreciation Method
Computer equipment	3 years	Straight line
Furniture and fixtures	7 years	Straight line
Leasehold improvements	Life of lease	Straight line
Office equipment	5 years	Straight line
Vehicles	5 years	Straight line

The preceding policy is highly recommended, and is used to keep the accounting staff from assigning special useful lives or depreciation methods to specific assets.

> **Policy:** The mid-month convention shall not be used when recording the depreciation for any fixed asset.

The preceding policy eliminates the use of a half-month of depreciation during the first and last months of depreciation for a fixed asset, which reduces the computational complexity of depreciation calculations.

If you are charging a natural resource asset to expense through a depletion calculation, periodically re-evaluate the estimate of the remaining amount of the natural resource to be extracted. The following policy controls the timing of this re-evaluation:

> **Policy:** The remaining recoverable quantity of any natural resources recorded as assets shall be reviewed at least once a year, as well as whenever the circumstances indicate a significant change in the most current estimate.

Adopt a detailed depreciation procedure that specifies exactly how to categorize each fixed asset and how to depreciate it based on the asset class to which it is assigned. The procedure for setting up depreciation for an individual fixed asset is:

1. Match the fixed asset to the company's standard asset class descriptions listed in the policies and procedures manual. If you are uncertain of the correct class to use, examine the assets already assigned to the various classes, or consult with the controller.
2. Assign to the fixed asset the useful life and depreciation method that are standardized for the asset class of which it is a part.
3. Consult with the purchasing or industrial engineering staffs to determine whether the asset is expected to have a salvage value at the end of its useful life. If this salvage value exceeds the company's policy for minimum salvage values, make note of it in the depreciation calculation.
4. Create the depreciation calculation based on the useful life and depreciation mandated for the asset class, using the asset cost less any salvage value.

The preceding procedure is based on the assumption that you are not using an integrated fixed asset software package that automatically creates a depreciation calculation when you have recorded the baseline data for a new asset. This procedure assumes that you are calculating depreciation separately (probably on an electronic spreadsheet), and so have to determine the correct depreciation type and duration for each individual asset.

The procedure thus far has only addressed the calculation of depreciation for a single fixed asset. Once each calculation is set up, you will not need to address it again until either the end of the useful life of the asset or when there is a change in estimate. However, you also need to deal with the aggregation of the depreciation for all fixed assets into a periodic journal entry, which is addressed in the following procedure:

1. Print the monthly depreciation report, sorted by asset class.
2. Compare the depreciation totals to the trend line of depreciation for the preceding periods to look for any unusual changes. Investigate and verify the calculations causing any such changes.
3. Scan the report to see if fixed assets appear to be assigned to the correct asset classes. Investigate and correct as necessary.

4. Create the monthly depreciation journal entry, using the standard depreciation template. The standard entry is to record a debit for the depreciation expense [in total or by department], and to record a credit to the accumulated depreciation account for each asset class. This information comes from the totals on the depreciation report.
5. Enter the journal entry into the accounting software.
6. Attach the depreciation report to the journal entry form and file it in the journal entries binder.

The preceding procedure assumes that you have a relatively small number of fixed assets, so that a brief review and comparison of assets as part of the depreciation calculation is cost-effective. If there are many fixed assets, skip the step to verify asset class assignments, and leave that task for the internal audit team or accounting staff to conduct at another time.

If you are using depletion to charge the cost of a natural resource to expense, the calculation is somewhat different from the normal depreciation procedure, as shown below:

1. Compute the depletion base, which includes the acquisition, exploration, development, and restoration costs associated with the asset.
2. Compute a unit depletion rate by subtracting the salvage value of the asset from its depletion base and dividing it by the total number of measurement units that you expect to recover.
3. Calculate the depletion to charge to expense by multiplying the actual units of usage by the unit depletion rate.
4. Record the depletion expense with a debit to depletion expense and a credit to the accumulated depletion contra account.

Impairment Policies and Procedures

Both GAAP and IFRS require that you periodically review fixed assets for impairment. This should be a formal, documented process that steps the user through the specifics of the required testing. Use the following policy to set the timing for impairment testing, as well as to limit the number of assets that are subject to the testing:

Policy: All fixed assets having a gross carrying amount greater than $____ shall be tested for impairment at least once a year, or when it appears that the carrying amount may not be recoverable.

The following procedure describes the basic steps to follow when reviewing fixed assets for possible impairment:

1. Sort the fixed asset register in declining order by net carrying amount (i.e., gross cost less accumulated depreciation and accumulated impairment).
2. Select for testing any fixed assets having a net carrying amount greater than $____. Export these items to a spreadsheet.

3. Determine the sum of the undiscounted cash flows expected from each asset over its remaining useful life and final disposition, and add this amount next to each asset in the spreadsheet.
4. If the cash flows total is less than the net carrying amount, the difference is an impairment. Note this amount in the spreadsheet.
5. Forward the spreadsheet to the controller, who will review and approve the calculations. The controller authorizes a journal entry to reduce the net carrying amount of the asset to its fair value, as represented by the remaining cash flows.
6. If impairment was recorded for an asset group, apportion the impairment amount among the assets in the group on a pro rata basis that is based on the carrying amounts of the assets.
7. Adjust the remaining depreciation on the asset(s) to reflect its (their) reduced carrying amount.

Asset Retirement Obligation Policies and Procedures

There is an obligation to record a liability for any asset retirement obligations, particularly under GAAP. This is an area that the accounting staff may miss, since it does not involve an up-front expenditure that would appear in the accounts payable system. Accordingly, consider using the following policy to force the accounting staff to consider the need for an asset retirement obligation.

> **Policy:** There shall be a formal evaluation of the need for an asset retirement obligation at the initial recognition of all fixed assets in the ____ asset classes. You shall also evaluate adjustments to these obligations at least annually, or whenever the circumstances indicate a potential change in the obligation.

Use the following procedure to initially account for an asset retirement obligation:

1. Determine whether there is an obligation to engage in asset retirement expenditures at the end of the useful life of the asset under review.
2. Estimate the number of years before which the company will engage in asset retirement activities and incur related expenditures.
3. Estimate the timing and amounts of the cash flows associated with any required asset retirement obligations. If there are a range of probabilities, incorporate them into a weighted-average estimate of cash flows.
4. Calculate the credit-adjusted risk-free rate.
5. Discount the estimate of cash flows to their present value using the credit-adjusted risk-free rate.
6. Record the present value of the asset retirement obligation as a credit to the asset retirement obligation liability account, and a debit to the fixed asset account to which the obligation relates.
7. Create a table for this initial liability layer that shows increases in the carrying amount of the liability over time, with the incremental increases

attributed to accretion expense. Include in the table the straight-line depreciation of the initial carrying amount of the liability.

8. Using the information in the table, set up accretion expense as a debit to the accretion expense account and a credit to the asset retirement obligation liability. Also, record the depreciation expense as a debit to the depreciation expense account and a credit to the accumulated depreciation account.

Intangible Asset Policies and Procedures

Most policies and procedures that apply to tangible fixed assets should also apply to intangible assets. One area that requires additional accounting effort is the proper valuation of an intangible asset, which is an area persistently targeted by auditors. Consider using the following policy, which incorporates the input of the auditors into the initial valuation of intangible assets, thereby reducing the risk of an auditor-mandated change in valuation at a later date:

Policy: The company's external auditors shall be apprised of the methodology used to assign values to intangible assets at the time of initial asset recognition, as well as the amount to be recognized.

Under IFRS, you are allowed to revalue intangible fixed assets under very limited circumstances. Use the following procedure to revalue such assets:

1. Consult the asset class revaluation schedule to determine when the next revaluation is to be completed.
2. Run a detailed schedule of the intangible assets within the asset classes to be revalued.
3. Hire an independent appraiser to conduct the revaluations, and forward the detailed schedule to the appraiser.
4. In cases where the appraiser is unable to derive a market valuation by reference to an active market, you cannot revalue the intangible asset. Stop any additional revaluation activities for these assets.
5. If there is an upward revaluation adjustment for those qualifying intangible assets, debit the fixed asset account for the amount of the incremental increase and credit a gain in other comprehensive income. If the increase reverses a revaluation decrease for the same asset, recognize the gain in profit or loss to the extent of the previous loss, and record any remaining gain in other comprehensive income.
6. If there is a downward revaluation adjustment for those qualifying intangible assets, recognize the loss in profit or loss with a debit, and credit the fixed asset account. If the decrease reverses a previous revaluation increase for the same asset, recognize the loss in other comprehensive income to the extent of the previous gain, and record any remaining loss in profit or loss.
7. If there is a revaluation adjustment, eliminate all existing accumulated amortization by debiting the accumulated amortization account and crediting the offsetting amount to the intangible fixed asset account.

8. If there is a revaluation adjustment, examine the amortization schedule being used for the intangible asset to see if its useful life should be changed. Because of the change in the carrying amount of the asset caused by the revaluation, the amount of prospective amortization expense recognized per period should change, even in the absence of any other changes in assumptions.

Transfer Policies

In a larger company with multiple locations, it is possible that some fixed assets may be transferred among the various locations. If so, it becomes difficult for the accounting department to keep track of the assets, which in turn makes it difficult for the auditors to verify that they exist. This is a lesser issue in smaller, one-location companies. If you find it necessary to formally document the transfer of fixed assets, consider using the following policy:

> **Policy:** The written approval of both the issuing and receiving managers are required for the transfer of fixed assets. These managers are defined as the persons who are relinquishing and accepting responsibility for the transferred assets, respectively. The accounting department shall be notified of all fixed asset transfers.

Disposal Policies and Procedures

There is a significant risk of fraud in the disposal of fixed assets, for employees may be able to sell assets without the approval of senior management, as well as pocket the proceeds. There should be a strict procedure in place for the disposal of fixed assets, which is supported by the following policy:

> **Policy:** The approval of the chief financial officer is required for all asset dispositions with a gross book value equal to or less than $____. The approval of the chief executive officer is required for all asset dispositions with a gross book value of greater than $____.

The disposal of an asset may require the participation of a number of employees in the accounting and purchasing departments, so a broad-based disposal procedure may require the use of several smaller procedures that are linked together to provide comprehensive coverage of the transaction. The following procedure assumes that a company is relatively small, so that only a few people are involved. It is written from the standpoint of a person in the accounting department.

1. Upon notification that an asset is to be sold or otherwise disposed of, send an asset disposal form to the person responsible for that asset, with instructions for how to complete it. A sample disposal form appears in the next section.
2. When the responsible person returns the form, verify that a designated manager has signed the form to indicate approval of the proposed transaction.

3. Forward the approved disposal form to the purchasing department, which handles the disposal.

4. Upon disposal of the asset, the purchasing manager signs the disposal form and returns it to the accounting department, along with a bill of sale and check payment (if sold), or a receipt from a charitable organization, or disclosure of any other disposal method.

5. If the asset was sold, forward the check payment and the bill of sale to the controller. The controller removes the asset from the general ledger, along with all associated accumulated depreciation, and records a gain or loss on the sale. The controller also notifies the fixed asset clerk to note the disposal in the detail record for the asset, and forwards the check to the cashier for inclusion in the daily bank deposit.

6. The controller files a copy of the journal entry and supporting documentation in the journal entry binder.

The Asset Disposal Form

The asset disposal form is used to formalize the disposition of assets. Ideally, the purchasing department should be involved in disposals, since it presumably has the most experience in obtaining the best prices for goods. Consequently, a large part of the form is set aside for the use of the purchasing staff, which describes how the asset is disposed of and the amount of funds (if any) received. There is space to state billing information, in case the buyer is to be billed. There is also a separate section containing a checklist of activities that the accounting staff must complete. A sample of the form is presented next.

Sample Asset Disposal Form

Asset Disposal Form

| Asset Tag Number | Asset Serial Number | Current Location |

| Asset Description |

Reason for Disposal

☐ No longer usable   ☐ Being traded in
☐ Past recommended life span ☐ Lost or stolen*
☐ Being replaced   ☐ Other _____

* Contact building security to file a police report

| Department Manager Approval Signature |

For Use by Purchasing Department

Type of Disposition   If buyer is to be invoiced, state billing information:

☐ Sold ($_____)
☐ Donated
☐ Scrapped   Buyer billing information
☐ Other _____

| Purchasing Manager Approval Signature | | Disposal Date |

For Use by Accounting Department

Accounting Actions Completed

Asset removed from general ledger	Initials	Date
Asset removed from fixed asset register	Initials	Date
Buyer billed for sale amount	Initials	Date
Cash receipt recorded	Initials	Date

Record Keeping Policies

There is a tendency to engage in the minimum amount of record keeping for fixed assets, usually just sufficient to record the amounts required under either GAAP or IFRS: the initial cost, asset retirement obligations (under GAAP), depreciation, impairment, revaluation (under IFRS), and derecognition. However, this level of record keeping ignores a number of other issues, such as who has responsibility for each asset, where it is located, its condition, and any active warranties. You can address this issue at a general level with the first of the following two policies, or in more detail with the second policy. The second version is perhaps too detailed for a policy, but has the advantage of mandating very specific types of record keeping.

> **Policy:** A detailed accounting and condition record shall be created and maintained for each fixed asset acquired.

> **Policy:** A detailed record shall be created and maintained for each fixed asset acquired, which shall include information about the assessed value, classification, cost, depreciation method, easements, impairment, location, supplier, useful life, warranties, and zoning associated with the asset.

If you are concerned about the risk of loss to key fixed asset records, you might also consider the following policy, which mandates off-site storage for certain types of records.

> **Policy:** Original title documents shall be stored in certified fire-proof bank vaults. Copies of purchase and disposal documents shall be maintained in off-site fire-proof storage facilities.

Given the high cost of fixed assets, there should be an especially robust document destruction policy for the documents related to them. These documents should not be commingled with other accounting records, and should require specific approval before being destroyed. The following policy addresses these issues:

> **Policy:** The records for fixed assets shall be stored separately from other accounting records, and their destruction must be approved in writing by the corporate controller.

Tracking Policies and Procedures

A major control weakness in many companies is that they do not have a system in place for reviewing the existence and condition of their fixed assets. Over time, a disparity may develop between management's perception of its fixed asset base and what actually exists. The following policy is useful for mandating a periodic review of the existence and location of fixed assets, but does not trigger any action to review the condition of equipment:

> **Policy:** An annual audit of all fixed assets exceeding a gross cost of $____ shall be conducted, and the results communicated to management.

You could use the results of the audit mandated in the preceding policy to generate a fixed asset location report, which could then be used to examine the condition of the assets. The following policy addresses this issue:

> **Policy:** An annual review of the condition of all fixed assets exceeding a gross cost of $_____ shall be conducted, and the results communicated to management.

In a larger business with multiple locations and many fixed assets, a fixed asset audit can be a large-scale endeavor that requires the full-time commitment of several people, as well as tight coordination between them to ascertain the existence and condition of fixed assets. The following procedure assumes that a larger-scale audit is needed:

1. Notify all department managers that you are freezing asset transfers between departments for the duration of the audit.
2. Verify that all asset transfer documents have been properly approved and entered into the fixed asset tracking database.
3. Print the fixed asset location report, sorted for the facility in which you plan to conduct the audit.
4. As you move through the facility, match the tag number and/or serial number of each asset to the report. Check off those found, and note their condition.
5. If you find what appear to be fixed assets that are not on the report, note their identification information and locations. See if these are leased assets or assets that are supposed to be in other locations.
6. Compile a list of exceptions and review them with the person responsible for the facility in which you conducted the audit.
7. Have the responsible persons report to you regarding missing assets, and verify their assertions.
8. Process the asset transfer documentation for any fixed assets that are proven to have been shifted to another location without any supporting documentation.
9. Report exceptions to the managers of the responsible persons for further action.
10. Notify the accounting department of any fixed assets that have been confirmed to be permanently missing, with a request to eliminate them from the general ledger, along with the recognition of any gain or loss, as needed.
11. Notify the internal audit staff of assets that have been confirmed to be permanently missing, as well as of any other control problems found, with a request for them to review the controls that caused these problems to arise.
12. Report to the chief financial officer, maintenance manager, and budget analyst the condition of all fixed assets found, which is used to update the forecasts for future asset purchases, as well as the need for additional maintenance.

This procedure works best if a qualified maintenance technician accompanies the auditor, in order to determine the condition of the assets found. If this is not possible, it may make sense to avoid tracking the condition of assets, on the grounds that the auditor is not qualified to do so.

The Fixed Asset Manual

If you have a large amount of transactional activity with the company's fixed assets, it may make sense to codify the preceding policies and procedures into a fixed asset manual, and issue it to all employees in the company who deal with fixed assets. This manual should contain the following items:

- *Responsibilities*. Describe who is involved with fixed assets. This includes the titles of the positions that are directly responsible for fixed assets, as well as contact information for the accountant responsible for fixed asset transactions, the budget analyst who handles capital budgeting proposals, and so forth. Also, describe the tasks of anyone who is assigned direct responsibility for specific fixed assets, such as reporting changes in location or missing assets.
- *Fixed asset policies*. Itemize all policies related to fixed assets.
- *Fixed asset procedures*. Itemize all procedures related to fixed assets, possibly including flow charts to visually illustrate the flow of transactions.
- *Fixed asset forms*. List all forms that users of the manual may need in order to complete various fixed asset transactions, such as a capital budgeting application form, asset transfer form, and asset disposal form.
- *Fixed asset reports*. Show examples of all reports related to fixed assets that are available in the accounting system, and how to obtain them. Such reports may include a depreciation report, audit report, responsibility report, asset replacement report, and maintenance report.
- *Asset tagging system*. If you use asset tags, describe who distributes and affixes tags, where to locate them on an asset, and how they are recorded.
- *Fixed asset account numbers*. List the account numbers in the general ledger in which fixed assets, accumulated depreciation, and depreciation expense are stored, and describe the transactions in which they are used.
- *Journal entries*. Though only for the use of a few people within the accounting department, it may be useful to include the standard journal entry templates to use for various transactions, along with examples of how they are used.
- *Glossary*. Include a list of all special terminology related to fixed assets, with definitions.
- *Feedback*. If users find a mistake in the manual, or want additional information included in future versions, there should be a name and address noted in the manual that they can contact with their feedback.

It is easiest to keep the fixed asset manual up-to-date by not issuing it in paper form at all – instead, post a link to a PDF version of the document on the company's website, and notify users whenever you have made a change to the document. Also, consider posting all forms related to fixed assets on the company website.

Summary

This chapter has presented a broad array of policies and procedures that can be used as guidelines for the development of your own fixed asset manual. However, please note that these are only guidelines. Every company has its own unique methods of operation, with a different blend of fixed assets, and may operate in an industry where there are varying concentrations of fixed assets. You may find that some policies and procedures are superfluous, while other areas require a greater degree of control. Thus, though the information in this chapter may form the basis for a fixed asset manual, expect it to be modified to a certain extent.

Chapter 15
Fixed Asset Tracking

Introduction

This chapter addresses the various options that are available for tracking and monitoring fixed assets. This may not seem like an issue, since fixed assets are, by definition, "fixed" and therefore require no tracking. However, in reality, a fixed asset is really an expenditure whose cost is greater than a company's capitalization limit, and which is expected to have a useful life of at least one year – there is no mention in this definition of a fixed asset having to be bolted in place. Indeed, the reverse may be the case for some assets; for example, a high-quality video camera may easily qualify as a fixed asset, and yet be designed to be ultra-portable. Thus, there are valid cases where fixed assets will be moved on a regular basis, and where you need to know where they are located. In addition, there are situations where you are less concerned with the location of an asset, and more so with its current operating condition. This chapter addresses how to track both the location and condition of fixed assets.

> **Related Podcast Episode:** Episode 196 of the Accounting Best Practices Podcast discusses fixed asset counting. It is available at: **accountingtools.com/podcasts** or **iTunes**

Tag Tracking

The traditional approach to tracking assets is to epoxy a metal tag onto each fixed asset. The tag has an asset number engraved on it; the asset number corresponds to a record number in a computer database or a manual record that itemizes the name, description, location, and other key information about a fixed asset.

The advantage of the metal tag is that it is almost indestructible and provides a unique identifier. However, a determined thief can remove the tag, and it may be considered a detriment to the resale value of an asset. Another problem is that the tag may be deliberately located in an inaccessible spot, where a thief would be less likely to look for it.

Some variations on the tag tracking concept that have differing advantages and disadvantages are:

- *Etching.* You can etch the asset number directly onto the surface of a fixed asset. This makes it nearly impossible to remove the asset number, but also defaces the asset, and may reduce its resale value.

- *Paper tags.* If you intend to resell a fixed asset at a later date and do not want to deface it with a metal tag, affix a plastic-laminated paper tag instead (or a paper tag that has been covered with tape). The lamination tends to reduce the amount of damage to the tag. The problem with this approach is that the tags may fall off, or can be easily removed by a thief.
- *Serial numbers.* If most fixed assets already have a manufacturer's serial number attached to them, use this information instead. Serial numbers are generally affixed quite securely, and so are a good alternative. However, they may be located in out-of-the-way places, and they may involve such long character strings that they do not fit in the tag number field in the company's tag tracking software.

Some companies do not bother with asset tagging, if their assets are few or so immovable that they are easily tracked without any identification method at all. Also, companies dealing with large numbers of low-cost fixed assets may view them as essentially office supplies that will be replaced every few years (such as laptop computers), and which are therefore not worth the effort of such a formalized tracking system.

Tip: If you expect to sell a fixed asset at the end of its useful life and applying a metal tag to it may impair its resale value, use the asset's existing serial number instead of an asset tag.

Bar Code Tracking

Some asset tags can contain quite a long string of digits, especially if you use the manufacturer's serial number as a substitute for an asset tag. It is easy to transpose these numbers when copying them down, which leads to identification errors. It is also a slow process to write down tag numbers. A faster, more efficient, and less error-prone technique is to instead track fixed assets using bar coded labels.

Bar code tracking involves printing a bar code that contains the tag number (and sometimes additional information), laminating the label to prevent tearing, affixing it to a fixed asset, and using a portable scanner to read the label. The person performing the scanning may also punch in a location code, and perhaps an asset condition code, and then uploads the record to the fixed assets database, where it is matched to the fixed asset record using the tag number.

Tip: Do not apply too many lamination layers to a bar code label, or else the bar code scanner will not be able to read the label.

It is possible for bar code labels to fall off an asset and be lost, and they can easily be removed by a thief. Thus, they do not necessarily provide a permanent tag. However, they present an extremely efficient method for quickly recording asset locations, as you may do during an annual fixed asset audit.

> **Tip:** If you use bar code tracking, put the bar code in an easily accessible part of the asset, so that you can access it with a portable bar code scanner. In addition, securely affix a metal asset tag in a less accessible part of the asset, where a thief is less likely to see it.

Bar coding is especially useful when you are dealing with large numbers of fixed assets that are not easily differentiated from each other, such as cubicle walls.

RFID Tracking – Active Transmission

The trouble with the bar coding solution just described is that someone needs to locate the asset, then locate the bar code on the asset, then scan it with a portable scanner, and then upload the contents of the scanner to the computer system in order to log the asset into the system. This means that you have to go to the asset in order to track it, which can be fairly labor-intensive. An alternative that eliminates these problems to a great extent is radio frequency identification (RFID).

In an RFID system, you affix an RFID tag to each asset, which periodically transmits its location through RFID receiving stations to a central database for viewing. The system determines the locations of assets based on their relative signal strengths as received by the RFID receiving stations that are located throughout the facility. The RFID tags have their own batteries, which can last as long as five years before requiring replacement. A variation on the RFID concept is the transmission of ultrasound signals. Ultrasound does not penetrate room walls, and so does not create the false-location signals that may sometimes arise in an RFID system.

If most of your fixed assets are bolted down or so heavy as to be essentially immovable, there is clearly no need to install an RFID tracking system. Instead, only use it to track those assets that will probably be moved from time to time, and for which there is an absolute need to know their locations (such as medical equipment in a critical care facility). In the latter case, the RFID system may actually *reduce* your investment in fixed assets, since you will be able to avoid purchasing additional fixed assets that might otherwise have been held in reserve to cover for assets that could not be located. An RFID system also makes it easier for the maintenance staff to locate equipment that is scheduled for maintenance, eliminates the time spent searching for equipment, speeds up the auditing of fixed assets, and prevents managers from hoarding equipment.

RFID Tracking – Passive Transmission

The RFID tracking system just noted incorporates battery-powered RFID tags that transmit their own signals to RFID receivers, so that a signal is being generated at regular intervals. An alternative system employs RFID tags that contain no batteries at all. Instead, these tags use the power from a nearby RFID transceiver to transmit a signal. These tags are less expensive, and also can potentially last for many years without replacement. This passive transmission system is ideal for monitoring the movement of fixed assets past a fixed point, such as a building exit door. If you place an RFID transceiver at that point, it can trigger an alarm when a fixed asset is moved past it, or activate a camera that photographs both the person moving the asset and the asset itself, along with a time and date stamp on any images taken.

This monitoring function is ideal for detecting the theft of assets. It also provides documentation of theft, which can assist in settling a claim with the company's insurer.

Use passive RFID tags on those fixed assets that are easily movable and which have a high resale value (such as laptop computers and other office equipment).

Wireless Monitoring

You may know exactly where your fixed assets are located, but are concerned with their ongoing condition, to plan for their timely replacement. The traditional approach is to have a periodic maintenance system in place, so that the maintenance staff provides feedback about the wear and tear on equipment. This approach may be sufficient, but what if equipment breaks down between periodic maintenance visits? Or what if maintenance is extremely rare, or if the equipment is so difficult to reach that maintenance requires disassembly of the machine? A possible solution is to install a wireless monitor. These monitors can be configured to continually review a number of factors, such as the inclination of a device, or its humidity, temperature, position, or pitch/yaw/roll. Any or all of these factors can indicate that a fixed asset should be replaced, and can provide immediate warning of the situation, since there is usually a noticeable change in such factors as temperature or vibration levels just prior to equipment failure.

The usual configuration of a wireless sensor system is to attach a sensor to the equipment to be monitored, and link it by a wireless router to the company's computer system. The monitor may be configurable to only sample at relatively long intervals, thereby saving on battery power, and then only transmitting a warning to the router when a measurement has exceeded a predetermined trigger point. The computer system then sends a warning e-mail to a designated recipient, who can take further action.

Creating a wireless monitoring system requires an initial investment, as well as the periodic replacement of monitor batteries, but it allows management to determine much more precisely the date on which it should replace equipment. Thus, some equipment replacements can be delayed, while there is also a reduced risk of sudden equipment failure, which would otherwise call for an expensive replacement on an emergency basis.

Summary

Which of the preceding asset tracking alternatives makes the most sense for your specific situation? It will depend on a variety of factors, such as:

- *Asset condition monitoring.* If you have assets that are at risk of failure, consider wireless monitoring. This system is most commonly used for larger industrial machinery where you have little concern about an asset being moved.

- *Fixed asset cost.* If you are dealing with fixed assets that barely exceed the capitalization limit, it may not make sense to monitor them at all. The key factor here is not the cost of the tags, but of the additional labor you expect to incur for subsequent monitoring of those tags. Thus, if you consider a fixed asset to be inexpensive and easily replaceable, a tagging system may be unnecessary.

- *High-usage assets.* If you have fixed assets that are heavily used, and which are typically moved among multiple locations, consider an active transmission RFID system. This is the most expensive tracking alternative, so evaluate how cost-effective it is before proceeding with an installation.

- *Periodic audits.* If you are mostly concerned about having an efficient method for compiling a fixed asset count, consider using a bar coded tagging system. This is the primary situation in which bar coding fixed assets makes sense.

- *Probability of theft.* If there is a reasonable chance that assets may be stolen, consider a combination of etching the asset number directly onto such assets, and affixing passive transmission RFID tags to them, with RFID transceivers mounted at the building exits.

Thus, the best method of asset tracking depends upon your circumstances – there is no single tracking method that is optimal in all situations.

Chapter 16
Fixed Asset Measurements

Introduction

It is useful for the accountant to be aware of a number of possible measurements related to fixed assets. These metrics are needed for a general understanding of the adequacy of a company's investment in fixed assets, as well as the return on investment from them, and whether they are being adequately utilized.

If you are deeply involved with the monitoring of individual assets you may not need these ratios, but consider using them when you need a fast opinion regarding the fixed assets of other companies, especially potential acquisitions where there is little time to conduct a detailed investigation into a business' fixed assets.

The ratios described in this chapter are clustered into three groups. The first group is used to investigate whether a business has an adequate investment in fixed assets or is maintaining them properly. The second group addresses the return on investment that a company is achieving from its fixed assets. The final group is primarily concerned with the level of asset utilization. All three groups of metrics can provide valuable insights into a company's fixed assets.

> **Related Podcast Episode:** Episode 30 of the Accounting Best Practices Podcast discusses asset utilization metrics. It is available at: **accountingtools.com/podcasts** or **iTunes**

Sales to Fixed Assets Ratio

It requires a large amount of fixed assets to compete in some industries, such as computer chips and automobiles. Use the sales to fixed assets ratio to determine how a company's expenditures for fixed assets compare to those of other companies in the same industry, to see if it is operating in a more lean fashion than the others, or if there may be opportunities to scale back on its fixed asset investment. This is quite useful to track on a trend line, which may show gradual changes in expenditure levels away from the historical trend. The ratio is most useful in asset-intensive industries, and least useful where the required asset base is so small that the ratio would be essentially meaningless.

The ratio can also be misleading in cases where a company must invest in an entire production facility before it can generate any sales; this will initially result in an inordinately low sales to fixed assets ratio, which gradually increases as the company maximizes sales for that facility, and then levels out when it reaches a high level of asset utilization.

To calculate the sales to fixed assets ratio, divide net sales for the past twelve months by the book value of all fixed assets. The formula is:

$$\frac{\text{Trailing 12 months' sales}}{\text{Book value of all fixed assets}}$$

The fixed asset book value listed in the denominator is subject to some variation, depending on what type of depreciation method is used (see the Depreciation and Amortization chapter). If an accelerated depreciation method is used, the denominator will be unusually small, and so will yield a higher ratio.

EXAMPLE

Mole Industries manufactures trench digging equipment. It has a relatively low sales to fixed assets ratio of 4:1, because a large amount of machining equipment is needed to construct its products. Mole is considering expanding into earth-moving equipment, and calculates the sales to fixed assets ratio for competing companies, based on their financial statements. The ratio is in the vicinity of 3:1 for most competitors, which means that Mole will need to invest heavily in fixed assets in order to enter this new market. Mole estimates that the most likely revenue level it can achieve for earth moving equipment will be $300 million. Based on the 3:1 ratio, this means that Mole may need to invest $100 million in fixed assets in order to achieve its goal.

Mole's CFO concludes that the company does not currently have the financial resources to invest $100 million in the earth moving equipment market, and recommends that the company not enter the field at this time.

Repairs and Maintenance Expense to Fixed Assets Ratio

When you are reviewing the potential acquisition of a product line or entire company, it is useful to review their ratio of repair and maintenance expense to fixed assets, especially on a trend line. If the ratio is increasing over time, there are several ways to interpret it:

- *Old assets.* The acquiree is relying on an aging fixed asset base, since it must spend more to keep them operational. This is the worst-case scenario, since the buyer may be faced with a wholesale replacement of the acquiree's fixed assets.
- *High utilization.* The acquiree is experiencing very high asset usage levels, which calls for higher maintenance costs just to keep the machines running fast enough to meet demand. You can spot this condition by looking for a high sales to fixed assets ratio (see the preceding ratio). A high profit level is also likely.
- *Preparing for sale.* If there is a sudden spike in the ratio in the recent past, it may be because the owner of the acquiree is simply preparing it for sale, and

so is either catching up on delayed maintenance or is bringing machinery up to a high standard.

- *Accounting changes*. It is possible that the repairs and maintenance expense has been moved among different accounts, such as from the cost of goods sold account or an overhead cost pool to its own account, which means that there could appear to be a sudden jump in expenses that is not really the case.

This ratio is least useful when the bulk of the repairs and maintenance expense is comprised of salaries paid to a relatively fixed group of repair technicians. In this case, the expense is essentially a fixed cost, and cannot be expected to vary much over time.

A problem that this ratio does *not* reveal is when an acquiree simply lets its machinery decline by not investing in repairs and maintenance; this means that the ratio would remain flat or could even decline over time. In this case, you must look elsewhere for an indicator, such as declining sales or an inability to meet customer delivery schedules.

To calculate the repairs and maintenance expense to fixed assets ratio, divide the total amount of repairs and maintenance expense by the total amount of fixed assets before depreciation. The amount of accumulated depreciation that may have built up on older assets would otherwise bring the denominator close to zero for some acquirees, so it is better not to use depreciation at all. The formula is:

$$\frac{\text{Total repairs and maintenance expense}}{\text{Total fixed assets before depreciation}}$$

EXAMPLE

Mole Industries is investigating the purchase of Grubstake Brothers, a manufacturer of backhoes. Its acquisition analysis team uncovers the following information:

	20X1	20X2	20X3	20X4
Sales	$15,000,000	$14,500,000	$13,200,000	$12,900,000
Profit	$1,000,000	$200,000	$(150,000)	$(420,000)
Repairs expense	$400,000	$240,000	$160,000	$80,000
Fixed assets	$5,400,000	$6,000,000	$6,050,000	$6,100,000
Repairs to fixed assets ratio	7%	4%	3%	1%

The information in the table strongly indicates that the decline in Grubstake's profitability over the past few years has led its management to cut back on repair and maintenance expenditures. Thus, if Mole elects to buy Grubstake, it can expect to invest a significant amount to replace fixed assets.

Accumulated Depreciation to Fixed Assets Ratio

If a company is not replacing its fixed assets, the proportion of accumulated depreciation to fixed assets will increase over time. The ratio is quite useful for analyzing prospective acquisitions, since it is an easy way to see if an acquiree is not reinvesting in its business. This information is especially useful when tracked on a trend line, since it shows gradual changes in the ratio that might not otherwise be immediately apparent.

There are several situations where this ratio is not useful. For example, a business may be using accelerated depreciation, which results in a large amount of accumulated depreciation despite having relatively new assets. The ratio can also be problematic if a company is not removing assets and accumulated depreciation from its books as soon as it disposes of them. It is also possible that a company has chosen to switch to leased assets under operating leases, where the fixed assets do not appear on the company's balance sheet. Finally, a company may acquire assets that have very long useful lives (such as hydroelectric facilities), where the gradual accumulation of depreciation is a natural part of the business. Be aware of these situations when deciding whether to use the ratio.

To calculate the accumulated depreciation to fixed assets ratio, divide the total accumulated depreciation by the total amount of fixed assets (before depreciation). The formula is:

$$\frac{\text{Accumulated depreciation}}{\text{Total fixed assets before depreciation deduction}}$$

EXAMPLE

Mole Industries is conducting an investigation of Vertical Drop, a heavy-lift helicopter company that installs cell towers and power poles, with the intent of buying the company. The primary asset of Vertical Drop is its fleet of Sikorsky helicopters, which must be properly maintained and replaced at regular intervals. Mole collects the following information about Vertical Drop's fixed assets:

	20X1	20X2	20X3	20X4
Accumulated depreciation	$4,900,000	$6,000,000	$9,400,000	$10,450,000
Fixed assets	$32,700,000	$33,400,000	$31,350,000	$29,875,000
Accumulated depreciation to fixed assets ratio	15%	18%	30%	35%

The ratio calculation in the table indicates that Vertical Drop essentially stopped purchasing replacement helicopters two years ago, which means that Mole may be faced with large-scale replacements if it buys the company.

Cash Flow to Fixed Asset Requirements Ratio

Does a company have sufficient cash to pay for its upcoming fixed asset purchases? The cash flow to fixed asset requirements ratio is useful both as a general internal analysis of a company's future prospects, and also as a means for determining the health of a possible acquisition. The ratio must be greater than 1:1 for a company to have sufficient cash to fund its fixed asset needs. If the ratio is very close to 1:1, a company is operating very close to the edge of its available cash flows, and should consider bolstering its cash position with a line of credit. The ratio is less useful if the company in question has substantial cash reserves, since it can always draw upon these reserves to fund its fixed asset requirements, irrespective of short-term cash flows.

To calculate the cash flow to fixed asset requirements ratio, divide the expected annual cash flow by the total expenditure that has been budgeted for fixed assets for the same period. Calculate the cash flow figure in the numerator by adding non-cash expenses (such as depreciation and amortization) back to net income, and subtracting out any non-cash sales (such as sales accruals). Also, subtract from the numerator any dividends and principal payments on loans. The formula is:

$$\frac{\text{Net income} + \text{Noncash expenses} - \text{Noncash sales} - \text{Dividends} - \text{Principal payments}}{\text{Budgeted fixed asset expenditures}}$$

EXAMPLE

Mole Industries has just compiled the first iteration of its budget for the upcoming year, which reveals the following information:

Budget Line Item	Amount
Net income	$4,100,000
Depreciation and amortization	380,000
Accrued sales	250,000
Dividend payments	100,000
Principal payments	800,000
Budgeted fixed asset expenditures	3,750,000

Based on this information, Mole's controller calculates the ratio of cash flow to fixed asset requirements as:

$$\frac{\substack{\$4,100,000 \text{ Net income} + \$380,000 \text{ Depreciation and amortization} \\ - \$250,000 \text{ Accrued sales} - \$100,000 \text{ Dividends} - \$800,000 \text{ Principal payments}}}{\$3,750,000 \text{ Budgeted fixed asset expenditures}}$$

$$=$$

213

$$\frac{\$3,330,000 \text{ Cash flows}}{\$3,750,000 \text{ Budgeted fixed asset expenditures}}$$

$$= 89\%$$

The ratio is less than one, so Mole will either need to draw upon its cash reserves to pay for the fixed assets, cut back on its fixed asset budget, or revise other parts of the budget to increase cash flow.

Return on Assets Employed

A common metric is the return on assets employed, which measures the return to investors on all of the assets in a company. Though this metric includes *all* assets, rather than just fixed assets, we include it here because fixed assets may be the predominant portion of all assets.

The return on assets employed measures how efficiently a company can use its assets to generate an adequate profit. A common result of using this metric is that management endeavors to shrink the amount of assets it uses; doing so releases the cash that would otherwise have been invested in the assets.

The return on assets employed metric is not especially useful for persistently low-profit companies, since the ratio will be subject to a great deal of fluctuation when the numerator is close to or below zero. Also, the fixed asset component of the denominator may not reflect the current value of the assets, since accelerated depreciation can yield an artificially low book value. Thus, if fixed assets comprise the bulk of the denominator and accelerated depreciation is being used, do not be surprised if a company is reporting an unusually high return on assets employed.

To calculate the return on assets employed, divide net profits by the total of all assets, where fixed assets are recorded net of all depreciation. The formula is:

$$\frac{\text{Net profit}}{\text{Total assets}}$$

EXAMPLE

Mole Industries has acquired Grubstake Brothers, a manufacturer of backhoes. Mole's CFO wants to know how much Grubstake's return on assets employed can be improved, so that Mole can generate sufficient cash to pay back its purchase price. The CFO examines the production bottleneck operation and concludes that $1,300,000 of fixed assets located downstream from the bottleneck represent unnecessary excess capacity, and can be safely eliminated. This change will yield the following alteration in the return on assets employed (ROAE) for Grubstake:

	Initial ROAE	Revised ROAE
Net profit	$200,000	$300,000
Total assets	$8,000,000	$6,700,000
Proposed fixed asset reduction		$(1,300,000)
Depreciation reduction from proposed fixed asset reduction		$(100,000)
Return on assets employed	2.5%	4.5%

Thus, the sale of selected fixed assets improves the return on assets employed, not only because of the asset reduction in the denominator, but also because of the related reduction in depreciation in the numerator that improves the net profit of Grubstake.

Return on Operating Assets

This metric is a variation on the return on assets employed that was just covered. The return on operating assets only includes in the denominator those assets that are actively used to create revenue. Thus, the formula is:

$$\frac{\text{Net profit}}{\text{Total assets used to generate revenue}}$$

There are several reasons for using this metric, which are to focus the attention of management on:

- Minimizing the number of assets needed to generate revenue
- Minimizing the total new investment in assets
- Spotting and eliminating those assets designated as not contributing to the generation of revenue

This metric can result in an interesting amount of political maneuvering, since managers may be tempted to exclude assets from the denominator in order to improve the results of the metric, but will then face pressure to dispose of the excluded assets.

EXAMPLE

The production facility for the Ditch Magic product line of Mole Industries has fallen on hard times. The facility used to have a sterling return on operating assets of 40%, but the metric has declined to an abysmal 5% after the manager of the facility added a number of automated machining stations that added a large amount of capital investment to the facility without much of an offsetting reduction in labor costs.

The CFO brings in consultants to investigate the situation. They recommend that the facility eliminate most of the automated machining stations and replace them with smaller, more flexible work stations that are both manually operated and more easily configurable. The current return on operating assets (ROA) and the projected calculation after these changes are made is noted in the following table:

	Initial ROA	Projected ROA
Net profit	$500,000	$700,000
Total assets	$10,000,000	$7,000,000
Proposed robot elimination		$(3,500,000)
Proposed work station additions		$500,000
Net change in depreciation		$(200,000)
Return on operating assets	5%	10%

The proposed changes should double the return on operating assets. In addition, they may introduce sufficient flexibility into the production process to generate enough additional profits to bring the facility back to the returns it generated in its glory days.

Bottleneck Utilization

In most production operations, there is a particular work station that is perpetually overworked, and which keeps the rest of the facility from maximizing its production potential – this is the bottleneck operation. A key focus of the manufacturing manager is to ensure that this work station is fully supported and utilized at all times, which makes the bottleneck utilization metric one of the more important performance measures that a company can track.

To calculate bottleneck utilization, divide the actual hours of usage of the operation by the total hours available. Depending on how closely management watches this metric, you may want to re-calculate it every day. The formula is:

$$\frac{\text{Actual hours of bottleneck usage}}{\text{Total hours in the measurement period}}$$

While important, the bottleneck utilization metric does not track the profitability of the work being run through the bottleneck operation. Thus, it could be utilized nearly 100% of the time, but with only low-profit items being manufactured, the company's profitability would still be low. Thus, this metric should be used in combination with an analysis of the profitability of products being scheduled for production.

EXAMPLE

Mole Industries runs a small production line that creates motorized tunneling devices for cable laying operations. The bottleneck in the production line is the paint booth. The paint booth runs for three shifts, seven days a week, while the rest of the production line runs for a standard eight-hour day, five days a week. Management is concerned that the paint booth will limit the production line's ability to expand, and wants to know what bottleneck utilization it has. The calculation is:

$$\frac{152 \text{ Actual hours of operation}}{168 \text{ Hours in a week}}$$

$$= 90\% \text{ Bottleneck utilization}$$

The calculation shows that there are only 16 additional hours of bottleneck time available, and it is likely that the paint booth staff will have a difficult time making those few additional hours available, given ongoing maintenance requirements. Thus, the management team needs to discuss whether it should invest in an additional paint booth or outsource some painting to a supplier. It may make more sense to build a new paint booth if there is an expectation of a large and permanent increase in sales (which would pay for the investment in a new paint booth), whereas outsourcing may be the better option if sales are not expected to increase much beyond the current level.

Unscheduled Machine Downtime

A properly managed production facility has a maintenance schedule for all of the equipment under its control, to which it closely adheres in order to ensure that all equipment is operational during planned production hours. When a machine requires unscheduled downtime for maintenance, this can be a warning flag that the machine in question is beginning to approach the end of its life span, and should be replaced. Otherwise, management will find that it requires an increasing amount of down time for additional unplanned maintenance, which in turn can interrupt the production schedule and jeopardize the timing of deliveries to customers.

The calculation of unscheduled machine downtime is the total minutes of unscheduled machine downtime, divided by the total minutes of machine time during the measurement period. It is best to run this calculation for each individual machine, so that you can more easily spot which ones may be in need of replacement. The formula is:

$$\frac{\text{Total minutes of unscheduled machine downtime}}{\text{Total minutes of machine time}}$$

It can be difficult to accumulate the information required for this metric. Machine operators tend to forget to record the information, and automated systems that track this information are quite expensive.

EXAMPLE

The controller of Mole Industries is compiling the budget for the upcoming year, and wants to know if any production equipment may require replacement. He compiles the information in the following table about a group of lathes for the preceding month:

	Lathe 1	Lathe 2	Lathe 3
Unscheduled downtime (hours)	7	21	112
Total machine time (hours)	720	720	720
Unscheduled downtime percentage	1%	3%	16%
Age of machine	4 years	6 years	11 years

The table provides two pieces of evidence in favor of replacing Lathe 3: its unscheduled maintenance percentage is eight times higher than the average downtime of the other two lathes, and it is by far the oldest machine in the group. The controller elects to make further inquiries targeted at the possible replacement of this lathe.

Summary

The determination of the adequacy of an investment in fixed assets is a difficult one to make just from ratio analysis. You really need to examine the capacity level of each machine, its age and maintenance record, and how it relates to the production flow to see if new equipment is needed. Still, if you are conducting a high-level examination of the fixed assets of a company, ratio analysis is a good way to obtain a general impression of the situation.

Some caution should be exercised when using any of the metrics related to the utilization of assets. If an asset is not being fully utilized, this is not necessarily bad – the asset should only be used to the extent that it is providing products that can be sold in the near future. If you use a utilization metric to argue in favor of increasing a machine's rate of production, you may only be forcing the company to create more inventory than it needs.

There is certainly no need to track all of the metrics described in this chapter, but you should select a few that most closely match your informational needs, and focus on tracking them over the long term.

Chapter 17
Fixed Asset Auditing

Introduction

If you are responsible for the accounting records of a company that pertain to fixed assets, you may be curious about how these records and related accounting systems are investigated by auditors as part of an annual audit. The following sections note the objectives that an auditor will likely pursue as part of a fixed asset audit, as well as the procedures he is most likely to follow, and the information that he will request from you.

Fixed Asset Audit Objectives

Before an auditor begins his audit procedures, he first decides upon the objectives that he wants to pursue through those procedures. The primary objectives related to fixed assets are:

- *Authorization.* Have the fixed assets been purchased under the correct company-specific authorizations? Fixed assets may be extremely expensive, so a purchase not made within the proper limits of authority may indicate a serious control problem.
- *Existence.* Are the fixed assets actually there? Even if all of the supporting paperwork is in order that appears to confirm the existence of a fixed asset, it is possible that the assets have been removed, so the auditor needs to visually confirm their existence.
- *Presentation.* Have all fixed assets been properly recorded in the balance sheet, and have all asset classes, asset retirement obligations, capitalized interest, depreciation, impairments, leased assets, and liens been properly disclosed?
- *Recordation.* Have all fixed assets been recorded as fixed assets? If the cost of some fixed assets were charged to expense as incurred, or if some costs under the capitalization limit were recorded as expenses, this can profoundly alter the profitability and asset levels of a company.
- *Valuation.* Have fixed assets been valued correctly? Valuation includes not only the initial cost applied to a fixed asset, but also any subsequent changes to that cost, impairments, and (if the IFRS framework is being used) revaluations.

The auditor then uses these objectives to design a set of audit procedures. These procedures are described in the next section.

Fixed Asset Audit Procedures

The exact audit procedures used will vary somewhat by audit firm, but you can expect to see some variation on the following procedures in a typical audit:

- *Discuss purchasing controls.* The auditors will discuss any changes since the last audit in your internal controls over the purchasing of fixed assets. They may ask about changes in the capitalization limit, as well as changes in the expenditure levels and types of expenditures at which fixed asset purchases are authorized. There may also be a discussion of the capital budgeting process, to the extent that it modifies authorization levels for fixed asset purchases.
- *Discuss leasing controls.* The auditors may discuss changes since the last audit in your controls over the leasing of fixed assets (irrespective of whether they are operating or capital leases). This topic may not arise if you do not lease assets.
- *Compare capital budget to purchases.* If there is a robust capital budgeting system in place, the auditors will compare the assets authorized through it to actual purchases, to see if there are any fixed asset purchases occurring without the formal review process.
- *Match supporting documents to register.* The auditors will likely trace supplier invoices to the costs listed in the fixed asset register for assets acquired during the accounting period being audited. They will also look for evidence that a person with the proper authority approved these invoices (which may include a review of the board of directors minutes), and that there is evidence of asset receipt. If the company obtained title to an asset, such as for land or a vehicle, they may want to see the title document.
- *Match register to assets.* The auditors may trace assets listed on the fixed assets register to the assets themselves by conducting a physical count of selected fixed assets. This count is likely to be targeted primarily at the highest-cost assets, with a few additional lower-cost items selected at random. The auditors may also review the condition of the assets, and any evidence that they are no longer in use.
- *Match assets to register.* During a physical count of fixed assets, the auditors may trace assets found back to the fixed assets register. This procedure uncovers undocumented assets.
- *Trace transfer documentation.* If fixed assets have been transferred between departments or subsidiaries, the auditors may examine the related transfer documentation to see if the transfers were properly authorized.
- *Review physical safeguards.* The auditors may review any safeguards the company has installed to prevent the unauthorized movement of fixed assets, or unauthorized access to them. This procedure may be minimized for those assets too heavy to be moved, but can be a major issue for highly movable assets, such as laptop computers.

- *Examine asset class assignments.* If you have standardized asset useful lives and depreciation methods based on the asset classes to which you have assigned fixed assets, expect the auditors to review the contents of each class to see if the fixed asset assignments are appropriate.
- *Verify depreciation.* The auditors will review your depreciation calculations to see if assets have been assigned the correct useful lives and depreciation methods (in comparison to the asset classes of which they are a part), and will want to see documentation of any salvage values that you have incorporated into the depreciation calculations. They may also manually re-compute some of the depreciation calculations, especially if the depreciation expense does not appear reasonable in comparison to the amount charged to expense in prior years.

Tip: Always use the same useful life and depreciation method for a fixed asset that is standard for all assets within its asset class. Otherwise, you will present the auditors with a broad array of depreciation calculations that are difficult for you to justify and for the auditors to verify.

If you have had large asset dispositions during the year, the auditors may also review your depreciation calculations for those assets through the disposal date.

- *Verify revaluations.* If you are using the IFRS framework, you have the option to periodically revalue selected classes of fixed assets. If so, the auditors will review your revaluation documentation.

Tip: If you engage in revaluations, always use a written valuation report from a third-party appraiser as the basis for the revaluations. Auditors consider this to be strong objective evidence of a revaluation.

- *Investigate impairments.* The auditors will review any documentation you have prepared regarding the impairment of fixed assets, and may also investigate declines in the market price of assets, any significant adverse changes in the extent of asset use, operating losses associated with assets, and physical damage to assets. If you are constructing assets, they may investigate whether there are significant cost overruns. They may bypass this procedure if the amount of fixed assets is quite small, on the grounds that any possible impairment would be immaterial.
- *Investigate asset retirement obligations.* The auditors will determine whether there is a legal obligation to incur material expenses to retire an asset, and whether the company has appropriately accounted for such asset retirement obligations.
- *Investigate held for sale assets.* If any assets have been classified as held for sale, the auditors will investigate the documentation supporting this classifi-

cation, as well as any revaluations of these assets, and whether they should continue to be classified as held for sale.

- *Investigate liens*. The auditors may investigate whether there are any encumbrances or liens on fixed assets that require disclosure.
- *Investigate lease agreements*. The auditors may examine any outstanding lease agreements to see if the underlying assets have been appropriately classified as operating or capital leases.

Tip: If the auditors want you to reclassify an operating lease as a capital lease, you may be able to protest that the extra accounting work associated with this changeover is not worth the effort, if there is no material impact on the financial statements.

- *Investigate repairs and maintenance*. The auditors will review the contents of the repairs and maintenance general ledger account to see if there are any items that had been charged to expense that should instead have been capitalized as additions to fixed assets.
- *Investigate groups of assets*. The auditors may choose to review situations where you have clustered together and capitalized groups of assets that would otherwise individually be below the corporate capitalization limit, and whether this treatment matches the company's capitalization policy for such situations.
- *Verify disposals*. The auditors will review the documented authorization for any asset disposals, as well as the proper recognition of any resulting proceeds from a sale. They will also investigate the derecognition of these assets from the accounting records, to see if any gain or loss on disposition was properly calculated and recognized. They may also ascertain if any assets disposed of had been used as collateral on existing loans.
- *Investigate gain and loss accounts*. The auditors may review the contents of the revenue, gain, and loss accounts in the general ledger to see if there were any transactions that indicate the sale of fixed assets, but for which the related assets and accumulated depreciation were not removed from the fixed asset records.
- *Calculate analytics*. The auditors will engage in analytical procedures to identify any fluctuations over time in the relationships between the various fixed assets and other accounts, and that appear to be inconsistent with other information. For example, they might calculate depreciation expense as a proportion of fixed assets on a trend line, to see if the proportion has changed significantly. They will inquire further if they spot any anomalies.
- *Review financial statement presentation*. The auditors will verify that all fixed assets have been properly recorded in the balance sheet, and that all asset classes, asset retirement obligations, capitalized interest, depreciation, impairments, leased assets, and liens have been properly disclosed in the accompanying footnotes to the financial statements.

Intangible Asset Auditing Activities

Since intangible assets are non-physical assets, verifying their existence and valuation can represent a challenge for the auditor. The following approaches may be used to do so:

- *Trace debits to supporting documents*. The auditors will trace all debits in the intangible asset accounts back to the supporting documents. They will look for evidence of payment by the company, as well as any documentation of the rights being conveyed to the company in exchange for those payments.
- *Review policies*. The auditors may review the company's amortization policies relating to intangible assets, noting if these policies have changed from prior years.
- *Review useful lives*. The auditors may compare the standard useful life for each intangible asset class to those used in the prior year, and investigate the reasons for any differences.
- *Compare amortization methods*. The auditors will compare the amortization methods used for each asset class to those used in the prior year, and investigate the reasons for any differences.
- *Calculation amortization*. The auditors will recalculate the amortization computations for a representative number of intangible assets.
- *Review for excess amortization*. The auditors may review the amortization calculations to see if there were any instances in which amortization was calculated past the useful life of an intangible asset.
- *Investigate unusual entries*. The auditors will examine the amortization expense and accumulated amortization accounts for any unusual entries.
- *Review retirement entries*. The auditors may review a sample of the entries used to remove retired intangible assets from the accounting records.
- *Examine write-downs*. The auditors may verify that any authorization to write down the value of an intangible asset was properly authorized.

Auditor Requests

The auditors will likely ask for several documents related to fixed assets, which are:

- *Fixed assets register*. This is a complete listing of every fixed asset owned by the company, including the cost of each item, its asset class, useful life, depreciation method, and salvage value (if any). If the assets are widely distributed through multiple locations, it is also extremely useful to include an asset location in the register, which the auditors can reference if they elect to physically review a selection of fixed assets. Be certain that the cost totals in the fixed asset register tie to the related account balances in the general ledger, or provide a detailed reconciliation that reveals (and justifies) any differences between the two.

> **Tip:** Matching the totals in the fixed asset register to the associated general ledger account balances should be a standard practice as part of closing the books every month. If you do not do so until the end of the year, you may be facing a mess that requires more investigatory time than you have available.

- *Purchases detail.* This is a binder in which you store copies of all supplier invoices for purchased fixed assets, which the auditors then trace back through the accounting records to verify that the amounts at which fixed assets were purchased are the amounts recorded in the accounting records. If the business has constructed assets, there should be an excellent organizational structure for the underlying purchase and labor receipts, with a summary page for each project that lists all costs incurred, and from which the auditors can trace a total project cost back to the accounting records.

> **Tip:** The auditors may spend a significant amount of time reviewing the fixed asset purchases binder, so help them be more efficient by using a highlighter to point out the amounts on supplier invoices that you capitalized. Also, if some explanation of capitalized amounts is needed, append a memo to the relevant documents, so the auditors can reconstruct your record keeping.

- *Fixed asset roll forward.* This is a summary table that begins with the totals for each fixed asset account at the beginning of the audit period, adds to it any changes during the period that related to asset additions and deletions, and then concludes with the ending balances for all of these accounts. The auditors will trace the beginning balances in this table to their audited financial statements from the preceding year, as well as the ending balances listed in their trial balance for this year, and all of the changes listed for the current period. This is a significant document for the auditors, so ensure that the information in it is correct and ties to all general ledger balances before giving it to them. An example of a fixed asset roll forward appears in the following exhibit.

Example of a Fixed Asset Roll Forward Report

Account Number	Description	Beginning Balance 12/31/20x1	Additions/ Deletions	Ending Balance 12/31/x2
Asset Categories				
1510	Computer equipment	$4,200,000	$380,000	$4,580,000
1520	Furniture and fixtures	350,000	(20,000)	330,000
1535	Land improvements	150,000	--	150,000
1545	Machinery	3,100,000	600,000	3,700,000
1550	Office equipment	200,000	40,000	240,000
	Asset totals	$8,000,000	$1,000,000	$9,000,000
Accumulated Depreciation Categories				
1610	Computer equipment	$(1,050,000)	$(500,000)	$(1,550,000)
1620	Furniture and fixtures	(160,000)	(50,000)	(210,000)
1635	Land improvements	(10,000)	(10,000)	(20,000)
1645	Machinery	(900,000)	(320,000)	(1,220,000)
1650	Office equipment	(30,000)	(20,000)	(50,000)
	Accumulated depreciation totals	$(2,150,000)	$(900,000)	$(3,050,000)
	Grand total fixed assets	$5,850,000	$100,000	$5,950,000

If there are a large number of additions to and deletions from the schedule, consider using a separate column to document each type of transaction, just to make the report easier to read and audit.

> **Tip:** If there are many fixed asset transactions, it can be difficult to update the fixed asset roll forward report for a full year. This is especially problematic when the audit is scheduled to begin shortly after the year closes. You can mitigate this issue by fully updating the report in the preceding month, so that it is accurate for 11 months of the year, and then conduct a minor additional roll forward for the final month of the year, thereby bringing it up to date for the auditors.

Summary

This chapter has outlined the basic steps that an auditor can be expected to follow in an audit that relates to fixed assets. However, the amount of effort expended may vary considerably, depending upon how much money the company has invested in its fixed assets. If there are few fixed assets, as is commonly the case in many services businesses, an auditor may conclude that the entire amount of fixed assets listed on a company's balance sheet is so minimal as to only require the briefest auditor attention. Conversely, in an asset-intensive business, the auditors may find it necessary to comb through the accounting records in great detail, given the impact on the financial statements of having incorrect account balances in this area. Thus, the information in this chapter *does* give an overview of the procedures that auditors follow, but *does not* give an indication of whether they elect to follow those procedures, or the intensity with which they choose to do so.

Appendix
Journal Entries

The following journal entries show the format you can use for most accounting transactions related to fixed assets. They are sorted in alphabetical order by type of activity.

Amortization. To record the amortization of intangible assets for a reporting period.

	Debit	Credit
Amortization expense	xxx	
Accumulated amortization		xxx

Asset exchange. To record the exchange of dissimilar assets. This entry also eliminates the accumulated depreciation on the asset being relinquished. There are line items in the entry for the recognition of either a gain or a loss on the exchange. You may need to add either a debit or a credit to this entry if cash is being paid or accepted.

	Debit	Credit
Asset acquired [state the account]	xxx	
Accumulated depreciation	xxx	
Loss on asset exchange [if any]	xxx	
Gain on asset exchange [if any]		xxx
Asset relinquished [state the account]		xxx

Asset held for sale #1 (initial reclassification). To record the reclassification of an asset to the held for sale asset class.

	Debit	Credit
Assets held for sale	xxx	
Asset [state the account]		xxx

Asset held for sale #2 (fair value decline). To record the decline in fair value of an asset classified as held for sale.

	Debit	Credit
Loss on decline of fair value of assets held-for-sale	xxx	
Assets held for sale		xxx

Asset held for sale #3 (fair value recovery). To record the recovery in fair value of an asset classified as held for sale.

	Debit	Credit
Assets held for sale	xxx	
Recovery of fair value of assets held-for-sale		xxx

Asset held for sale #4 (sale of asset). To record the sale of an asset classified as held for sale. The entry includes line items for a gain or loss on the sale transaction.

	Debit	Credit
Cash	xxx	
Accumulated depreciation	xxx	
Loss on asset sale [if any]	xxx	
Gain on asset sale [if any]		xxx
Assets held for sale		xxx

Asset impairment. To record the reduction in an asset's book value to its fair value when the fair value is less than its book value.

	Debit	Credit
Impairment loss	xxx	
Accumulated impairment		xxx

Asset retirement obligation #1 (initial recognition). To record the initial liability for an asset retirement obligation.

	Debit	Credit
Asset [state the account]	xxx	
Asset retirement obligation liability		xxx

Asset retirement obligation #2 (accretion expense). To record the periodic accretion expense associated with an asset retirement obligation liability.

	Debit	Credit
Accretion expense	xxx	
Asset retirement obligation liability		xxx

Asset retirement obligation #3 (depreciation expense). To record the periodic depreciation expense for the asset of which the asset retirement obligation is a part.

	Debit	Credit
Depreciation expense	xxx	
Accumulated depreciation		xxx

Asset retirement obligation #4 (settlement). To record the settlement and derecognition of the asset retirement obligation. There are additional line items for the recognition of a gain or loss on the settlement, depending upon the amount of expenditures actually incurred.

	Debit	Credit
Accumulated depreciation	xxx	
Asset [state the account]		xxx
Remediation expense [if any]	xxx	
Loss on ARO settlement [if any]	xxx	
Gain on ARO settlement [if any]		xxx

Asset revaluation #1 (accumulated depreciation elimination). To record the elimination of accumulated depreciation associated with a fixed asset prior to its being revalued under IFRS.

	Debit	Credit
Accumulated depreciation	xxx	
Asset [state the account]		xxx

Asset revaluation #2 (gain on revaluation). To record a revaluation gain under IFRS. An additional line item is included for the reversal of a loss on revaluation in a prior period (if any).

	Debit	Credit
Asset [state the amount]	xxx	
Loss on revaluation [a reversal, if any]		xxx
Other comprehensive income – gain on revaluation		xxx

Asset revaluation #3 (loss on revaluation). To record a revaluation loss under IFRS. An additional line item is included for the reversal of a gain on revaluation in a prior period (if any).

	Debit	Credit
Loss on revaluation	xxx	
Other comprehensive income – gain on revaluation [a reversal, if any]	xxx	
Asset [state the account]		xxx

Capital lease. To record the initial acquisition of a leased asset that is classified as a capital lease.

	Debit	Credit
Asset (capital lease)	xxx	
Capital lease obligations		xxx

Component replacement. To record the replacement of a component. This entry eliminates the original asset and any accumulated depreciation, while a second entry records the replacement component. There is a loss on asset derecognition stated in the entry, on the assumption that the asset being replaced has not yet been fully depreciated as of the replacement date.

	Debit	Credit
Loss on asset derecognition [if any]	xxx	
Accumulated depreciation	xxx	
Asset [being replaced, state the account]		xxx

	Debit	Credit
Asset [state the account]	xxx	
Cash or Accounts payable		xxx

Depreciation. To record the depreciation expense incurred for a reporting period. Many line items are presented for the accumulated depreciation for different types of asset classes. You may also apportion the depreciation expense among departments or subsidiaries.

	Debit	Credit
Depreciation expense	xxx	
Accumulated depreciation – Buildings		xxx
Accumulated depreciation – Computers		xxx
Accumulated depreciation – Equipment		xxx
Accumulated depreciation – Furniture		xxx
Accumulated depreciation – Software		xxx
Accumulated depreciation – Vehicles		xxx

Derecognition (sale). To eliminate a fixed asset from the accounting records upon its disposal through a sale to a third party. The entry provides for recognition of either a gain or loss on the transaction.

	Debit	Credit
Cash	xxx	
Accumulated depreciation	xxx	
Loss on asset sale [if any]	xxx	
Gain on asset sale [if any]		xxx
Asset [state the account]		xxx

Donated asset #1 (related to major activities). To record the receipt of a donated asset by a not-for-profit entity, where the donated asset is related to the entity's major activities.

	Debit	Credit
Asset [state the account]	xxx	
Revenue		xxx

Donated asset #2 (related to peripheral activities). To record the receipt of a donated asset by a not-for-profit entity, where the donated asset is related to the entity's peripheral activities.

	Debit	Credit
Asset [state the account]	xxx	
Gain on contributed assets		xxx

Interest capitalization. To capitalize the interest cost associated with the construction of a fixed asset.

	Debit	Credit
Asset [state the account]	xxx	
Interest expense		xxx

Glossary

A

Accretion expense. The expense arising from an increase in the carrying amount of the liability associated with an asset retirement obligation. It is not an interest expense. It is classified as an operating expense in the income statement.

Accumulated amortization. The sum total of all amortization expense recognized to date on an amortizable intangible asset.

Accumulated depreciation. The sum total of all depreciation expense recognized to date on a depreciable fixed asset.

Accumulated impairment. The cumulative amount of impairment charged to a fixed asset.

Active market. A market in which the items being traded are homogenous, there are willing buyers and sellers, and prices are available to the public.

Amortization. The write-off of an intangible asset over its expected period of use.

Assessed value. The valuation assigned to a property by a government appraiser. This valuation is used as the basis on which property taxes are calculated.

Asset class. Assets of a similar nature and use that are grouped together. Examples of asset classes are land, buildings, machinery, furniture and fixtures, and office equipment.

Asset group. The unit of accounting for one or more fixed assets, which is the lowest level at which you can identify cash flows that are independent from the cash flows of other asset groups.

Asset number. A unique identification number that is typically etched into a metal plate and affixed to a fixed asset. It may be the primary form of identification in the fixed asset database.

Asset retirement obligation. A liability associated with the retirement of a fixed asset.

B

Balance sheet. A report that summarizes all of an entity's assets, liabilities, and equity as of a given point in time, which is usually the end of an accounting period.

Book value. An asset's original cost, less any depreciation that has been subsequently incurred.

Boot. The cash paid as part of an exchange of assets between two parties.

C

Capital expenditure. A payment made to acquire or upgrade an asset. You record a capital expenditure as an asset, rather than charging it immediately to expense. Instead, you depreciate it over the useful life of the asset.

Capitalization. When you record an expenditure as an asset, rather than an expense. This usually occurs when the amount of an expenditure exceeds a company's capitalization limit, and it has a useful life of greater than one year.

Capitalization limit. The amount paid for an asset, above which an entity records it as a fixed asset. If an entity pays less than the capitalization limit for an asset, it charges the asset to expense in the period incurred.

Capitalization rate. The rate you use to calculate the amount of interest to be capitalized.

Carrying amount. The recorded amount of an asset, net of any accumulated depreciation or accumulated impairment losses.

Cash-generating unit. The smallest identifiable group of assets that generates cash inflows independently from the cash inflows of other assets. Examples are product lines, businesses, individual store locations, and operating regions.

Chart of accounts. A listing of all accounts used in the general ledger, usually sorted in order by account number.

Collateral. An asset that a borrower has pledged as security for a loan. The lender has the legal right to seize and sell the asset if the borrower is unable to pay back the loan by an agreed date.

Commercial substance. A condition that arises when an entity's future cash flows are expected to change significantly as a result of a transaction. A cash flow change is considered significant if the risk, timing, or amount of future cash flows of the asset received differ significantly from those of the asset given up.

Conditional promise to give. A promise to contribute that is dependent upon the future occurrence of a specific future event whose occurrence is uncertain.

Cost to sell. The costs incurred in a sale transaction that would not have been incurred if there had been no sale. Examples of costs to sell are title transfer fees and brokerage commissions.

Custodian. The person who is responsible for a fixed asset. Also known as the *responsible party.*

D

Depletion base. The natural resource that is to be depleted as an asset. It is comprised of the acquisition, exploration, development, and restoration costs associated with the asset.

Depreciation. The gradual charging to expense of an asset's cost over its expected useful life.

Derecognition. The process of removing a transaction from the accounting records of an entity. For a fixed asset, this is the removal of the asset and any accumulated depreciation from the accounting records, as well as the recognition of any associated gain or loss.

Discount rate. The interest rate used to discount a stream of future cash flows to their present value. Depending upon the application, typical rates used as the discount rate are a firm's cost of capital or the current market rate.

Disposal group. A group of assets that you expect to dispose of in a single transaction, along with any liabilities that might be transferred to another entity along with the assets.

E

Easement. The legal requirement to allow access to a property by third parties for a specific purpose.

Executory costs. The transactional and operational fees associated with a lease, which includes such items as insurance, maintenance, and taxes.

Expenditure. A payment or the incurrence of a liability by an entity.

F

Fixed asset. An expenditure that generates economic benefits over a long period of time. Also known as property, plant, and equipment.

G

General ledger. The master set of accounts that summarize all transactions occurring within an entity.

Gross carrying amount. The total cost of a fixed asset prior to any reductions for depreciation or impairment.

H

Held for sale. A designation given to assets that an entity intends to sell to a third party within one year. You do not depreciate a fixed asset that is designated as held for sale.

I

Impairment. When the carrying amount of a fixed asset exceeds its fair value. The amount of the impairment is the difference between the two values.

Income statement. A financial report that summarizes an entity's revenue and expenses, as well as its net income or loss. The income statement shows an entity's financial results over a specific time period, usually a month, quarter, or year.

In service date. The date on which an asset is brought to the condition and location for which it was intended. This is the point at which cost accumulation and interest capitalization ends, and when depreciation begins.

Intangible asset. An identifiable, non-monetary asset that has no physical substance.

Intangible asset class. A group of intangible assets having similar characteristics and usage. Examples are brand names, licenses, and copyrights.

Interest. The cost of funds loaned to an entity by a lender, usually expressed as a percentage of the principal on an annual basis.

L

Lessee. The party in a leasing transaction that contracts to make rental payments to a lessor in exchange for the use of an asset.

Location code. An abbreviation of the address and room within which a fixed asset is located.

O

Other comprehensive income. A separate section of the income statement that follows the profit or loss section. It contains various items of revenue, expense, gains, and losses that do not appear within profit or loss.

P

Periodic depreciation. The amount of depreciation recorded in the current accounting period.

Profit or loss. That portion of the income statement prior to other comprehensive income. It contains the results of operations, plus finance and tax expenses, and the effect of discontinued operations.

Property, plant, and equipment. An expenditure that generates economic benefits over a long period of time. Also known as a *fixed asset.*

Purchase cost. The installed cost of an asset.

R

Recoverable amount. The higher of an asset's fair value less any costs to sell, and its value in use. Value in use is the present value of any future cash flows you expect to derive from an asset.

Reporting unit. An operating segment or one level below an operating segment. An operating segment is a component of a public entity that engages in business activities and whose results are reviewed by the chief operating decision maker, and for which discrete financial information is available.

Residual value. The estimated amount that you would currently obtain upon the disposal of a fixed asset at the end of its estimated useful life. Also known as *salvage value.*

Responsible party. The person who is responsible for a fixed asset. Also known as the *custodian.*

S

Salvage value. The estimated amount that you would currently obtain upon the disposal of a fixed asset at the end of its estimated useful life. Also known as *residual value.*

Serial number. A unique number assigned to a fixed asset by its manufacturer. The serial number may be used in place of a company-assigned asset number.

Supplier. The entity from which a company purchases a fixed asset. Can also be identified as the manufacturer or vendor.

T

Temporary difference. The difference between the carrying amount of an asset or liability in the balance sheet and its tax base.

Throughput. Revenues minus totally variable costs. Totally variable costs are usually just the cost of materials, since direct labor does not typically vary directly with sales.

U

Unconditional promise to give. A commitment that only requires the passage of time or a demand by the receiving entity for the commitment to be realized.

Useful life. The estimated lifespan of a depreciable fixed asset, during which it can be expected to contribute to company operations.

V

Value in use. The present value of any future cash flows you expect to derive from an asset or cash-generating unit.

W

Warranty period. The time period during which the manufacturer will pay for repairs to equipment, or its replacement.

Z

Zoning classification. The type of use to which a property may be put, as per the guidelines issued by the government having jurisdiction over the property. Examples of zoning classifications are agricultural, commercial, industrial, open space, residential, and retail.

Index

Made in United States
Orlando, FL
01 June 2022

18401015R10141